AMERICAN *angels*

CultureAmerica

KARAL ANN MARLING   ERIKA DOSS

Series Editors

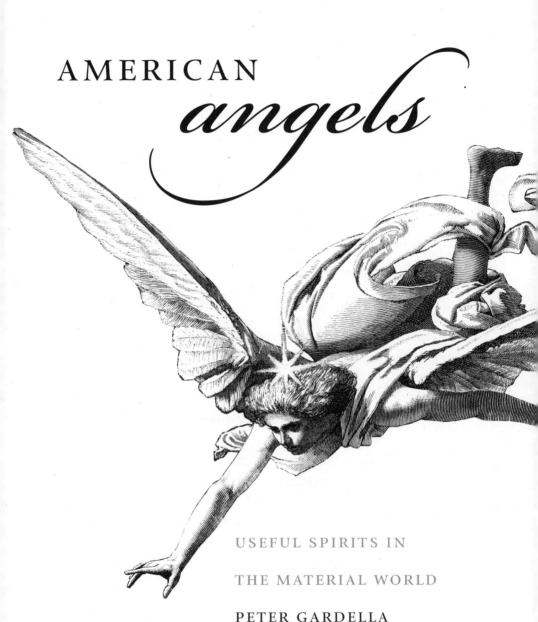

AMERICAN *angels*

USEFUL SPIRITS IN

THE MATERIAL WORLD

PETER GARDELLA

UNIVERSITY PRESS OF KANSAS

Published by
the University
Press of Kansas
(Lawrence, Kansas
66045), which
was organized by
the Kansas Board
of Regents and
is operated and
funded by Emporia
State University,
Fort Hays State
University, Kansas
State University,
Pittsburg State
University, the
University of
Kansas, and
Wichita State
University

© 2007 by the University Press of Kansas

Library of Congress Cataloging-in-Publication Data
Gardella, Peter, 1951--
     American angels : useful spirits in the material world
/ Peter Gardella.
          p. cm. — (CultureAmerica)
     Includes bibliographical references and index.
     ISBN 978-0-7006-1537-7 (cloth : alk. paper)
     1. Angels—Miscellanea. 2. United States—
Civilization—21st century. I.Title.
     BF1623.A53G37 2007
     202'.150973—dc22   2007028197

British Library Cataloguing-in-Publication
Data is available.

Printed in the United States of America

10 9 8 7 6 5 4 3 2 1

The paper used in this publication is recycled and
contains 50 percent postconsumer waste. It is acid free
and meets the minimum requirements of the American
National Standard for Permanence of Paper for Printed
Library Materials Z39.48–1992.

FOR WILLIAM GARDELLA

collaborator, critic, beloved son

Contents

Acknowledgments

This book would not exist without Colleen McDannell, the Sterling Mc-Murrin Professor of Religious Studies and Professor of History at the University of Utah, who suggested me to the University Press of Kansas for the project and usefully critiqued early drafts of two chapters. Before I began my work on angels, Colleen helped my scholarly career in many ways. Although younger than I, she has been a mentor.

Three students at Manhattanville College did internships that involved work on this book and made distinctive contributions. Lauren Fisher, who has also inspired me as a good student in several classes, told me about the Victoria's Secret advertising campaign featuring the theme of angels and commented on the text. Trisha Murray led me to Thomas Cole's paintings and set an example of thoroughness in art history that I have tried to follow. Joanna Becker read everything with a discerning eye, chased down artists for permissions to reproduce images of their work, and found images of angels online. Their faculty supervisor in art history, Professor Gillian Greenhill Hannum, also deserves thanks for sending her students to me.

Among family and friends, my niece Molly Taylor Greenhouse brought me closer to the creative edge of culture by alerting me to phenomena like the angels and demons of Allison A. Carmichael on the Web (at mangapunksai.com) and to the new television series *Fallen*. My son William read several chapters and contributed his thoughts, particularly influencing my thinking about angels and empire. When the book needed an indexer, he took on that task. Professor Cecilia Winters and her daughter Svetlana told me about Angel Oracle Cards and shared their set before I bought my own. Professor Theresa Sanders of Georgetown, who once spent a year with us at Manhattanville, gave me strong encouragement about my introduction. Professor Robert Orsi, an old friend from grad school, suggested that I look again at his latest book. He turned out to be right about its relevance to the topic of angels.

Nancy Jackson, my first editor at the University Press of Kansas, was very helpful in working with the book proposal and outline, and my second editor, Kalyani Fernando, helped to bring the process to completion, providing encouraging responses to the text and solving the persistent problem of the title. Editorial assistant Hilary Lowe and editor-in-chief Michael Briggs also kept my spirits up during the publication process. Without the support and advice of Susan McRory, the production editor who suggested Photofest as a source for pictures and gave her advice about many images, the final text would not be nearly as inviting as it is. Kathy Streckfus went far beyond the normal job of a copyeditor, not only correcting grammar and enforcing consistency but asking for more content, especially with regard to evangelical Christians.

Reacting to the proposal as an outside reader, Professor David Morgan urged that the book treat art and material culture as sources rather than using art as illustration, and I have attempted to follow this advice. Professor Morgan also offered helpful suggestions for organization while responding to the full text. As the book went through drafts, CultureAmerica series coeditor Erika Doss made detailed and useful criticisms, sharpening my focus on the connections of angels with American social and cultural history. The other coeditor of the series, Karal Ann Marling, reminded me of some topics I had forgotten, including Disney's *Night on Bald Mountain,* which resulted in a much-improved ending for chapter 3.

The librarians at Manhattanville and at Yale acted as angels at many points during the research stage of this project. Yale's policy of allowing alumni to buy circulation privileges made my job much easier. Susan Burdick at the Yale Divinity Library helped me keep track of materials and provided technical assistance. At Manhattanville, Elizabeth Gallagher helped me scan photographs, and another librarian, Marianne Irmler, supplied the book on angel artist Andy Lakey that informed my thinking for chapter 2. The staff at Hank Paper's Best Video Store, especially Mike Wheatley and Tyler Barger, helped me find angel movies.

Before all these scholarly helpers stands my wife, Professor Lorrie Greenhouse Gardella of Saint Joseph College (Connecticut), who is herself a scholar in social work and cultural history. She gave me Gustav Davidson's classic book *A Dictionary of Angels* twenty years ago. She hung pictures of Hamaliel, angel of August, and Verchiel, angel of July, on a wall in our house to remind me and William that our birth months are cared for. She is always the first editor of my writing, but in this case I cannot help but feel that she started the project before me.

Finally, let me offer thanks to my guardian angel, who has probably kept me safe as I drive along I-95 and the Merritt Parkway more often than I would like to know.

CHAPTER 1

Useful Spirits of American Culture

 It took me more than a year after starting my re-
search on angels in American culture to realize
that I had to look not just at Christian bookstores
or the New Age sections of Barnes and Noble, but
also at greeting card shops. It took more than two
years for me to break down and buy some angel
figurines, with the excuse that I had to get their
pictures taken for this book. Emerging from a Hallmark store with three
angels in packages, I felt an unaccountable lifting of my spirit. In part,
the feeling may have arisen because this was my last errand before going to visit my son in college, but after finishing my research, it is hard
for me to say that my happiness had nothing to do with the presence of
angels.

As angel experts commonly advise, surrounding ourselves with images of angels helps us to sense their healing presence.[1] That may explain why, before beginning my last weeks of work on *American Angels*
(revising the copyedited manuscript, finding the last pictures, checking
some facts), I felt moved to place the angel figurines called "Courage"
and "Angel of the Spirit" on top of my computer, with Courage facing
me and the other angel kneeling before my statue of the Hindu god Ganesha, who has been sitting on my computer since I wrote my last book.
However well or badly my work may proceed, it does seem to me that
the proximity and arrangement of these figures generates energy.

Although this book attempts to describe and analyze the angels of
American culture, not to show people how to reach their angels or to
explain how I sought mine, in religious studies there is always some
byplay between the scholar and the believer or practitioner. Chapter 4
does include my account of participating in an angel channeling session,
asking angels to speak to me. Though I must confess that I have never
seen or conversed with an angel, I do believe in them, and in God, and
I have frequently felt what American philosopher William James called
the "something more" that religious experience discloses to ordinary

consciousness. It seems reasonable to me, as it did to James, to argue that ordinary consciousness is connected to another dimension, and that our account of the world cannot be complete if we eliminate mystical experience. Following more recent philosophers of science, I would also argue that we know no more about consciousness than a twelfth-century scientist like Albertus Magnus knew about the nature of fire.[2] It feels exciting to me to live in an age when the most basic investigations of both physics and psychology raise more questions than they answer about the nature of the world, ourselves, and whatever consciousness has to do with what might be called energy or even spirit.

I also believe that the angels of America are best understood through an approach to American religious history that has been disparaged as "exceptionalist"—in other words, an approach that sometimes uses the word "America" for the United States and concentrates on the United States as a unique event in history. What we call "America" is, after all, not a natural nation but a movement. The United States results from many journeys away from Europe (and other Old Worlds) and toward the consummation of history, or at least the future.

The angels that flourish in American culture inhabit a unique spiritual landscape where, as atop my computer, they share space with Ganesha and many other spirits. America, with less commitment to any native or Old World culture than any other nation (even the other nations of the Americas), provides a free space in which angels can connect many forms of religion and spiritual practice. As Diana Eck, the founder of Harvard's Pluralism Project, has written, the United States can claim to be "the world's most religiously diverse nation," and the development of religious pluralism may be "the greatest form of lasting leadership we can offer the world."[3]

Within this context, I value the angels of America as signs and agents of a new form of American faith, neither monotheistic nor polytheistic, but transtheistic, which emerged in American culture more than a century ago and exploded into prominence in the past twenty years. Though this book will criticize some aspects of the religion of angels that sometimes embodies transtheistic faith, I hope that the story told here will read on the whole as an affirmation. I also hope that *American Angels* will help all its readers, believers and nonbelievers and all those in between, to appreciate how others in our history have experienced and thought about angels and how those experiences and thoughts have affected many aspects of life, from movies and television to real sex and war, in the history of the United States.

Americans from Cotton Mather to Walt Disney and from Frank Capra to Tony Kushner have loved angels. Their place in the culture has expanded from Mather's Latin diaries, which recorded his private vision of an angel in 1685,[4] to Kushner's play *Angels in America* in the 1990s and its screening on the HBO television network in December 2003. Though angels have retained their importance as cultural icons over this broad sweep of American history, the American angel has of course undergone some changes. The gender of angels, for example, has shifted: Puritan Cotton Mather and Mormon prophet Joseph Smith both saw very masculine angels in their visions, but since Victorian times, female angels have prevailed. Their descendants now walk fashion runways as "Victoria's Secret Angels." In the past two decades, androgynous angels have become much more prominent. Gabriel was played by actress Tilda Swinton in the 2004 film *Constantine*, and Tony Kushner's angel, who is called the "Continental Principality of America," could copulate with a gay man and give two women orgasms. Instead of serving as messengers and guardians assigned by God to humans, angels have become subjects of public entertainment and tools in corporate marketing strategies. Throughout the gender shifts and the move from private to public, however, American angels have retained one consistent characteristic: They have been useful. Their utility has given rise to an informal but coherent American religion of angels, a religion shaped in part by market forces in the United States.

Defining the Religion of Angels

Asserting that the United States has given birth to a religion of angels raises questions about what the word "religion" means. Derived (by the Roman philosopher Lucretius) from the Latin verb *ligare*, or "to bind," and the prefix *re*, for "again," religion implies something binding or obligatory.[5] William James defined religion as "the feelings, acts, and experiences" of people who "apprehend themselves to stand in relation to whatever they may consider the divine."[6] Whether "the divine" meant a single God, many gods, or a nontheistic principle like the Tao or the simple Awareness of some Buddhists did not matter to James; he dealt only with solitary "feelings, acts, and experiences." More recently, cultural anthropologist Clifford Geertz defined religions as systems of meaning, and historian of religion Robert Orsi as networks of relationships "between heaven and earth."[7] In my own work, I have defined religion as any "system of nonrational commitments that holds life together."[8] That definition includes the commitments of groups or individuals about almost anything, including work, food, exercise, and holidays, as long as such commitments actually hold life together (*ligare*) for those who maintain them.

Such a broad definition does not mean that everyone has a religion. Just as some people love no music, others have no deep commitments of any kind. For some, life does not hold together. A few maintain a commitment to conscious rationality, calculating costs and benefits and cultivating no rituals, symbols, or other nonrational elements. But for most people, certain objects, stories, names, sounds, and images give shape to the world to such an extent that life without them, or in opposition to them, would be empty of positive feeling or meaning.

To say that a religion of angels has emerged in American culture means that angels have become important objects of commitment for many Americans, but not that anyone commits to angels exclusively. Angel enthusiasts sometimes relate primarily to angels but often also belong to Christian churches or other formal religious groups. Like almost all Americans, they participate in what sociologist Robert Bellah identified in 1967 as the "American civil religion," the system of government-sanctioned holidays, historical sacred texts, and values to which citizens of the United States pledge allegiance.[9] Those who speak with their angels, collect angel figurines, and read books or watch movies about angels also take part in the "domestic religion," the network of private values and rituals that historian of American religion Colleen McDannell identified in Christmas celebrations and that I tried to describe further in *Domestic Religion* (1998).[10] Although there are core groups of angel activists, no firm line separates angel believers from other Americans. We all live in the culture that puts angels in the shopping mall and atop the Christmas tree, sets huge wings on lingerie models, and makes both angels and demons into characters in movies.

Formal religions surround this cultural religion on four sides. On the right are the conservative Protestant, Roman Catholic, and occasional Jewish and Muslim thinkers who write books about angels based on Scripture and tradition.[11] On the left, taking more daring stances and appealing to experience, are writers and practitioners of New Age religions such as Elizabeth Clare Prophet's Church Universal and Triumphant or the Spiritualists and Swedenborgians who flourished in the nineteenth century.[12] Below are the exorcists, concerned with demons and Hell, many working in churches but often in semisecrecy, and the vanishingly few outright Satanists.[13] Meanwhile, the Mormons, who teach that all redeemed humans become angels and gods, might be said to stand above the center of popular culture.[14] Between these positions lies the subject matter of this book: the movies, plays, songs, and television shows about angels (and demons); the angel statuary of public parks and cemeteries; the angels and demons of spiritual warfare, whether seen by players of computer games or by generals on battlefields in the Middle East; the angel pins and figurines for sale at Hallmark stores; and the angel therapists who teach people to converse with their personal guardian angels.

Alongside the angels have come many similar spirits. American culture abounds in superheroes who wield angelic powers in comic books; science-fiction characters who travel at speeds faster than light and intervene from heavenly vehicles; demigods with origins in Egypt, Africa, Greece, northern Europe, Persia, India, China, and Japan; and New Age visions of the spirits of dolphins, whales, elephants, or Gaia the Earth herself. In the cosmos inhabited by such spirits, the new form of faith that I have called transtheistic, involving a provisional acceptance of many spiritual powers with an assumption of some underlying unity, becomes possible. Angels were the first objects of this transtheistic faith, and angels continue to connect it with the traditions of Judaism, Christianity, and Islam.

The religion of angels makes a difference not only across all of American culture but also in the formal religions, because angels mediate divine power. But angels by definition are not God. Their name in Western religions means "messenger" (Greek *angelos,* Hebrew *malakh,* Arabic *malik*),[15] and they function in monotheistic scriptures as messengers from God to people. In any culture where angels become prominent symbols, the focus is shifting from God to humanity.

This is so particularly in America, where the religion of angels is a cultural phenomenon arising from the marketplace and the media rather than from institutions of formal religion. The rise of angels in America also indicates a shift in religious power from clergy to laypeople. This phenomenon may be seen as both a fulfillment and a contradiction of the "secularization" that sociologists of religion since Max Weber have been describing. In classical social theory, "secularization" refers to a loss of authority by religious officials over areas of life such as marriage, inheritance, and education. It also means the advance of reason over religious or magical thinking with regard to the world, the "disenchantment" of nature and society.[16] In the angel movies, songs, and collectible statues of American culture, laypeople have certainly used angels to validate their feelings about ultimate questions and to claim a realm of religious practice for themselves. These expressions of belief in angels have at the same time contradicted secularization by reasserting the power of the nonrational in supposedly secular realms like political and social action, ecology, psychotherapy, and medicine.

Uses of American Angels

Angels have always been mediators. Once they were also rulers, moving the heavenly spheres that moved the planets. In the Bible, angels executed judgment: The Torah showed them sent to destroy Sodom and Gomorrah, and the Christian book of Revelation predicted that they would pour wrath upon the Earth. But in the United States, angels have become servants of humanity and symbols of a new unity.

Today, at a Mobil station selling quick oil changes and car washes, Americans can buy Guardian Angel pins for $7.95. The same rack offers Casino Angel pins in two models, winged figures holding cards or working slot machines. The Barnes and Noble bookstore has Angel Oracle Cards for $15.95, complete with a Tarot-like instruction book and a deck of angels that range from the traditional Michael, Raphael, and Uriel to Shanti, Merlina, Bethany, Akasha, and Athena; the same publisher also sells Archangel Oracle Cards. Clairvoyant counselors not only write books on how to communicate with angels but also hold evening and weekend workshops and run websites devoted to receiving and promulgating angel messages. Over the past seven decades, movies from *It's a Wonderful Life* to *Angels in the Outfield* (in two versions), television shows like *Touched by an Angel,* and innumerable Christmas specials have taught Americans that angels either exist to serve human purposes or can be made to do so. As befits the nation that nurtured the philosophy of Pragmatism, the United States has reduced angels from the awesome status of creatures who proclaim the most significant events in history or impart visions to prophets to mere helpers in ordinary life, sidekicks to more heroic humans. Angels in these roles resemble EMS workers, psychotherapists, or comic foils more closely than they do messengers of God. Rather than saying "Fear Not!" to calm the awestruck subjects of their visitations, angels like Clarence from *It's a Wonderful Life* or Monica from *Touched by an Angel* have to convince people of their status.

On higher levels, American culture has also demonstrated the enormous potential of angels to mediate between religions and between cultural and religious practices. People pray to, through, and with angels, both in traditional churches and in New Age contexts. Roman Catholics and other Christians often treat the angels Michael, Gabriel, and Raphael as saints, naming churches, schools, and hospitals for them and putting paintings and statues of them near altars. Yet Americans make movies even about these saintly angels, including *Gabriel over the White House* (1933) and *Michael* (1996), in which the archangel Michael (played by John Travolta) became a sexual partner for humans. The angel Gabriel turned bad in *The Prophecy* (1994) and appeared again as a villain in *Constantine* (2004). Though Hollywood occasionally produces a devotional film about a saint, a biblical figure, or another religious hero, the film industry never puts saints or biblical people into the comedies, romances, melodramas, science-fiction epics, and holiday movies where angels abound.[17] Saints and the Bible divide the audience on the basis of religious affiliation, while angels unite believers in Judaism, the various branches of Christianity, and Islam and avoid offending humanists (at least those who can tolerate fantasy). Angels seem both less substantial and less serious than saints or biblical figures.

Beyond the phenomena normally thought of as belonging to religion, the wild variety of angel metaphors in American culture reveals how angels mediate by crossing boundaries. For example, the motif of angels appears in the names of the Hell's Angels motorcycle club, the Guardian Angels neighborhood watch group, the female detectives called Charlie's Angels on television and in movies, and the Blue Angels team of navy precision pilots. In each of these cases, the word "angel" imparts an unofficial quality, a quality of not being (or pretending not to be) exactly what they are. The Guardian Angels and Charlie's Angels aren't "really" police or detectives but a special category, volunteer police or beautiful female detectives (it's easy to forget how startling it was in 1975 to see women carrying guns on television). The Blue Angels aren't normal combat fighter pilots but a flying team for air shows, and the Hell's Angels aren't just a motorcycle gang or a club, but *the* motorcycle gang exalted into a cult or way of life. In a sense, the concept of "angel" undermines the concepts of motorcyclist, watchman, detective, and fighter pilot. Scholars of religion describe the dimension that the word "angel" suggests as liminal, a word rooted in the Latin *limen*, or "threshold."[18] Liminal experiences (which include sex, intoxication, war, and dying) test limits and suggest the possibility of transcendence, and angels are liminal creatures by nature.

This liminality of angels makes them available to artists and writers and even to engineers, working in many genres. In the 1980s, a series of movies called *Angel* featured a high school honor student who dressed as a prostitute at night and killed criminals. Television heroine Buffy the Vampire Slayer had a boyfriend named Angel, a vampire who had turned good and renounced human blood; this Angel later had his own TV series. Jessica Alba's television series *Dark Angel* featured a genetically engineered woman fighting for justice and acceptance by normal humans. Meanwhile, demons appear not only in horror movies like *Rosemary's Baby* and *The Exorcist* but also in the programs of our computers, where "daemons" awaken as we boot up and wait to be "summoned" when we need them. Angels connect the world of appearances to a hidden realm of realities.

Playwright Tony Kushner used angels to seek effects that recalled the religious role of drama in ancient Greece. *Angels in America* functioned not just as a play, nor simply as the "gay fantasia on national themes" promised in its subtitle, but as a religious ritual in the form of a drama, a play that attempted to evoke the powers it depicted in order to save the nation. In the climactic scenes of the play, an angel's blessing delays the death of the hero from AIDS; spirits of those who have died from that plague join hands to restore the ozone layer; and representatives of some of the most deeply divided religious communities, cultural groups, and geographical regions of the nation (Mormons and Jews, African Americans and liberal Protestants, straight and gay, Salt Lake City and New York City) come together at the statue of the Angel of Bethesda in Central Park. Among all of the possible symbols of religions, only angels could work for all the parties within such a ritual drama. Only angels, with their lack of commitments to dogma and their ambiguous gender, could integrate gay sex, gay love, and gay rights into solemn statements about the mission of America and the meaning of history. And yet—fulfilling the American tendency to transform angels into servants of humanity—the humans of *Angels in America* dominate the angels and ultimately use them for their own purposes. The human prophet of the play refuses the message of the angel who comes to him, seizes the angel to get the blessing of more life, and tells the angel principalities of the seven continents what to do about their abandonment by God.

Structure of This Book

This book attempts to participate in the angelic capacity to transcend categories. In particular, it blurs the boundaries normally separating disciplines like the history of religion, cultural studies, art history, gender studies, and philosophical theology to explore the role of angels in American culture at many levels. Chapter 2, "Angels in the Material World," takes a general survey of how angels move in material forms through the American marketplace. Among the angel products it considers are Victoria's Secret bras, collectible figurines from Precious Moments and Willow Tree, and Hallmark Christmas decorations. The chapter also looks at angels in folk art by Howard Finster and Andy Lakey and at a series of guardian angel murder mysteries. In the course of this survey, it should become clear that the American religion of angels has a material and institutional basis in thousands of retail stores, in the manufacturing and distribution network for angel products, and in the work of countless commercial artists. This religion does not grow

The Continental Principality of America, as portrayed by Ellen McLoughlin (facing page) on Broadway and Emma Thompson in the HBO television production of Angels in America, *crashes through the roof of an apartment to call a gay man, dying of AIDS, to his prophetic vocation. The character of Prior Walter (facing page) was played by Stephen Spinella. (Photofest/Photofest; Joan Marcus/HBO)*

from traditional American sources of cultural power in the Northeast but from the South and West, with its center in the neighborhood of Kansas City (home of Hallmark and Walt Disney).

The third chapter, "Angels Come from Persia," travels to prebiblical times to describe the origins of angels. It then passes quickly through the Middle Ages and the Renaissance to focus briefly on the American colonies, which were established at a time when a burst of interest in angels and in warfare with demons was gripping both England and Spain. During the nineteenth and early twentieth centuries, angels gradually moved from formal and sectarian religion into the new mass culture of the industrial world, descending from the paintings and statues of churches and the words of sermons into the pages of literature and the public art of cemeteries and war memorials. The writers who contributed to that story ranged from Herman Melville, Henry Wadsworth Longfellow, and Walt Whitman to Spiritualist best-seller Elizabeth Stuart Phelps, whose movement was mercilessly parodied in the angel stories of Mark Twain. The most prominent American painters and sculptors of that era, from Thomas Cole and Abbott Thayer to Horatio Greenough, Emma Stebbins, and Daniel Chester French, also took part. By the end of the journey from ancient Persia to the modern Midwest, the normal sex of angels in art had changed from male to female.

In "Angels, Therapists, and Exorcists," chapter 4, the focus shifts to the angel explosion of the late twentieth century, when books on encounters with angels and instructions on contacting angels proliferated. Seeking the roots of angel therapies, this chapter considers several angel movies, such as *It's a Wonderful Life*, that have presented influential models of the angel as therapist. The story of angel therapy also includes a wave of concern for demonic possession that preceded and followed *The Exorcist* and a new set of angels and demons on television shows like *Highway to Heaven* and *Touched by an Angel*.

Women wrote most of the angel books and suffered most of the demonic attacks in this period, but the women of angel therapy were not often romantically involved with spirits. The fifth chapter, on "Angels, Love, and Sex," deals with romantic stories of angels. It begins with biblical accounts of angel/human marriage and proceeds to the flirtations and deeper encounters of angels and humans in American novels and films, from *The Bishop's Wife* and its remake, *The Preacher's Wife*, to

Jack Nicholson's Satan in *The Witches of Eastwick* and John Travolta's *Michael*. The chapter also considers how angels have figured in popular love songs, from *Teen Angel* and *Johnny Angel* to the music of Jimi Hendrix, Sarah McLachlan, and the Goo Goo Dolls.

Chapter 6, "Angels of War and Apocalypse," starts with the usefulness of angels to leaders of the War on Terror. It explores the roles of angels in American wars against a background beginning with war stories in the Bible and extending through colonial wars, the Civil War, and World War II, citing movies like *A Guy Named Joe* (1944) as well as recent evangelical fiction. Especially vivid imagery of fighting angels appears in the novels of Frank Peretti from the 1980s and the *Left Behind* series of Christian bestsellers that blossomed around the year 2000. Considering the association between angels and the end of the world, the chapter draws a distinction between angels of prophetic and apocalyptic literature and ends with the angels of apocalyptic comedies like *The Horn Blows at Midnight* (a Jack Benny movie of 1946) and *Dogma* (1999).

Finally, chapter 7, "New Angels and Superheroes," attempts to synthesize trends that continue to shape the American religion of angels today. As Western history moves full circle to its Mesopotamian roots, movies like *Crash* (2004) and *Prairie Home Companion* (2006) show American angels becoming more multicultural, more physical, and more intimately engaged with humans. Angel believers from New Age and evangelical camps share equally in these trends. Although the sides of the culture war denounce each other as satanic, and Satan increasingly appears in our political discourse, scholars like Lynn Schofield Clark and David Chidester have noticed that those who see Satan and other angels share some common ground. According to my reading of popular culture, a new mythology has emerged in comic books, science fiction, and fantasy, from *Superman* to *Star Trek* to *Charmed* to the angels of anime and artistic websites, where superheroes develop into angel substitutes and technology endows humans with angelic powers.

The book concludes after reviewing theories of angels developed by American philosophers like William James and Mortimer Adler, adventurous clergy such as Andrew Greeley and Matthew Fox, and scientists with New Age inclinations. Here I add my own theory to the mix. Together, these American theories amount to a pragmatic gospel of angels that inspires both hope and fear. Some readers may suspect it is an example of the "different gospel" that Paul warned the Galatians should be rejected, even if "we, or an angel from heaven, should preach" it (Gal. 1:8).

In all parts of this story, Americans find angels very useful. Responding to the abundant evidence for Americans using angels to serve their human needs, one of my editors for this book asked why people in the United States seem to need so much help that they would develop a religion of angels. The answer may relate to the definitions of religion itself. If religions are systems of meaning and/or relationships that hold life together, the act of coming to America surely weakened such systems for many. The endless mobility of Americans, who change home addresses an average of eleven times in their lives,[19] weakens them further. An American social ideology of self-reliance and individualism also isolates people and, ironically, contributes to the need for supernatural help. Angels may well be the last resort, an insubstantial and infinitely malleable source of community and commitment that remains after most of the networks and traditions of formal religions are lost.

The usefulness of this book will be measured by how well it uses angels to explore the mix of religion and culture in the United States. Scholars have just begun to acknowledge the spiritual effects of a popular culture that has become so saturated with religion that rock stars have taken to singing about their faith and athletes are constantly praying in public. The religious world has become so thoroughly entangled in popular culture that movies like *The Exorcist* and *Star Wars* and *Dogma*, television shows like *Touched by an Angel* and *Charmed*, and novels like *The Celestine Prophecy* and *Left Behind* have caused millions of people to think differently about their formal religious beliefs and even to change their practices, at least as such things are measured by polls and targeted by marketers. Angels are the best exemplars of a culture in which, contrary to the hopes of secularists and fundamentalists, religion and entertainment and art are increasingly one.

 About a thousand malls and shopping districts in the United States hold both a Victoria's Secret lingerie shop and a Hallmark store selling cards and collectible gifts. Because these stores have been filled with angel-themed products for the past decade, they provide useful sites from which to sur-to survey the American religion of angels. The basic, physical presence of angels in contemporary American life is perhaps most obvious in the malls and card shops and toy stores, but it extends to folk art and advertising. New attitudes toward the physical world have become embodied in the angels that move through the country's marketplaces. Though these angels have biblical precedents, they evoke actions and attitudes that theologians have often dismissed as pagan. Reverence for human emotions and for nature is consistently expressed by the material angels of the United States. Usually, the angels who teach this reverence for nature and emotions are ideal images of women and children, though they can also be scruffy men or even animals.

Angels of the Mall

In every Victoria's Secret lingerie show since 1999, models have walked the runway (or descended from the ceiling, as Heidi Klum did in 2003) in scant underwear and huge wings. The most prominent models are known as "Victoria's Secret Angels." Many of the bras belong to a collection called "Angels," the store's cosmetics are named "Dream Angels," and customers can use "Angel credit cards" to buy everything.

These winged models echo a painting by Abbott Thayer (1849–1921), a great American artist who portrayed his daughter Mary as an angel in 1889 and later in a dozen other paintings, at least partially in response to the death of his wife. The first of Thayer's paintings of Mary, simply called "Angel," was popular from its first exhibition, has been widely reproduced as a poster, and appeared on the cover of the best-selling

Abbott Henderson Thayer,
Angel, *1887. Oil on canvas.*
36 1/4 x 28 1/8 in. (92 x 71.5 cm).
(Smithsonian American Art
Museum. Gift of John Gellatly)

book *Ask Your Angels* in 1992. Both Thayer's angels and the Victoria's Secret models combine beauty and innocence. As Thayer said, wings create "an exalted atmosphere." A contemporary critic commented that there was "a lovely hint of the human and intimate" in Thayer's angels. "Yet they are not of this earth," he said. "They have a mystic air, and a glance that fathoms the beyond."[1]

Wings, however, also belong to animals. In the male gaze of a patriarchal culture, delicately dressed women with lithe bodies and wings bring together physical and spiritual appeal, embodying the American sexual ethic that I have called "innocent ecstasy."[2] Such angels promise transcendence within the body, offering a taste of Heaven without the need to die. They suggest feeling beyond the limits of human capacity, with freedom from guilt and hope for eternity (which, capitalized, becomes Eternity, the name of a Calvin Klein perfume). By bringing spirit into the marketplace and into the bedroom, the angels of Victoria's Secret and Abbott Thayer fulfill the basic mission of angels, to mediate between matter and spirit. Like most American angels, they take part in the American dream of making *this* world a sacred place, at least a Magic Kingdom if not a Kingdom of God. Not that these two dream kingdoms should be entirely equated—the angelic Mary Thayer wore loose tunics,

Heidi Klum, from The Victoria's Secret Fashion Show *on CBS, 2003. (Photofest)*

not seamless underwire Angels bras—but humans need earthly symbols for their heavenly aspirations.

Americans buy angel figurines and jewelry in almost 6,000 Hallmark stores, and stores without the Hallmark name selling the company's cards and other products number in the tens of thousands. Angel bras and Dream Angel perfume are available in about 1,000 Victoria's Secret lingerie shops across the United States, and through the Victoria's Secret catalog and website. Representations of angels elsewhere range from female figurines and babies wearing wings to movie characters like Clarence, the guardian angel from the 1946 film *It's a Wonderful Life*, who appears as a genial, white-haired man. Angels for children include the Care Bears, whose videos and picture books show them descending from the heavenly Care-A-Lot to free the frozen victims of Professor Coldheart. Adolescents can follow the exploits of Archangel, a winged mutant hero among the X-men, and use Angel of Wrath and Exalted Angel cards to play "Magic: the Gathering." In the online role-playing games "Diablo" (1997) and "Diablo II" (2000), players meet archangels Tyrael, Inarius, and Izual and battle seven demons, from Duriel, Lord of Pain, to Baal, Lord of Destruction, before they face Diablo himself.[3] On the websites of a popular artist named Allison Carmichael, the angels Michael and Gabriel, Azrael, Lucifer, and Satan appear as lovely, squabbling teens.[4]

From Wal-Mart to Barnes and Noble to Blockbuster, angel figurines, books and movies about angels, Angel Oracle Cards, angel pins, and products advertised by angels move steadily through the marketplace, adding notes of purity and hope. Even in the National Cathedral of Washington, D.C., a site dedicated to the formal religion of Christianity in the Anglican tradition and to the American civil religion (as the site for the 9/11 memorial service and services after the deaths of presidents), the bookstore during the Christmas season of 2006 stocked volumes called *Angel Cats: Divine Messengers of Comfort* (2004); *Angel Dogs: Divine Messengers of Love* (2005); and *Angel Horses: Divine Messengers of Hope* (2006).[5] The generic spirituality of angels enables them to take every form and to enter every setting in American society without giving offense or detracting from the process of buying and selling. At Christmas, Nativity scenes rarely appear in the mall, but angels always do. The angels of material culture unify the whole spectrum of religions and attitudes toward religion—not only Protestant, Catholic, Jew, and Muslim, but also New Age, Neopagan, Goth, Punk, and "spiritual"—in the United States.

To approach the angels of American culture, one must first renounce the retreat to abstraction, the attitude of scorn for the market and even for the physical world, which scholars have inherited from theologians. Theology teaches that angels have no bodies. Following Aristotle, the Jewish thinker Moses Maimonides and the Christian Thomas Aquinas divorced angels from the world of matter in the 1200s. By that time, Muslims had already distinguished the angels, whom they saw as creatures of light, from the genii, or *jinn,* who are creatures of fire;[6] the angels of Islam have neither bodies nor emotions and never fail to carry out their missions from God. The notion of an angel like Clarence from *It's a Wonderful Life* trying to earn his wings by helping a human is alien to orthodox Jewish, Christian, and Muslim angelology. What would Maimonides or Aquinas say of a culture so prolific in angels that it tells children inspirational stories about teddy bears who live in Heaven while at the same time using a fat, unshaven, incompetent guardian angel to market Capital One credit cards?

An average Hallmark store stocks angel statues and pins in at least a dozen forms, most prominently as collectible figurines from brands like Willow Tree, Precious Moments, Boyd's Collectibles, Serenity, and several other sources. These angels are sometimes crafted to mark events like birthdays and weddings, but more often to convey emotional messages like Gratitude, Love, or Peace. Some can be quite mundane: The Boyd's collection has a "retired" figure (no longer made, but still sold, so that its value increases) called Mrs. Fries, the Guardian Angel of Waitresses, who holds an enormous platter of food. Hallmark's own brand of collectible Christmas tree ornaments (released in mid-July, as it is every year) for 2006 featured Veronica, a white-haired little girl with small white wings, who is standing on a cloud and playing a flute. Veronica was the nineteenth in a series called Mary's Angels after their creator Mary Hamilton, who has worked for fifty years designing Hallmark cards and began designing angels in 1988. The ornaments for 2006 also included a repainted version of Hamilton's first angel ornament, now called Angelica (the original was named Buttercup). Other designers contributed angel ornaments with names like All Is Calm (a Black

Willow Tree Angel of Grace *(kneeling) and* Courage, *by Susan Lordi.*
(Collection of Peter Gardella, photo by William Gardella)

female angel, dressed entirely in white, holding a white dove and an
olive branch); The Gift of Love (a blonde angel in a green and white
dress with small white wings, holding a green sphere by a golden ribbon); and Angel of Life (another blonde, reclining against huge white
wings, wrapped in a pink shawl, with very red lips and holding a branch
with green leaves).

The most popular form of angel figurine in Hallmark stores, usually
found in a display near the cash register, is the Willow Tree line of angels
without faces designed by Susan Lordi. Carved from clay, replicated in
resin, and costing as little as twelve dollars in their smallest (four-inch)
forms, these angels first appeared in 2000 in a Nativity set that included
fifteen angels. Their bodies look and feel porous and organic, in contrast
to most figurines. In place of facial features Lordi uses bodily posture,
hand and arm positions, and held objects to express spiritual and emotional states. Her first creation was an Angel of Healing, who holds a
bird in her hands as she bends gently to the right, inclining her head
toward the bird. "I was thinking about the idea of fragility and how we

need to heal our inside—our soul," Lordi is quoted as saying on a Willow Tree website.[7] Her other angels include Angel of the Spirit, Serenity, Angel of Grace, Angel of Remembrance, Welcoming Angel, Angel of the Garden, Angel of the Kitchen, and Angels of Summer, Autumn, Winter, and Spring. All these angels are female and most are white, with the exception of the very pious Spirit (who kneels) and Grace, who have dark, blank faces. Their wings are sixteen loops of wire rusted to a dark brown, with eight loops on each side, arranged in groups of three on the outside, two in the middle, and three closest to the angel's back. As Lordi has said, the wire wings "have lightness" and "add visual movement and at times seem to flutter" while remaining "very simple and humble."

Although these simple bodies, with what one of my students has called "coat-hanger wings," provide easy targets for mockery, they have an undeniable power for those who allow themselves to see. Their facelessness causes the viewer to "become a participant in the understanding of the piece," as Lordi has said. She was inspired by dolls sewn by Amish women, who do not make faces because their religion prohibits idols. Facelessness also links the Willow Tree angels with Neopagan poppets, used in magic, and with the Muslim tradition of never painting the Prophet Muhammad's face.

Judging by the market penetration of the Willow Tree angels, they succeed in bridging religious groups normally separated by broad gaps of doctrine and practice. Susan Lordi traces her emotional inspiration to "growing up in a very huggy, extended Italian family." Though Lordi and her sister deny any Catholic affiliation or inspiration,[8] the figures certainly express a Catholic sense that bodies and emotions can be sacramental. Lordi also drew on the very reserved German Protestant tradition of the Amish, not only in making her angels faceless but also in making them in clay and resin and muted colors rather than in the brightly colored and polished surfaces of many other angels found in Hallmark stores. These angels are also marketed across religious divisions: Calls to several Hallmark stores indicated that Willow Tree is the best-selling angel line in the Mormon capital, Salt Lake City, just as it is in Connecticut. More surprisingly, Lordi's angels are sold in the Deseret Book Stores run by the Mormon church, even though Mormon doctrine holds that angels have no wings. The Deseret stores generally stock specifically Mormon statues like the Angel Moroni blowing his trumpet or the prophet Joseph Smith. A web search under "Susan Lordi Catholic" shows that many stores specializing in Roman Catholic books and religious articles also stock Willow Tree angels. Meanwhile, people who practice astrology, acupuncture, and T'ai Chi are also sending Serenity or Grace to their friends in the form of a Willow Tree angel. Browsing the newsletter of an evangelical Episcopal church in San Antonio, one finds the "Chi Rho Bookstore" of the church announcing in May 2005 that it had stocked "several new additions to the immensely popular Willow Tree line," including Happiness, Thank You, Joy, and New Life. The story rejoiced that "pet lovers have not been overlooked," because "now you can find a puppy among the angels."[9] Over the years Lordi has added many nonwinged figurines to her line, but the concept of angels as personified emotions still animates the group. With Willow Tree, the creation and selling, exchanging and displaying of material angels has become a remarkably ecumenical form of religious practice.

More specifically Christian and more intense in their effects, the Precious Moments figurines designed by Missouri artist Samuel Butcher are often called "the number-one collectible in the United States." The teardrop-shaped eyes of these children are far more familiar to Americans than Susan Lordi's faceless figures, in part because Butcher has been drawing and marketing them in many forms, including greeting cards and cartoon versions of Bible stories, since 1974. The first time he saw one of his drawings made in a three-dimensional form, according to the Precious Moments website, "Sam was so overwhelmed . . . that he fell to his knees and wept." That account concludes that "it was the beginning of a phenomenon for both Sam and the gift industry."[10]

More than 1,500 Precious Moments figurines have been marketed since that dramatic moment in 1978. The smallest of the porcelain versions sell for about thirty dollars, and many cost twice or three times that much. In Hallmark stores, they are kept in locked glass cases against a wall. Although all of the figures derive from the tradition of *putti*, or baby cherubs, that began in the Renaissance, only a small subset of the Precious Moments figures in stores are angels with wings. The wings are usually white and short, and very short in the case of the baby angels, who also wear robes with a patch or two to make them look poor and humble. Gold, tubular halos often sit at odd angles on their heads.

Safely Home, *a Precious Moments figurine by Samuel Butcher. (Collection of Peter Gardella, photo by William Gardella)*

Because the Precious Moments figures are children (or babies taking childlike poses) they have become associated with the right-to-life movement opposing abortion rights, participating in the same aesthetic as the "precious feet" pins directly sold by right-to-life groups. They express nostalgia for babyhood that suited the demographic moment of their introduction, the "baby bust" of the mid-1970s when the U.S. birthrate reached a low point equaled only at the bottom of the Great Depression.

Precious Moments angels have something no other collectible angel has—a sacred site of their own, called Inspiration Park.[11] At Carthage, Missouri, near the geographic and population center of the United States, Samuel Butcher opened the Precious Moments Chapel in 1989. Approached by a path lined with small angel statues blowing trumpets and marked by colorful angels on signs, the chapel holds no actual services but receives about 400,000 visitors per year. They enter through a bronze door that features three Precious Moments child angels, one holding a cross, with words from the prophet Habakkuk—"The Lord is in his holy temple; let all the earth keep silence before him"—in all caps across the top. In one sense, the chapel is a monument to deceased children. The front wall is covered by a painting called Hallelujah Square, in which the risen Christ—the only adult in the chapel—receives winged children into Paradise. The side walls are lined with paintings that show Precious Moments children in robes carrying lambs and taking part in other scenes that reference the parables of Jesus and the Psalms of David. On the ceiling is a fresco of blue sky and clouds, with Precious Moments child angels flying and playing among them. After leaving the main room of the chapel, visitors pass into the Memorial Rooms, one of which replicates the room that the artist's son, who was killed by a drunk driver at age twenty-seven, lived in as a seven-year-old. Large memorial books are available to visitors to write the names of deceased loved ones. Outside the chapel is a Resurrection Cave, with a Precious Moments angel at the entrance to represent the angel who told the disciples that Jesus was not in the tomb. Celebrating Christ's victory over death, a Fountain of Angels in another building features tiers of angels under jets of water that soar to a height of 80 feet, accompanied by a light show and music by the London Symphony Orchestra. Inspiration Park also includes a wedding chapel for those who wish to marry at the sacred site; a gallery museum illustrating the history of Precious Moments; and a store that stocks the largest selection of Precious Moments figurines in the world.

Beyond Willow Tree and Precious Moments, Hallmark stores carry many other versions of angels. The same company, Demdaco, that distributes the Willow Tree line also offers Journey of Grace angels by Nancy Carter, whose figures are female heads framed by wings. These angels have expressive, somewhat cartoonish faces and bear names of emotional states like "Effortless Joy," "Nurturing Kindness," and "Dream's Possibility." Those who seek a more traditional style may prefer Seraphim Classics angels, made from resin "fortified with both porcelain and marble," according to the manufacturer's website. These elaborate female figures, modeled on "the greatest artistic achievements of the Renaissance Masters" by Seraphim's chief sculptor, Gaylord Ho, have large wings and gracefully flowing robes. Their names and titles include "Vanessa—Heavenly Maiden" and emphasize nature and emotions, with such characters as "Ariel—Heaven's Shining Star"; "Harmony—Love's Guardian"; "Emily—Heaven's Treasure"; and "Alyssa—Nature's

Angel." A more modern and casual version of the same lovely-woman-with-wings motif is offered under the title of Charming Angels by Boyd's Collectibles. Among the Charming Angels are Alessandra, Guardian of Hope; Amissa, Guardian of Friendship; Aurora, Guardian of Dreams; Oceania, Angel of the Seas; and Christiana, Guardian of Secrets. Both Seraphim Classics and Charming Angels run around thirty dollars each. For fifteen dollars, the Pavilion Gift Company offers Kneeded Angels, softer figures whose designs are "handmade from bread dough" by artist Carol A. Graziano and translated into plastic, with fabric wings.[12]

More explicitly religious angels are available in the Foundations series by artist Karen Hahn and in the Heartwood Creek stone resin figures by artist Jim Shore. Shore's Heartwood angels are the largest in most stores, measuring ten to thirteen inches in height; some stores stock them only for Christmas. These angels normally stand quite straight and wear large skirts on which elaborate pictures, such as Jesus kneeling in the garden of Gesthemane, a Nativity scene, or a gathering of angels in Heaven, may appear. Stylistically, the patterns and colors of the Heartwood angels combine the effects of "folk art" and quilting with the texture of wood, though the figures are actually cast in stone resin. Shore also does angels with scenes of the seasons, and even his most Christian messages have a natural rather than a cultivated look. In the less folksy Foundations series, Karen Hahn uses the skirts of her angels (which are also stone resin, but glazed rather than wooden in texture) to display religious quotes. Her Angel of Peace, for example, releases a dove with one hand while her skirt proclaims the prayer of St. Francis of Assisi, "Lord, make me an instrument of your peace." Foundations angels sometimes quote the Bible, but more often figures from Christian history.

Underlying the collectible angels is a corporate structure and a set of artists centered in the American heartland around Kansas City. Demdaco, the owners of Willow Tree and Journey of Grace, is headquartered in Stilwell, Kansas, and distributes from a warehouse in north Kansas City. Susan Lordi, the Willow Tree artist, is identified on the Willow Tree website as living in Kansas City. Samuel Butcher's Inspiration Park lies near Joplin, Missouri, less than three hours' drive south of Kansas City. Corporations like Enesco, on the other hand, which bought the land for Inspiration Park and which has distributed Heartwood Creek and Foundations angels, and Roman, Inc., the manufacturer of

Seraphim Classics, are headquartered near Chicago. Sometimes corporate relations between the Kansas City and Chicago companies have proved stormy. After sales of Precious Moments figurines fell from a high of $206 million in 1996 to $55 million in 2004, Samuel Butcher ended his licensing of Precious Moments figures to Enesco and began using his own company to distribute from closer to Inspiration Park in Carthage, Missouri; however, Butcher and Enesco have more recently made a new agreement.

The most constant factor in the Kansas City base of angel manufacture and sales is Hallmark Cards, Inc., the company whose building defines the skyline of Kansas City and whose stores serve as missionary chapels for tens of millions who take part in the informal religion of angels. Founded in 1910 by Joyce C. Hall, the son of a Methodist preacher who started his career as a child distributing literature in Nebraska for his grandfather, an advocate for prohibition, Hallmark has maintained a culture of commitment to high-minded sentiment.[13] The founder introduced the company slogan, "When you care enough to send the very best," in 1944 and ran the company until 1966, when his son Donald J. Hall succeeded him. Company management went to a third generation when Donald J. Hall, Jr., took over leadership in 2002. Hallmark reported net revenues of $4.2 billion in 2005, with 18,000 employees worldwide and 4,500 at the Kansas City headquarters.[14] If each of the more than 5,600 Hallmark stores in the United States sold just one angel figurine per day, the chain would distribute about 2 million angels per year. When one considers Hallmark alongside Precious Moments, the Demdaco corporation, and Walt Disney, who also came from Kansas City, and whose Walt Disney World hosts a Precious Moments Weekend every September, it seems easy to fix the geographic center of the American religion of angels. The only rabbi to contribute to the spate of popular angel books of the 1990s was Morris B. Margolies, who served as rabbi of Congregation Beth Shalom, a Conservative synagogue in Kansas City.[15]

Just as the religion of angels stems from the center of the continental United States, so the Victoria's Secret shops that began in San Francisco, with allusions to Victorian England, have gravitated to the center of American culture since their acquisition by The Limited, a company headquartered in Columbus, Ohio. Although marketing sexy underwear seemed edgy when Victoria's Secret started in 1977, the brand long ago entered the mainstream, and to do so it employed a metaphor of angels. In an average Victoria's Secret store, as of 2006, many products called "Angels" are gathered at the center of the store. The space nearest the door is filled with Pink, a line of bras and underwear, tops, and sleepwear directed at college-age women. At the back are items branded as Sexy Little Things and Very Sexy, designed for special occasions and for women who, in the words of a clerk at one store, have the bodies of dancers. In the center are Angels bras, including Ipex Angels, Angels Secret Embrace, and many other varieties, along with Angels tops and nightwear, all targeted at the central customer demographic, women between twenty-five and forty-five years old and their husbands and friends. The appeal of the whole Angels line is that the items are pretty and flirtatious but demure, emphasizing pastel colors rather than the dark shades of the "sexy" outfits at the back of the store or the hot pink clothing at the front. Allied with the Angels clothing is the line of cosmetics, body lotions, and perfumes called Dream Angels, introduced in 2005.

Victoria's Secret began to market Angels bras in 1999, but angels in lingerie represent an idea that was always central to the business. Founded by a Stanford graduate and San Francisco entrepreneur named Ray Raymond in 1977, Victoria's Secret was intended from the beginning to project an atmosphere of refined and elevated sensuality.[16] Raymond found the attitudes of lingerie saleswomen too clinical—or too embarrassing for male shoppers looking for gifts for their wives or girlfriends—and the products available in department stores either too frilly or too conservative. His use of Victorian boudoir furnishings in his first store, along with an emphasis on seductive styles, led to sales of half a million dollars in the first year, immediate expansion, and appropriation of the concept by The Limited in 1982. By the mid-1990s, Victoria's Secret had become the largest lingerie retailer in the country, but sales were beginning to stagnate. The introduction of Angels, the first line of seamless and label-free "enhancer" bras, revivified business. The new bras were introduced on a Valentine's Day webcast in 1999 that was called "An Evening of Fantasy and Myth." This was the first show that featured models with wings (designed by Martin Izquierdo, a costume and scene designer noted for work in ballet and on Broadway). Wings have since appeared in every Victoria's Secret show through the summer of 2006, when models Gisele Bundchen, Karolina Kurkova, and Adriana Lima designed wings for themselves and auctioned them on eBay to benefit Free Arts New York, an art education program for at-risk children.[17]

Art depicting angels often connects with charity in American popular culture, further linking angels to the improvement of the material world. One line of statuettes in the Hallmark stores, "Sarah's Angels," is sold in packaging that briefly tells the story of a woman named Sarah Lee, who died at forty years of age from cancer after a remission of several years that was promised her by angels; part of the proceeds from these angel figurines is said to be donated to "a cancer fighting cause." Each major brand of angel figurines makes some gesture in the direction of charity, such as dedicating proceeds from one of its figures to breast cancer research. As a spokesman for Roman Seraphim Angels, Ross Bainbridge, wrote on his website, "collectors like knowing that their purchase is going towards a worthy cause," and so "Roman donates tens of thousands of dollars" each year to several named charities.[18]

Angels and toys come together in the Care Bears, the stars of several movies and a television show in the 1980s. These characters live on in Care Bear products today, providing an example of angels emerging entirely from the marketplace. To discover the angelic character of Care Bears, one needs only read the package copy from the VHS of their first movie: "Way up high where the clouds and rainbows live, the Care Bears watch over the Earth and make sure everyone is kind and friendly to one another." When they notice things going wrong, as when an Evil Spirit from a book of spells lures a lonely young man to cast a spell that takes away people's feelings, or when Professor Coldheart literally freezes people, they come to the rescue. The bears also accomplish cosmically angelic tasks, such as replacing stolen stars and redirecting a Cloud Worm that threatens to eat their homes in Care-A-Lot. After being sent to a cloudy area, the Worm helps people there to have sunny days. The primary weapon of the Care Bears is to stand together (there were originally ten Care Bears, with names like Tenderheart Bear and Share Bear, Funshine Bear and Wish Bear, and a comic relief figure named Grumpy Bear) and do the "Care Bear Stare," projecting love from the symbols on their stomachs. This weapon is stronger if more bears do it, of course. While the stories inculcate various lessons, like not running away from home, the primary lesson is always to care for others, and even for those who make things difficult.

The Care Bears began to appear in 1981 as greeting card characters drawn by artist Elena Kucharik for American Greetings, a competitor of Hallmark based in Cleveland. Founded in 1906 by Jacob Sapirstein (1885–1987), a Russian-Polish immigrant who was the son of a rabbi, American Greetings is the largest publicly owned greeting card company in the world and employs about as many people as Hallmark.[19] Like the family-owned Hallmark, the company is still run by direct descendents of the founder. American Greetings has stores that sell Willow Tree angels and Precious Moments figurines just as Hallmark does. The story of American Greetings provides ample evidence that the American marketplace for angels is not by any means just a Christian or even a New Age phenomenon. The market is truly ecumenical and includes Jews from the broadest level of merchandising to the highest levels of culture, as demonstrated by Tony Kushner and his *Angels in America.* Other Jews work with the images of angels at every level in between.

As a distributor not only of cards but also of toys made from artificial fur and plastic, American Greetings showcases the many new materials used in the manufacture of contemporary angels. Instead of Abbott Thayer's oil paints, or the marble and bronze of angel statues, mass-produced collectibles are made of various resins and plastics. French philosopher Roland Barthes noted in the 1950s that the whole hierarchy of materials traditionally used in the manufacture of goods was being replaced by a single category, "plastic," from which everything could be made. Barthes also pointed out how often the scientific names of new materials had names that evoked Greek myth (for example, "polystyrene"). Historian of religion David Chidester has more recently written about "plastic religion" and the twentieth-century "Age of Plastic," which has culminated in an age of silicon and infinitely malleable bodies based on nothing but information.[20] In such an age, anyone can make a religious image that everyone can share, and the whole world of images can be absorbed into a system and interpreted as revelation.

Direct intervention of angels in the marketplace took place in a story by Joan Wester Anderson, a prominent religious author who contributed *Where Angels Walk* to the angel therapy books. In "Miracle at Wal-Mart," Anderson recounted the story of Ruby Whitehurst, a woman who used the Wal-Mart sale after Thanksgiving to seek Christmas gifts for the children of a poor woman from Puerto Rico who worked with her. The woman had told Whitehurst that her daughter wanted a Cabbage Patch doll and her son a remote-control truck, but neither item appeared at the Wal-Mart on Thanksgiving Friday. Whitehurst bought other gifts and went home, but then began to feel restless. "My spirit was telling me to purchase the Cabbage Patch baby and two remote control trucks," Whitehurst told Anderson. She returned to Wal-Mart for the second time on that crowded shopping day, and by the front door she found "a stack of very nice Dodge Ram remote control trucks" that had not been there earlier. Then she saw a shelf containing Cabbage Patch babies, but it came to her that she wanted a Hispanic doll to give to the Puerto Rican girl. Finding no such doll among those on the shelf, she put a different doll in her cart, but still felt unsatisfied. An older woman who noticed her dilemma told her about another shelf of dolls at the back of the store. She went there, prevailed on a reluctant clerk to get a particular doll she could not reach, and got one with a birth certificate (a distinctive feature of Cabbage Patch dolls) that read "Consuelo Tavia." Whitehurst exulted, "Brown skin, brown eyes. . . . A Hispanic baby for a Hispanic child. And the only one there." Thrilled by her success, she went home, but she returned the following Saturday to get presents for others on her list. She found no bin of remote-control cars, no shelf of Cabbage Patch dolls on the back wall, and no clerk who remembered either. Only angelic intervention could explain the sudden appearance and disappearance of the toys. "I think the angels are taking very good care of me this Christmas," Whitehurst told Anderson. "And why not?" the author commented. "Her generous soul receives its own gifts."[21]

Angels in Visionary Art

Some of the most important American angel art of the past few decades has arisen directly from religious experience. And some claim that this work also has the power to heal as people look at or touch the angels within the pictures. The angels of Howard Finster (1915–2001), a Baptist preacher from Georgia, and Andy Lakey (b. 1959), a former car salesman from California, express a range of sentiments, from evangelical to New Age. Beginning at either end of that religious spectrum, Finster and Lakey have contributed to an American drive to sacralize the material world.

Finster began his career in 1919 at the age of three, when his beloved fourteen-year-old sister, Abbie, died after being bitten by a rabid dog. Shortly thereafter, wandering lost amid tomato plants while looking for his mother on the family farm in Alabama, the toddling Finster looked into the sky and saw his sister "about the height of a house," wearing a long white robe over a familiar skirt and descending to him on a series of steps. Abbie did not tell him where his mother was, but she said, "Howard, you're gonna be a man of visions." Finster called this experience "the foundation for my visions" and "the hard rock o' my faith in my visions."[22] His visions included Heaven and Hell, and therefore angels and demons, but also many other, especially allegorical, scenes. After being called to preach at the age of fifteen, Finster proclaimed his call at a revival. He preached in the self-taught Baptist tradition for decades, moving from one church to another and sometimes working odd jobs to support himself.

In 1976, Finster discovered that only one of those gathered for an afternoon service could remember what he had preached in the morning. He then became inspired to dedicate himself entirely to sacred art. Using found materials, from Coke bottles to parts from automobile wrecks and old bicycles, he created a 4-acre theme park called Paradise Gardens, located about 100 miles from Atlanta. The curator of the American Folk Art Museum visited in 1978 and called it the most satisfying work of art he had ever seen, and the park continued to grow for years thereafter. Finster became famous, went on Johnny Carson's *Tonight Show*, and gained a reputation among art critics and broad influence in the art world; he has been called "the Elvis of folk art."[23] Some have testified that the art had the effect that Finster intended, because their lives were changed by visiting Paradise Gardens or looking at his other drawings or painted objects. Although Paradise Gardens fell into disrepair after Finster died in 2001, there is a nonprofit organization seeking to restore the site. A local museum also features Finster's work, and some of his angels have found their way to the Smithsonian in Washington, D.C., and to galleries in New York.

Finster's depictions of angels merged the angelic and the human. In Paradise Gardens, a human-sized guardian angel made of wood flies

Howard Finster made many versions of this basic angel form and gave or sold them to many people. This angel was given by Finster to Frederica Mathewes-Green, a Christian activist and writer. (Courtesy of Frederica Mathewes-Green)

over the path, wearing long black hair and a long white robe, and its wings contain scores of names of people Finster knew and thought of as friends. Two of Finster's other angels have wings containing the images of human faces. Many Finster angels are flying, bodies parallel to the ground and heads held up and smiling. In another mode, Finster put wings on full-length portraits of people, including himself and Elvis Presley.[24] He came (after a vision in 1977) to believe that he had lived on many other planets and had been sent by God to preach on Earth. Elvis, he thought, had been meant to spend the last years of his life preaching.

When Howard Finster told his wife that he had lived on other planets, she urged him not to tell anyone else, but the vision actually fit into a consistent worldview. Finster combined an old-time Baptist emphasis on escaping Hell and damnation with a sense of unity between the human and divine that resembled the doctrines of the Mormons, the perspectives of some American New Age writers, and the visions of the Swedish scientist and mystic Emanuel Swedenborg (1688–1772), who also saw angels. Heaven and Hell were not incorporeal states of mind but physical planets for Finster. When Jesus spoke of new heavens and a new earth, he was referring to a new planet, Finster said, and Finster believed that his visions revealed what happened on many planets. In one painting, called *This Board Shows a Speck of God's Endless Space*, Finster showed more than two dozen planets inhabited by people and angels of various kinds. One of these planets had angels who went up and down between the surface and the interior, where they lived, in long "silos,"

Finster's visions included whole worlds and scenes in which angels acted out the drama of salvation. Howard Finster, The Lord Will Deliver His People across Jordan, *1976. Enamel on fiberboard. 30 1/8 x 29 5/8 in. (76.4 x 75.1 cm). (Smithsonian American Art Museum. Gift of Herbert Wade Hemphill, Jr.)*

from which they emerged to "fly" by skating on a surface of ice. Another planet had people who moved in similar silos to the interior and came to the surface to travel on streets "twenty-five or thirty thousand miles long."[25] By locating angels so vividly in physical worlds, Finster united the genre of science fiction, with its normally world-transforming visions, with the otherworldly message of his faith.

On New Year's Eve of 1986, less than ten years after Finster saw other planets and angels in silos, a young car salesman in California partied too hard. His drinking, combined with freebasing and snorting of cocaine, left him in a seizure on the floor of the shower in his apartment with his heart nearly failing. After he begged God to let him live, he sensed seven angels swirling around him and merging into one. The angel then held his body at the level of his heart and lifted him into another dimension, which he saw in a vision that resembled Finster's. "There were a thousand planets with ten thousand poles of light extending through them and into the void," Lakey wrote. Angels entered the poles of light and moved in them toward a center. But unlike Finster, who went into the silos on two planets and moved up and down with the angels and people who lived there, Lakey could not enter these transportation beams: "I was rejected, bounced off the poles and out of the dimension," he later wrote.[26] He woke up in an emergency room.

Three years of failed attempts to draw what he had seen followed. After a second visit from angels, this time without the mediation of cocaine, in 1989, Lakey began to paint his drawings with thick acrylic squeezed out of tubes, on canvas stretched over wood to hold the weight of the paint. The resulting works had dramatic textures. The subject at first was always angels, and angels of the same sort: lozenge-shaped bodies with stubby arms held straight out, and elongated oval heads floating just above the bodies. Complexity grew from the lines inside the angels' bodies or from lines in their surroundings. Eventually other figures—celestial doors, abstract landscapes, humans—joined the angels, but Lakey was on an artistic mission. His angels had charged him in 1989 to complete 2,000 angel paintings by the year 2000, and he reached that goal with a year to spare, on New Year's Eve of 1999. Lakey's numbering of his angel paintings again paralleled the story of Howard Finster, who was "impressed by God" to do 5,000 paintings after being told to make sacred art in 1976.[27]

Success came to Lakey through a friend who let him hang his work in a bank, where an art dealer saw it, and by 1992 Lakey angels were hanging in the collections of former president Jimmy Carter, actor Ed Asner, and Pope John Paul II. When a friend suggested that even blind people could enjoy these angels because of their extreme texture, Lakey contacted Ray Charles and Stevie Wonder, both of whom liked his work. Ed Asner gave a painting to the Lighthouse School for the Blind in New York. Lakey then held what has been called the first exhibition of paintings specifically for the blind. That exhibit caught the attention

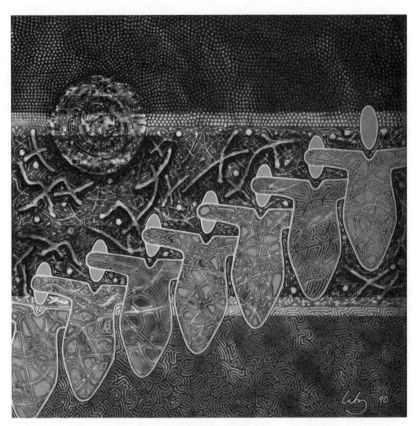

When a car salesman named Andy Lakey nearly died in a drug overdose, he had the experience of being saved by seven angels. After years of work, he produced this depiction of his experience; he went on to create 2000 angel paintings by the year 2000. Andrew Lakey, My Seven Angels, *1990. Acrylic on canvas over wood. 48 x 48 inches. (Collection of the artist, reproduced by permission.)*

of Oprah Winfrey, and Lakey appeared on Winfrey's show in 1994, sharing the story of his rebirth with the world. He still claims to donate 30 percent of the revenue from his art to charities, and especially to charities for the blind.

Now the stories of healing began. An operating-room nurse from San Diego, recovering from a divorce and from chronic pain after a car accident, touched a Lakey painting in a gallery and "felt an intense, hot vibration." She bought the painting and found her pain relieved. A

Seattle postal worker was cured of depression after seeing the first angel painting, *My Seven Angels,* which author Eileen Freeman had used as the frontispiece of her 1993 book, *Touched by Angels.* In Oregon, a dying man bought a small Lakey angel and kept it with him at every moment until his death. A woman who had lost her niece to AIDS found that a Lakey angel channeled the dead girl, who told her that "everything will be all right." Another woman succeeded in becoming pregnant, after years of failed medical interventions, when she purchased a Lakey miniature. Both a psychologist and a New Age healer reported powerful effects from Lakey paintings in their offices.[28]

The artist denied that he possessed any psychic powers but began to paint angels in response to people's specific requests for help. He called these works "healing paintings" and reported that he "felt guided" when he made them. Thinking about how the healings worked, he denied that power inhered in the paintings but claimed that they acted as catalysts that caused those who saw or touched them to "release the spiritual energy that people already have within them." In other words, Lakey claimed that his angels bridged the realms of body and spirit and transformed the material world.

Having been saved and inspired in his art by angels, Andy Lakey found himself becoming an angel channeler and an angel therapist (categories that will be explored more fully in chapter 4). He described the channeling as "an out-of-body experience, as if I'm watching myself paint," and said that he completed his elaborately balanced and detailed patterns "in seconds," not only without a plan but without thinking about them while they took shape. "There's an even number of lines and curves, the dots are placed like they're supposed to be there, it's balanced, but I don't even pay attention to it. . . . The angels go where they want to go."[29] His openness to the angels extended to his communication with humans. Lakey accepted phone calls from women who were mourning the death of a child. For those who sent photographs of their deceased children, he painted what he saw when the photo was taped under the canvas. He called the results "energy paintings," and said of his interactions with the women, "I'm like a pillow for their grief."[30]

While many angel therapists work by consulting their own angels and the angels of their clients, as we will see later, Lakey claimed no such power but worked through the material world. Angels and substances

Another part of Lakey's vision involved angels entering a world to which he was denied access. Andrew Lakey, Angel #840, *1994. Mixed media on canvas over wood. 60 x 72 in. (Collection of the artist, reproduced by permission)*

lay at the heart of his story. Angels had delivered him from substance abuse and imminent death to a life immersed in tubes of thick paint, which he used to make tangible angels in which he and others felt spiritual power.

Ironically, tragically, or (as he might see it) as an opportunity to develop his spiritual life, Lakey fell victim to substances in another way. His painting technique and his production of 2,000 angel paintings during the 1990s resulted in his developing such severe allergic reactions that he has endured five surgeries on his sinuses and now has to paint (when he paints at all) in a haz-mat suit. The works from 2006 displayed on his website were done in colored pencil. As a person rescued by angels, however, Lakey still draws them, despite his difficulties.

Material Angel Helpers

Dramatic material circumstances and material solutions dominate the stories of rescue by angels that have become so prominent in American culture over the past century. In *It's a Wonderful Life*, the Frank Capra movie that resurfaces every Christmas, not only is angel Clarence physical enough to jump into a river, but the peril from which Clarence saves George Bailey, played by Jimmy Stewart, is a suicide in that same river. George Bailey's salvation appears when his friends and neighbors arrive at his home with money, food, and drink on Christmas Eve. Charles Lindbergh won a Pulitzer Prize in 1954 for a book that describes, among other things, the angels who helped him stay awake to fly *The Spirit of St. Louis* on his 1927 transatlantic flight. Evangelist Billy Graham's book *Angels* begins with stories about angels intervening at the Battle of Mons in World War I and angels piloting RAF fighter planes in World War II. Andy Lakey's wife, Chantal, met her angels as they led her down a cliff where her first husband had just fallen to his death. During the 1990s, books crammed with stories of angels rescuing people in peril from automobile crashes, sinking boats, and murderers and rapists on city streets flew off the shelves and to the tops of best-seller lists. Two authors whose works appear in my chapter on the angel therapies of that decade, Sophy Burnham and Doreen Virtue, claimed to have written their books because they were saved by angels from a ski accident and a carjacking, respectively.

Here again, the useful angels of American culture updated biblical precedents. The prophet Elijah, ready to die in the desert as he fled a persecuting king, was fed by an angel in 1 Kings 19; the book of Daniel tells the story of Shadrach, Meshach, and Abednego, who were saved by an angel from the fiery furnace (Dan. 3:25). In the New Testament, angels help Jesus as Elijah was helped in the wilderness (Matt. 4:11), and Peter is set free from prison by an angel who breaks the chains that had bound him (Acts 11:7). Of course, in these biblical cases, angels rescued people who had some purpose of God's to carry out in the history that the Bible was narrating. The American stories might lead one to question why angels catch some people who are falling off cliffs but not others. Often, writers advance the theory that angels respect human freedom and can help only those who call on them for help.[31]

A far milder and more domestic, but still quite physical, sort of angel rescue appears in an ongoing series of mysteries by Mignon Ballard, an American writer who sets her stories in the South. In Ballard's books, the heroine has typically lost her husband or lover to death, divorce, or estrangement and returned to some location of her childhood, where she discovers a murder. The angel who helps solve the case introduces herself as Augusta Goodnight. A middle-aged woman who favors long skirts and beautiful jewelry, she helps not by wielding lightning bolts or flaming swords but by making muffins for breakfast, serving them on the good dishes, and cleaning up. The heroines are skeptical at first. "Was I actually in my grandmother's kitchen having a conversation with some weirdo who claimed to be my guardian angel?"[32] But they soon become appreciative: "Augusta whisked the dishes to the sink, and in seconds they were clean, dry, and put away."

As angel Augusta explains, she is there not so much to intervene as to support. "We can't change things . . . we seek to guide you as best we can—if you let us." While Augusta Goodnight does not know who the villain is, she helps the heroine straighten out her life, mostly by listening and advising as she provides food and keeps house. In the process, she reveals how involved angels are in their own material happiness. For example, Augusta tends strawberries in heavenly gardens when not on assignment. This explains why she tends to leave a faint scent of strawberries behind her in her missions on Earth. She may be the most practical angel among all the spirits of American culture. Mignon Ballard has so far published seven Augusta Goodnight mysteries, and the two most recent, *Too Late for Angels* (2005) and *The Angel and the Jabberwocky Murders* (2006), include appendices with "heavenly recipes" for meals that Augusta made.

A comprehensive call for material help from angels came from the San Francisco rock group Train in 2005. In "Calling All Angels," sung as stanzas of fairly rapid chanting separated by a wailing chorus, Train seeks help with everything from marital strife to environmental crisis. The chanting parts of the song complain about "the atmosphere," invoke a vision of humanity "drowning in a sea spilled from a cup," and worry about television, "marriage lies," and children who have to "play inside so they don't disappear." For all these troubles and more, angels are presented as the answer. Angels can provide "a sign" that help is available, give reassurance that existence has meaning, and, above all, supply someone to answer the repeated "I . . . I'm calling all angels" of the chorus.

"Calling All Angels" violates what evangelical writers on angels have often pointed out (with some justification) as a biblical standard: that people should not pray to angels but only to God. Roman Catholics have always allowed prayers to angels, as to saints (and to some, like St. Michael, who are both angels and saints), and in this song American practice regarding angels resembles the Catholic more than the biblical. The song reveals the character of the American religion of angels not simply in being a prayer, however, but also in the way the prayer focuses on ecological and other material conditions. In typically American fashion, Train calls on angels not just for spiritual aid, but for material and practical help to restore this world.

Another dimension that distinguishes American stories of angel rescue is the explicit role of the marketplace. After all, the suicide from which Clarence saves George Bailey in *It's a Wonderful Life* was provoked by a run on Bailey's building and loan company, so that Bailey's salvation is financial and material. The therapists and doctors who have reported wonderful healing effects on their patients who have touched Andy Lakey's paintings had to first purchase these paintings for their offices. According to angel therapist Doreen Virtue, people should buy plenty of angel art to help them stay in touch with their angels. "Surround yourself with reminders, such as angel statues and posters," Virtue advised, "so you won't forget to call upon your heavenly friends for help and assistance."[33]

Virtue edited selections of angel art into a boxed set called *Messages from Your Angels Oracle Cards*. The first deck of forty-four cards represents work by eight different artists who depict angels that include the traditional Michael, Raphael, and Uriel but change Gabriel to Gabrielle (a frequent choice in contemporary culture) and extend the list to angels known as Athena, Caressa, Chantall, Maya, Merlina, Oceana, Omega, and Shanti, among others. Only one of the nontraditional angels, Daniel, is male. With the cards comes a book of instructions on how to lay out and read spreads of three, four, five, and six cards after asking questions. Categories of questions include soulmates, new love, life purpose, abundance, healing, contacting guardian angels and deceased loved ones, finding out what the angels are trying to tell us, or looking to the future. The effect is much like that of using a Tarot deck, but with no negative images like the Hanged Man. One need not worry about placing the cards wrong, Virtue assures the reader, because "the angels are supervising the process, and their power prevents an incorrect reading."[34] While some of the angels on the cards are depicted as beautiful women in sensual clothing and poses, the messages associated with them, both on the card and in the book, are all very positive and innocuous. At the back of the book are instructions for contacting the artists who designed the cards so that those who like a particular picture can acquire it in a different form or see other angels by the artist that they might wish to buy.

In a culture more directly shaped by capital than any other in history, this connection between angels and the marketplace was probably inevitable, and it has produced phenomena that both charm and repel the critical observer. In the midst of the angel craze of the 1990s, a book called *Angels, Angels, Angels* came out under the name of Andy Warhol, even though the artist had been dead for seven years.[35] It seems that Warhol did many sketches of winged creatures, most of which he called "faeries," during the 1950s. He did draw and label two as angels. In 1994, scores of these pictures were collected into a book along with Warhol quotes, mostly about living for the moment and not judging others. Though on one hand the project seems exploitative, on the other the pictures are lively and the message uplifting.

Dawn Dacus, Chantall, *from Doreen Virtue,* Messages from Your Angels Oracle Cards *(Carlsbad, CA: Hay House, 2002). Chantall's message reads, "New romance is imminent—either with a newcomer; or through reignited passion in your existing relationship. Be open to giving and receiving love." (Copyright Dawn Dacus, reproduced by permission)*

Physical Angels in History and Theory

The physical angels of American religion have precedents in the Bible, where angels often appear to have bodies. Not only do the "sons of God" marry human women and cause them to conceive children in Genesis 6 (a story that receives more attention in chapter 5), but angels visit Abraham and eat with him in Genesis 18, and an angel wrestles with Jacob and puts his hip out of joint in Genesis 32. A seraph, one of the six-winged angels who surround the throne of God, touches the mouth of Isaiah with a live coal that the seraph has to hold with tongs in Isaiah 6. Ezekiel sees angels in the forms of animals, including a lion, an ox, and an eagle (Ezek. 1), and later an angel puts a scroll into that prophet's mouth (Ezek. 3). More than 500 years after Ezekiel, the Christian author of the book of Revelation wrote about seeing the same animal angels (Rev. 4) and of receiving a scroll from an angel and eating it (Rev. 10). Far from working as mere ghosts or insubstantial spirits bearing messages from God, biblical angels participated fully in the material world. For the apostle Paul, writing in his letters to the Galatians (4:3, 9) and Colossians (2:8, 20), the angels were equivalent to "elemental spirits of the world" (or "of the universe") who ruled the physical creation.

America's angels stand closer to the physical presences of the Bible than to the abstract angels of philosophical theology. As cultural critic Harold Bloom has pointed out, Americans prefer a generalized "biblical religion," inspired by stories of ancient Israel and the first Christians, to the more elaborate forms of Judaism and Christianity that developed in Europe.[36] Bloom found this American focus on the Bible among many disparate churches and movements, including Mormons, Christian Scientists, Seventh-Day Adventists, Jehovah's Witnesses, Pentecostals, Southern Baptists, and African American Protestants. Amid all these attempts to get back to the Bible, it is not surprising that biblical models prevail when Americans think about angels.

As the range of America's Bible-based movements indicates, the Bible offers broad resources for spiritual seekers. Just as the people who wrote the Bible had more intimate contact with their pagan neighbors than later Jews and Christians did, so the stories and laws of the Bible show more visible connections with polytheism and the gods of nature than later Judaism and Christianity. Americans have drawn many ideas about the relations of angels to the material world from those that appeared in the millennia during which the Bible was written and edited.

For example, as a later chapter will describe, Americans have focused on several Bible passages that imply that every nation has an angel and that these angels fight each other during earthly wars (Deut. 32:8, Ps. 82, Dan. 10:13–14, Rev. 17:14). Many evangelicals in the United States have rediscovered this concept and applied it in the world-transforming prayer and missionary activities that they call "spiritual warfare." One liberal theologian, Walter Wink, has seen the idea of national angels as an affirmation of the spiritual dimension of history; playwright Tony Kushner dramatized national angels in the character of the Continental Principality of America and other members of the heavenly court (who represent the other continents, not the planets) in *Angels in America.*

Recovering another biblical doctrine, over the decades since *The Exorcist* (1973) appeared on movie screens Americans across the spectrum of religions, from evangelical to New Age, have revived the biblical practice of building the kingdom of God by casting out demons (as in Acts 19:13, among many other places). Since the 1990s, other Americans have appealed to angels in the effort to cure disease and to maintain health (following John 5, in the King James Version). Meanwhile, in the arts, American culture has produced the first representations of sex between angels and humans since the Bible suggested such misbehavior in the book of Genesis (and in the apocryphal books of Enoch). As the chapter on "Angels, Love, and Sex" will argue, Americans have used stories of sex between humans and angels to challenge sexual limits and roles.

Nowhere have Americans returned with more enthusiasm to the biblical model than in making physical replicas of angels. Angels provided a curious exception to the prohibition of idols in the Hebrew Scriptures. The Torah commanded Israel to "make two cherubim (shining ones) of gold" at each end of the ark containing the tablets of the Law given on Mt. Sinai. The ark was to support a "mercy seat," or symbolic throne of God, and the cherubim were to face each other and "spread out their wings above, overshadowing the mercy seat with their wings" (Exod. 25:18–20). These cherubim more closely resembled the winged lions of Assyria than the "cherubic" infants that became popular in the Renaissance. In 2 Samuel 22 and in Psalm 18, God rides to battle on cherubim. In Isaiah 6, they crouch under his throne while seraphim fly above. Other angels take vivid physical form in Numbers 22 (as a man holding a sword) and Ezekiel 10 (as flying wheels with wings and faces).

Many pagans, of course, also made images of heavenly beings, not only for their temples but for their homes as well. One of the most serious incidents of opposition to the mission of Paul, the Christian apostle, occurred in Ephesus, a city of Asia Minor, where the silversmith Demetrius complained that Paul's preaching had endangered the trade of artisans like him who made replicas of the large statue of the goddess Artemis in the temple. Demetrius inspired the crowd in a theater to chant, "Great is Artemis of the Ephesians," and Paul was prevented from speaking to them (Acts 19).

If Demetrius could have traveled through time to visit the United States today, he would have seen that his concern was in the long run entirely misplaced. His beloved Artemis has simply been transformed into an "angel," both in the *Dark Angel* television series (now in reruns) and in the music of the group "Artemis" (which has a song called "Angel"). If he worked for Boyd's Collectibles, he could make an angel named Athena (a colorful, winged woman with birds on her shoulders, sometimes described as "The Wedding Angel"). As a silversmith, he would find a market for many types of silver guardian-angel pins—some holding birthstones of the different months, others dedicated to police officers, firefighters, skiers, automobile drivers, or even gamblers.

Art historians have pointed out that angels became more solid and human, developing feet and muscles and casting shadows, as art moved from the Middle Ages through the Renaissance. In the United States, angels have become even more integrated with humanity than they were during the Renaissance, when they appeared only in formal settings like churches, public squares, and the palazzos of the powerful and rich. Angels now take shape in an array of common materials and in identities as undignified as "Mrs. Fries" and those angel pins for gamblers. They are displayed in settings from the child's bed to the kitchen shelf to the computer screen. That screen may show everything from paintings by Giotto, Raphael, or Abbott Thayer to models in wings from the Victoria's Secret runway; angels and demons from the game Diablo;

or the gender-bending, cute but Punk images of Michael, Gabriel, Lucifer, and Satan by Allison Carmichael at her mangapunksai.com website. Such new forms often seem to have degraded angels, making them commodities and even cheap or vulgar commodities, but they have also taken part in a process of religious change that has spiritualized the material world.

In a book called *Visual Piety: A History and Theory of Popular Religious Images*, David Morgan said nothing about angel art or angel collectibles, focusing primarily on Warner Sallman's paintings of Christ. But Morgan did grapple with the issues of exploitation and aesthetics involved in discussing any art made not for museums but for commercial sale and devotional use. He concluded that popular religious art does embody an aesthetic, a theory of beauty, but that this aesthetic differs from that applied by critics and consumers to "high" or socially elite art. As Morgan pointed out, theorists since the eighteenth century have emphasized detachment, objective proportionality, and intellectual originality in judging high art. Morgan's correspondence with consumers of popular religious art, however, led him to identify factors like recognition, interactivity, empathy, and sympathy as crucial to their judgments of the beauty and appropriateness of a piece of art.

Applying these criteria to America's material angels and angel art, it could be said that they are usually judged by the popular standards, which may account in part for their neglect by scholars. In practice, however, the criteria are frequently mixed. The same Serenity Classic angel can be praised for its resemblance to the work of "Renaissance Masters" and named "Alyssa—Nature's Angel" for those who seek to evoke the Earth. The wings worn by model Adriana Lima in a Victoria's Secret lingerie show can represent not only the best work of the leading costume designer on Broadway but also the fulfillment (as she avowed in an interview) of her girlhood dream to have wings. The same wings also engage the fantasies of various observers, even as they echo a prehistoric image of the bird goddess. Mixing the elite, the popular, the fantastic, and the archetypal belongs to the realm of all religions, including the American religion of angels. And as Morgan concluded, "Sacred images—whether Sallman's or [the Renaissance master] Brunelleschi's—are those that make belief work."[37]

Energy and Angels

No physically visible or audible angel had to descend into Wal-Mart for Ruby Whitehurst to attribute her shopping success to angelic guidance. For angel believers and many modern theorists, the whole material world is a realm of revelation, saturated with spirit. At the end of Andy Lakey's book, the artist recounts seven lessons he has learned from his encounters with angels, and the fifth is "There are no coincidences." Literally everything happens for a reason, he believes, and so he urges everyone to "Listen to your inner voice, and look for the meaning in unexplained events." James Redfield, who wrote a preface for Lakey's book, began his main character's adventure in *The Celestine Prophecy* (a religious novel from 1993 that stood atop the New York Times best-seller list for more than two years, while receiving almost no notice from scholars in religion or other commentators on culture) with the lesson of following the guidance of apparent coincidence. The aim of life, according to Redfield's book, is to rise to higher and higher levels of energy, or "vibration," until one's body can literally fly and one can appear or disappear at will. In other words, by following the steps of the prophecy, people would become like angels.

When Redfield pronounced that everything was energy, so that all forms of life stood on a continuum from plant to angel, he was taking part in a tradition with a long history, and many recent manifestations, with regard to angels in the United States. Andrew Greeley's novel *Angel Fire* (1988) featured a female Angel Gabriel who was really an energy being, not supernatural but trammeled like the rest of us by death and the speed of light. According to Robert Sardello, a psychologist who edited an anthology called *The Angels* in 1994, angels at the level called the Thrones, the third after Seraphim and Cherubim, continually create the material world, and particularly the world of minerals and crystals, which reflect God better than humanity does because a mineral is "desireless, and as such is the perfect reflection of the Creator's desire."[38] Another author who contributed to *The Angels*, physicist Donald Cowan, sees angels as inhabitants of the original void that expanded in the Big Bang. They are therefore able to move faster than light in the universe that has grown within that original void.[39] A medical doctor,

Larry Dossey, wrote in the same anthology that angels emerge during the process of "involution," whereby Spirit creates the material world by forgetting itself, or withdrawing.[40] In a book called *The Physics of Angels* from 1996, which arose from the collaboration of a former Dominican and then Episcopal priest, Matthew Fox, with biologist Rupert Sheldrake, angels are understood not as bodies but as fields, on the analogy of the gravitational and magnetic fields of the Earth. A center for research in gardening and agriculture based on efforts to communicate with the spirits who inhabit plants and landscapes has thrived since 1976 in the foothills of the Blue Ridge Mountains in Virginia. Its founder, Machaelle Wright, was inspired by practices discovered by a Canadian, Dorothy Maclean, and first employed at Findhorn, in Scotland. Wright named her center in Virginia "Perelandra," recalling the title of a C. S. Lewis novel in which angels—on Venus—figure prominently.

Behind these American visions of angels exerting force on the material world stand many historical figures. Robert Sardello's thinking about the Thrones and crystals stems directly from Rudolf Steiner (1861–1925), an Austrian philosopher who claimed to see angels. A great deal of angel mysticism came to the United States through John Chapman (1774–1845), also known as Johnny Appleseed, a missionary who in his travels across the country sowed not only seeds but also books describing Swedenborg's visits with angels. To explain how angels have become so cheap and plentiful, and matter so spiritual, in the United States today requires a quick turn through ancient and modern history, which the next chapter attempts to provide.

But before we take that historical trip, it may be useful to reflect once more on the connection of angels to the material world. As mentioned in chapter 1, at the end of *Angels in America* Tony Kushner brought the main characters of his play to the Angel of Bethesda Fountain in Central Park. There, the character called "the Prophet" gives a speech about the paradoxes of angel statues: "I like them best when they're statuary. They commemorate death but they suggest a world without dying. They are made of the heaviest things on earth, stone and iron, they weigh tons but they're winged, they are engines and instruments of flight." Besides this speaker, whose "real" name is Prior Walter and who represents an ancient line of English forebears, the group at the fountain includes a Jewish pseudo-intellectual who was once Prior Walter's gay lover, an

African American nurse who is a former drag queen, and a middle-aged Mormon mother who came to New York to save her son. A material angel, in Kushner's vision, brings Americans together. The angel statue around which these characters stand celebrates healing; it is a larger cousin of Susan Lordi's first angel in the Willow Tree line of figurines.

Some problems in this healing vision become apparent when history is taken into account. The idea of the angel of Bethesda comes from John 5, a story in which a crippled man is lying by a pool in Jerusalem that is said to heal all illness for the first to enter when an angel stirs its waters; he has not been healed because someone always reaches the water before him. Jesus comes by and heals him by the power of his words. Inspired by this story in the seventeenth century, the American colonial minister Cotton Mather entitled the first medical text written in this county *The Angel of Bethesda*. When American biblical experts created the Revised Standard Version of the New Testament in 1946, however, they relegated the angel from the story of Bethesda to a footnote, leaving only the pool, the crippled man, and Jesus in the main text. The statue in Central Park was fortunately erected long before the Revised Standard Version was published, but it also exemplifies an elided history. Its creator, Emma Stebbins, stood among the transformative artists of the nineteenth century who made the angels of American parks, town squares, public murals, and cemeteries predominantly female. Stebbins was also one of a group of female sculptors of that time whose memory and works have been largely forgotten and sometimes lost. Because gay history is being recovered, dueling websites now contest the issue of whether Stebbins was gay. But most people ignore, take for granted, or react against the revolution of religious symbolism in which she took part, and which continues to give rise to countless material angels and many movements of the spirit in our day.

From Stone Age bird goddesses to the winged deities of Egypt, Greece, and India, the visual and spiritual relatives of angels abound in many cultures. A more direct story illustrates how angels came to the United States. The story begins in the heavens over Mesopotamia and Persia and continues through Israel, transplantation across the Atlantic by conquerors from Spain and England, and shifts of gender and identity (broadening to include dead humans and gods of other cultures) during the Victorian era. By the first half of the twentieth century, artists in many genres—including painters Thomas Cole and Abbott Thayer, sculptors Emma Stebbins and Daniel Chester French, writers from Emerson and Longfellow to Mark Twain and H.D. (Hilda Doolittle), and filmmakers Walt Disney and Frank Capra—had begun to use angels to invoke new visions of the cosmos.

From Planets to Angels

The angels of American culture descend from spirits of the Persian Empire. Persia once linked Israel and Greece to Mesopotamia, where people first recorded their knowledge of the heavens. In Mesopotamia, the seven visible "planets," or moving heavenly bodies—the sun, the moon, Mercury, Mars, Venus, Jupiter, and Saturn—each had a god or goddess to govern it. Sometime between 1500 and 600 B.C.E, the Persian prophet Zarathustra transformed the seven planetary gods into four sons and three daughters of a single creator God, seven beings who personified Wisdom, Truth, Kingship, Devotion, Integrity, Immortality, and Obedience. Later, in the Jewish book of Tobit, the archangel Raphael introduced himself as "one of the seven angels who stand ready and enter before the glory of the Lord" (Tobit 12:15). At the end of the first century after Jesus was born, the Christian book of Revelation reported that "the seven angels who stand before God" received seven trumpets

Winged spirits such as this genie from Assyria became angels of the creator God in ancient Persian religion and proliferated in the Bible and in other Jewish writings after the Persian Empire dominated Judea for two centuries. Relief depicting a human-headed genie watering a sacred tree. *Near Eastern, Assyrian (from the palace of Assurnasirpal II at Nimrud), 883–859 B.C.E. Gypseous alabaster with traces of paint. 88 1/2 x 72 3/4 in. (224.8 x 184.8 cm). (Yale University Purchase. Courtesy Yale University Art Museum)*

to usher in the end of the world (Rev. 8:2). The seven great male and female spirits of Persia became all male, or sexless beings referred to with male pronouns, as they passed into Judaism and Christianity. Only in the nineteenth century, and especially in the United States, were angels again commonly seen as female. In America, angels appeared in more human forms as they came down from the heavens and became more practical. Spirits that had started as embodiments of cosmic order began to represent change.

Below the seven immortals, Persian religion included many spirits, such as Vayu (Wind), Mithra (the Warrior), and Haoma (a plant spirit, possibly ephedra), who served the creator, and others who rebelled against God.[1] The angels of Persia showed that monotheism could subsume ancient gods and goddesses. Among the spirits who worked their way through the Persian Empire to modern America was Pazuzu, the demon who possessed Linda Blair in *The Exorcist*.[2] Pazuzu began as the four-winged spirit of the southwest wind and protector of women in childbirth; his statue stood at Nineveh (the capital of Assyria, whose ruins lie near Mosul in Iraq) 3,000 years ago.

Jews exiled to Assyria, Babylon, Egypt, and Persia, or traveling as merchants to these regions (all of which, along with Judah itself, formed part of the Persian Empire for two centuries), gradually added more spirits to their scriptures. Jews saw some angels as messengers of God and gave them Hebrew names like Gabriel ("Strength of God") and Michael ("Who is like God?"). On the negative side, the Hebrew Scriptures told of *bnai elohim* ("sons of god"), who mated with human women in Genesis 6, and of Satan (whose name derives from a Persian word meaning "accuser"), who charged Job with hypocrisy. Most biblical angels had no wings, but the seraphim ("burning ones") that the prophet Isaiah saw each had six. According to Isaiah 6, in the year 738 B.C.E. ("the year that King Uzziah died"), a priest named Isaiah entered the inner sanctum of Solomon's Temple in Jerusalem, where the Ark of the Covenant was kept, and there he "saw the Lord sitting on a throne, high and lofty." Though Isaiah did not describe the Lord, he went into some detail about other spirits. "Seraphs were in attendance above him; each had six wings: with two they covered their faces, and with two they covered their feet, and with two they flew." These seraphim called out to each other in a chant that has echoed through thousands of years of Jewish and Christian worship: "Holy, holy, holy is the Lord of hosts; the whole earth is full of his glory." When Isaiah feared that he could not see God and live, a seraph flew to him and touched his mouth with a burning coal from God's altar, enabling him to receive and speak God's word as a prophet.

Later prophets, like Ezekiel and Daniel, had even more elaborate interactions with angels. Ezekiel saw angels as animals, people, and wheels of fire moving through the sky; Daniel held long conversations with Gabriel about events that concluded with Michael fighting Israel's enemies. All these prophets worked in the centuries after 800 B.C.E., when Israel and Judah were in most intimate contact with Assyria, Babylon, Egypt, and finally the whole Middle East in the context of Persia, the homeland of angels. During the Jewish exile to Babylon after 586 B.C.E., the scribes who compiled Hebrew traditions into the Torah made angels very prominent. Angels of the Torah (which later became the first five books of the Christian Old Testament) guarded the gates of Eden, visited Abraham and announced the birth of Isaac, destroyed Sodom and Gomorrah, wrestled with Jacob and named him Israel, and led the nation of Israel through the desert to the Promised Land.

As Judaism spread throughout the Mediterranean civilization that arose after Alexander the Great destroyed the Persian Empire, angels emerged as one of the most distinctive Jewish contributions to the world's religions. Angels offered a Jewish solution to the problem of the apparent separation between eternity and time, the changeless God and a changing world, linking the realms of Heaven and Earth. Angels served as the Jewish (and ultimately Western, Christian, and Muslim) version of Hindu savior gods and Buddhist bodhisattvas. By the time of Jesus and the New Testament, good and evil angels had become the constant friends and adversaries of Jewish believers, and God had ceased to speak or to appear directly to prophets. The winged figure that the Greeks called Nike and the Romans Victory was appropriated to represent angels in early Christian art.[3] Six centuries after Jesus, Muslims announced that God had spoken again through the Prophet Muhammad, and that God's messages had been brought to Muhammad by the same angel Gabriel who had visited Daniel and the Virgin Mary.

In the Middle Ages, angels became tools of theological inquiry. Christian thinkers from Origen (185–254) and Augustine (354–430) through Anselm of Canterbury (1033–1109) and Thomas Aquinas (1225–1274) explained the existence of evil in the world, the nature of humanity, and even the purpose for which people were created by reference to angels. Adam and Eve sinned through the influence of Satan, also known as the angel Lucifer ("Light-bearer"), who had already chosen evil in the exercise of his own free will. People could repent, but angels could not, because our material bodies meant that we lived in time, while the immaterial angels constantly chose good or evil in their own dimension and only entered time to visit us. After death, those humans who were saved by Christ would join the ranks of angels and replace the fallen angelic followers of Satan, who would torture their human victims in Hell forever. Although Jews did not join Christians in their theory of the Fall, Jewish philosophers such as Maimonides (1135–1204) saw angels in every transaction of energy between humans and God. Every *mitzvah*, or good deed, that a Jew performed gave birth to an angel, and these angels would eventually reunify the shattered world into a single realm of light. Medieval science, whether among Christians, Jews, or Muslims, continued the Mesopotamian tradition that angels were the governors of stars and planets, adding that the angelic spheres conveyed motion to the changing world by their attraction to the Unmoved Mover, God.

Belief in Gabriel, Michael, and even Satan still unifies billions of people on every continent who disagree about Jesus, Muhammad, Moses, Israel, the meanings of the scriptures, and the nature of God. Since the words most commonly translated into English as "angel"—*angelos* in Greek and *malak* in Hebrew and Arabic—mean "messenger," a consensus has emerged among monotheists that good angels bring messages from God, while demons, or fallen angels, attempt to deceive. Speculation on the roles of angels in creating the world and moving the planets has receded, but concepts about angels governing the nations, recording history, and protecting individuals from harm continue to appeal to new generations in many cultures around the world.

Nowhere does the power of angels make itself felt more strongly or more often than in the United States, where Mormons put statues of the angel Moroni on every new temple, and a television show called *Touched by an Angel* ran from 1994 to 2003, featuring a team of angelic therapists, often drawing more viewers than any other dramatic series. The American attraction to angels began early. As Increase Mather preached in colonial Massachusetts, "Angels cannot be seen, though they stand by. . . . This Assembly is full of them at this hour, yet we see them not."[4] Despite Puritan resistance to graven images, Puritan gravestones frequently featured a head—at first a skull, but later a cherubic face—with wings.[5] The shift from skull to cherub signified a change. Instead of emphasizing the departed soul and death, the depiction of an angel stood for resurrection to new life. On these gravestones, colonial Americans began to identify dead humans with angels. Winged heads on gravestones continued until the mid-1700s in New England; in the rural cemetery movement of the 1800s, they were displaced by elaborate guardian angel statues and friezes. On the other side of the continent, the Catholics of New Mexico carved no saint as often as the archangel Michael.[6] Protestant missionaries who met the Navajo saw their sand paintings as pictures of demons.[7]

Colonial Angels

A common Spanish and English root for the American preoccupation with angels and demons has lately been revealed by Jorge Cañizares-Esguerra in his book *Puritan Conquistadors* (2006). As Cañizares-Esguerra documents, both through texts and copious reproductions of illustrations from books, many versions of a "satanic epic" in which the Spanish conquests of the New World were presented as contests with the Devil (who was alternately pictured as possessing the Indians and the Spanish, depending upon an author's point of view) were translated and published in the England of Queen Elizabeth and after. He speculates that this Iberian, satanic epic influenced English literature from Edmund Spenser's *Faerie Queene* through William Shakespeare's *The Tempest* and John Milton's *Paradise Lost,* and he establishes convincing parallels between the Spanish accounts of combat with Satan and English histories like John Smith's *Generall Historie of Virginia* (1624) and Edward Johnson's *Wonder-Working Providence of Sion's Savior in New-England* (1654).[8] Following the traumatic slaughters of English colonists and natives in King Philip's War (1675–1676), the New England Puritans located Satan firmly among the Indians and the Spanish and saw God's angels fighting on their own side. As chapters 6 and 7 will show, the American pattern of seeing history as a war with Satan persists into the twenty-first century.

Whether in peace or war, Americans have tended to see angels as servants of humanity rather than as messengers of God. Increase Mather's *Angelographia* (1696) approved of stories like that of Samuel Wallis, who was said to have been confined to his home by illness for thirteen years until an angel cured him with a potion of "Blood wort and Red sage, steeped in small Beer." Mather warned, however, that angels of inspiration, from "Mahomet's" Gabriel to the angels who visited Hildegarde of Bingen, Savonarola of Florence, English Quakers, or French Huguenots, were all devils. Scriptures recorded no case in which a good angel became a familiar spirit to a human, visiting that person often, Mather noted, but many in which demons possessed people and remained with them. As for the visions that familiar spirits brought, there would be no revelations beyond the Scriptures,[9] so such visions must also be false.

Statues such as this one from New Mexico, depicting St. Michael the Archangel in the courtly garb of the Renaissance, were among the first sculptures made by Christians in America. Rafael Aragon (1795–1862), Saint Michael the Archangel. *Painted wood. 86 x 51.4 cm. (Private collection. Photo by Michael O'Shaughnessy, reproduced courtesy of The Palace of the Governors History Library)*

Portrayals of Michael the Archangel and other angels spread into Protestant contexts and became more Nordic and more medieval in spirit as the Gothic style prevailed. This version of Michael appears in the Tiffany windows of the First Presbyterian Church of Pittsburgh, which was dedicated in 1905. Female angels feature prominently in many windows of that church. (Photograph by William Gardella)

The American preference for practical angels resulted in part from intellectual trends of the era when Europeans first came to the land that would become the United States. After the Copernican revolution in astronomy, the world was no longer thought to be surrounded by spheres of heavenly crystal containing the stars. Then Galileo's telescope made the planets look like rocks rather than habitations of gods, and Newton's laws explained planetary movements as factors of blind force rather than expressions of intelligent purpose. Angels no longer needed to govern the heavens or stand in ranks between humanity and the realm of God beyond the stars.[10]

At the same time, the new human ability to penetrate heavenly secrets and to travel the world gave Europeans an exalted sense of human power that could extend to power over angels. Increase Mather told of a witch executed at Hartford, Connecticut, who commanded fallen angels and "Employed Evil Spirits to be Revenged on several." According to Mather, even "the Indian Pawaws (i.e., Wizards)" had often "by the hands of Evil Angels murdered their Neighbours." Meanwhile, good angels constantly served humans without delivering any messages. When we reached Heaven after death, according to Mather, angels would "tell us wonderful things, concerning what they have done for us, which we little think of now; how they delivered us at such a time, how they were with us at such a place, how they prevented such and such designs from taking effect against us."[11]

Perhaps because of this shift in the role of angels from Heaven's messengers to Earth's helpers, a revival of philosophical and literary interest in angels took place in England as the English colonies in America took root during the middle decades of the seventeenth century. John Milton's epic poem *Paradise Lost*, with its extensive roles for Raphael, Satan, and many other angels, was apparently influenced by this revival. According to the research of one Milton scholar, the years between 1640 and 1665, when Milton completed the manuscript of his poem, saw "several dozen fairly substantial works dealing wholly or predominantly with angels" published by English authors.[12] Within these books, Neoplatonist philosophers like Henry More argued (especially against Roman Catholics) that angels must have bodies because they have effects in the material world. Even Thomas Hobbes, the political theorist, who was frequently called an atheist, included a chapter on angels in the *Leviathan*, where he backed the physical reality of angels. When Milton pictured Raphael eating with Adam and Eve in Eden and blushing when he discussed how angels made love, or reported conversations between Satan and Belial on angelic lust for human women, he was working in the midst of a widespread discourse and making his own position clear.

Across the Atlantic in colonial Boston, Increase Mather scorned speculation about the metaphysical nature of angels, the extent of angelic knowledge, or the free will of angels, saying that to offer discourse on such subjects would be to feed his people "with Stones instead of Bread." Yet he paused over theory long enough to reject the medieval tradition that saw nine ranks of angels. Those ranks had names based on biblical terms as they were arranged in a sixth-century book, *The Celestial Hierarchy*, which had gained authority from its attribution to Dionysius, a convert of the apostle Paul. In descending order from God, the Pseudo-Dionysius had listed seraphim, cherubim, thrones, dominions, virtues, principalities, powers, archangels, and angels. A slightly different ranking appeared in the *Divine Comedy* of Dante (1265–1321). Both in Dionysius and in Dante, these hierarchies taught the superiority of contemplation over action. Upper ranks of angels surrounded and praised God, middle ranks handled cosmic matters, and only the lowest ranks interacted with people. In America, however, Mather was more concerned with Earth than Heaven. He preferred the four angelic ranks listed by Paul in Colossians 1:16 (Thrones, Dominions, Principalities, and Powers), and he interpreted Paul's ranks as analogues of the British colonial government under which he lived. Where Colossians spoke of Thrones, Mather saw kings. Dominions were equivalent to princes and dukes, Principalities were governors of colonies, and Powers were magistrates in towns. The mystery of why Satan and his demons should be chained for a thousand years (as Revelation 20 predicts) before being judged could also be understood by analogy with the English system of justice, in which criminals might be "committed to Prison . . . there to lye in Chains, until the *Sessions* comes."[13] Medieval angelology described a choir with ranks stretching from Earth to Heaven, but the American Puritan wanted angels to be an efficient set of officials organized to govern humans and to eradicate evil.

Unfortunately, the millennium of Satan's imprisonment had not yet arrived in 1693, when Cotton Mather (the son of Increase) wrote

The Wonders of the Invisible World to defend his role as an expert in the Salem witch trials. As the younger Mather exclaimed, "When we are in our Church-Assemblies, O how many Devils, do you imagine, croud [*sic*] in among us!" Devils rocked some of the congregation to sleep, Cotton Mather warned; they distracted others, and made "another, to be pleasing himself with wanton and wicked Speculations."[14] Between angels and demons, it seems wonderful that the churches of Boston had enough room for people. Scholars have long suggested that the Mathers used the assaults of demons in witchcraft to assure New Englanders that they were not alone.[15] As the end of the Puritan era threatened to turn New England into a colony of merchants and farmers without a religious mission, both devils and angels served as allies of preachers.

Tides of rationalism, revivalism, and revolution swept through American religion in the eighteenth century, but angels retained their prominence, and Americans continued to see angels in practical and human terms. As Jonathan Edwards (1703–1758), the great evangelist and theologian, reflected, "The angels of heaven, though a superior order of being, . . . are yet all ministering spirits sent forth to minister to them that shall be the heirs of salvation; and so in some respect are made inferior to the saints in honour."[16] Edwards also subordinated angels to humans by repeating an argument that had appeared in John Milton's *Paradise Lost*, which said that the fallen angels had gone into rebellion because they objected to God's plan to become incarnate as a human. Edwards added the idea that good angels were not confirmed in their salvation until Jesus ascended to Heaven in a glorified human body after his resurrection.

As the French and Indian War raged in 1755, minister Joseph Fish encouraged the church at Westerly, Rhode Island, with his vision of *Angels Ministering to the People of GOD, for Their Safety and Comfort in Times of Danger and Distress*. The occasion was a day of fasting and prayer "for Success to our Armies" in an expedition of New Englanders against Quebec, and Fish was ready to cite the angels who came to rescue Daniel. Like Edwards, Fish stressed that "notwithstanding the Dignity of their Nature," angels "are all ministering Spirits" employed by God to "tend upon their younger Brethren, the Sons of Adam." Where medieval Catholics had distinguished nine ranks of angels and assigned most to direct contemplation and worship of God, and Jewish thinkers saw ten ranks of angels who mediated the powers of God in creation, the American listed ten kinds of *service* that angels performed for humans. Angels could serve as messengers; prophets, as in Daniel or Revelation; warners of "impending Danger"; comforters in affliction; guards against enemies; deliverers out of danger; executors of judgment on sinners; fellow-worshippers at prayer; guides for the souls of the dead; and gatherers of people for the Last Judgment. According to Fish, angels surrounded even the most degraded human beings. "A Beggar on the Dunghil [*sic*], polluted with Sores, and neglected by Men, is visited by Angels. . . . Yea, the highest Angel in Heaven is pleas'd with the Command, to come forth and serve him." The preacher concluded that New England's Yankees need not fear the French or their Indian converts to Catholicism, for "what will their Numbers, Strength, and Subtilty [*sic*] avail, against an innumerable Company of Angels?"[17]

Up to this point, writers and preachers maintained a firm distinction between angels and humans. Anselm of Canterbury (1033–1109) had suggested that humans were made to fill up the ranks of fallen angels, but even he saw the two orders of being as distinct in origin. As the eighteenth century moved toward revolutionary climaxes in America and France, however, the line between angels and humans came under attack. According to *Heaven and Hell*, a tour of the afterlife by Emanuel Swedenborg, all angels were former human beings who continued to grow spiritually.[18] Human free will was actually maintained by the counterbalancing attractive forces of angels, who loved God and others, and demons, who loved the world and themselves. Though many denounced the visionary as a madman, books based on his visions sold widely for more than a hundred years; they were distributed across America along with apple seeds by "Johnny Appleseed," a follower of Swedenborg, and they gave rise to a small Christian denomination, the Church of the New Jerusalem, which continues as the Swedenborg Society. More importantly, Swedenborg contributed to a merging of angels and humans that would also take place in Mormon and Spiritualist churches and then spread into American popular culture. By the time the apprentice angel Clarence won his wings by saving George Bailey in *It's a Wonderful Life*, many Americans had forgotten that theologians had ever made any distinction between angels and the dead.

Humans and Angels

Nineteenth-century Americans made the identification of angels with humans the subject of explicit struggles. For followers of Mormon prophet Joseph Smith, the young man in upstate New York who claimed to have found the buried Book of Mormon in 1823, formerly human angels mediated every event in religious life. Moroni, son of Mormon, revealed his father's book by appearing to Joseph Smith in shining garments, without wings but floating just above the floor of the prophet's room.[19] The Jesus whose visit to America was described in the Book of Mormon was himself an angel, as was God the Father before He created the world. All people could complete a process of preexistence, earthly life, and glorification after death that included exaltation to angelic and then to divine status, when we might serve as messengers to and even creators of other worlds. Although many who heard this gospel rejected its unification of human and angelic realms, Mormons contributed much to the American view of angels. The closer approach of angels to humans and the importance of angels in American life are in part legacies of Mormon thinking. As Mormon theorist Oscar W. McKonkie asked in 1973, "Could you really accept a religion as the true way of God without God's personal messengers in it?" McKonkie went on to quote Mormon visions of angels by leaders including Brigham Young, Heber C. Kimball, Heber J. Grant, Parley P. Pratt, David O. McKay, Harold B. Lee, Alexander Neibaur, and his own grandmother Emma Somerville McConkie, whose "angel" was the child Jesus. The frequency of Mormon visions of angels led McConkie to conclude that the religion was true. "If angels minister to a people, they are the Lord's people. If angels do not minister to a people, they are not the Lord's people," he wrote. "When judged by this standard, it is not difficult to find which of all churches is true."[20] With the Mormons' pragmatic approach to angelic visits, distinctions between angels and humans, or between messages from God and human projects, were almost entirely obliterated.

Meanwhile, the emergence of Christmas as the major holiday of American culture also brought angels into greater prominence. The story of the birth of Jesus in the gospel of Luke featured angels who told shepherds what was happening. Inspired by that version of the Nativity, a Unitarian minister named Edmund Hamilton Sears wrote one of the first popular Christmas carols, "It Came Upon a Midnight Clear," in 1849:

> It came upon a midnight clear,
> That glorious song of old,
> From angels bending near the earth,
> To touch their harps of gold:
> "Peace on the Earth, goodwill to men
> From Heaven's all gracious King!"
> The world in solemn stillness lay
> To hear the angels sing.

The second verse makes angels even more prominent ("Still through the cloven skies they come, / With peaceful wings unfurled") and emphasizes the continuing presence of angels, in the present, "O'er all the weary world":

> Above its sad and lonely plains
> They bend on hovering wing,
> And ever o'er its Babel sounds
> The blessed angels sing.

Evangelical Christians have criticized the song for its lack of emphasis on Jesus, but it gave Unitarians like Sears a way to celebrate what was rapidly becoming a universal holiday in the United States. As nineteenth-century Americans adopted the German and English (originally Norse pagan) custom of bringing the cosmic tree Yggdrasil into their parlors, they often Christianized the pagan symbol by putting an angel on top. Christmas continues to make Americans think of angels today.

Around the same time that Sears wrote his lyrics, strange rappings were being heard at the home of the Fox sisters in Hydesville, New York. These mysterious sounds, reported in 1848, marked the beginning of a movement called Spiritualism, which for half a century realigned relations between angels, humans still living, and "the so-called dead," as the Spiritualists termed them. Former slave and abolitionist Frederick Douglass, writer Harriet Beecher Stowe, newspaper magnate Horace Greeley, and President Abraham Lincoln were among those who participated in Spiritualist séances. Inventions like the telegraph, photography, and the telephone made the idea of communicating with the dead by means of invisible energy seem scientific. Perhaps the medium at a séance acted as the telegraph key. People wondered if photography could record the presence of spirits; or if some sort of equipment, like the telephone, could convey spirit voices.[21] All these possibilities implied that spirits could have bodily effects, and if angels were spirits, perhaps they had bodies too. Many tried Spiritualist practices without leaving their traditional churches. Through Spiritualism, the congruence of humans and angels penetrated further into the religious mainstream.

Some clergy advanced a more human model for angels while rejecting the idea of pursuing communications with the dead. In *Abaddon, and Mahanaim; or, Demons and Guardian Angels* (1856), the Rev. Dr. Joseph F. Berg, a prominent Dutch Reformed pastor in Philadelphia, dismissed séances as "the merest tricks of mountebanks who have imposed on popular credulity" but at the same time warned "that a real demoniacal influence may, in many instances be put forth" at such events. The best cure for attacks by demons, which Berg predicted would increase as the climax of world history approached, was to take recourse to good angels, such as the camps of angels Jacob saw in the book of Genesis when he named a place "Mahanaim," or "two camps." According to Berg, God does not give just a single guardian angel to every believer but "gives a host": "Yea, he gives two camps. . . . He protects the children of Jacob from Esau on the one hand and from Laban on the other. He maketh his angels ministering spirits . . . to them that are heirs of salvation." Good angels often "assumed bodies and appeared in human form" to help people in the Bible, but they probably had bodies of their own, he theorized: "Angelic beings may have bodies peculiar to their nature, and similar . . . to the resurrection bodies of the saints." According to Berg, angels may even eat: "It may have been with reference to this . . . that the Psalmist says, alluding to the manna which supplied the Israelites in the desert, 'Man did eat angels' food.'"[22] When another mainstream Protestant, the Rev. Dr. Lewis R. Dunn, inveighed against "the wild dreams and vagaries of modern spiritualism, with its table-turning, its writing of bad grammar and worse sense," as "the devil's agency for blinding the hearts and minds of men," and protested against confusing dead humans with angels, he nevertheless accepted the Spiritualist premise "that all the angels, and all redeemed spirits" have some kind of body or "investiture . . . in which it appears before God." However "ethereal" the bodies of angels may be, Dunn said, angelic bodies were likely "an organic vehicle suitable to their nature and employments."[23]

Though modern Christians ridiculed the supposed arguments of medieval theologians over angels dancing on the head of a pin, the jokes reflected a real dispute over whether angels had bodies and therefore took up space. The question of angelic bodies entailed further questions, such as whether angels could have memories or simply active knowledge; whether angels could have sex (with other angels or with humans); and whether angels were by nature immortal or subject to death. For Roman Catholics, the Fourth Lateran Council in 1215 decided that angels were incorporeal, invisible, and immortal; but Catholics like the Franciscan John Duns Scotus (1265–1308) argued otherwise. Americans of the nineteenth and twentieth centuries tended more and more to think of angels as spirits with subtle (or not so subtle) bodies.

Angels and Gods of Literature

Great American writers used angels to express doubts and also transgressive hopes about religion and the meaning of life. Here they followed the example of John Milton, the English Puritan poet who made daring speculation about angels and demons central to the plot of his masterpiece, *Paradise Lost* (1667). In that poem, Satan, flying from the outer darkness to tempt Eve on Earth, passes the sun and its angel Uriel, who tells the demon where to find his prey but then warns Gabriel, the guardian of humanity, who drives Satan away for a time. Raphael goes to Eden to instruct Adam and Eve; and after the Fall, Michael expels the unhappy couple from the garden. Scores of other good and evil angels figure in the plot and dialogue of the poem. Milton depicted the angels living very human lives filled with pride and anger and regret. As many have noted, the portrait of Satan in *Paradise Lost* has so much power that a reader can wonder which side Milton favored; but the poet's lifelong affiliation with the Puritan cause, and his service in Oliver Cromwell's government, made his reputation unassailable among Puritans and their heirs. American writers who wanted to fictionalize angels had Milton's authority to legitimize their task and his lists of heavenly and demonic hosts to draw upon, and they began to do this in the nineteenth century.

In *The Divinity School Address* (1838), Ralph Waldo Emerson concentrated on God and presented the unity of the world in positive terms, assuring newly graduated ministers "that the Ought, that Duty, is one thing with Science, with Beauty, and with Joy." In the poem *Uriel* (1846), however, he used an angel to put a negative twist on unity. Jewish and Christian traditions knew Uriel as the angel whose name means "fire of God"; he is often identified with the sun, and sometimes charged with guarding the gates of Hell. In Emerson's poem, Uriel throws Heaven into confusion when he speaks "against the being of a line":

> Line in nature is not found;
> Unit and universe are round;
> In vain produced, all rays return;
> Evil will bless, and ice will burn.

According to Emerson's Uriel, the straight "line," which he equates with a direct contradiction between good and evil, is a fiction of geometry that does not really exist; everything in nature is a curve. With these words, Uriel withdraws from Heaven. The other angels try to forget his message, but sometimes, when they see "the good of evil born," they remember, and tremble without knowing why.[24] The involvement of angels in the mystery of why God should permit evil was invoked by Emerson in a more personal way than it had been by Milton. Milton's powerful Satan proved the need for a powerful God to contain him, but Emerson's critical Uriel suggested that evil might have rights equal to the rights of good, within the same system.

At the end of *Moby Dick* (1851), Herman Melville brought good and evil together with the symbols of war in Heaven. After Captain Ahab's harpoon line drags him after the whale, nearly sinking his ship, a bird is nailed to the mast where a sailor is trying to nail a flag. Now Melville evokes the scene from Revelation 12, where Michael the Archangel casts Satan out of Heaven, but with a different result: "So the bird of heaven, with archangelic shrieks, and his imperial beak thrust upwards, and his whole captive form folded in the flag of Ahab, went down with his ship, which, like Satan, would not sink to hell till she had dragged a living part of heaven along with her." There is no victory for good this time, "and the great shroud of the sea rolled on as it had five thousand years ago."[25]

Satan gains another victory in Walt Whitman's *Chanting the Square Deific* (1865), where he appears alongside gods and demigods like Jehovah, Brahma, Saturn, Kronos, Hermes, Hercules, and Christ. In this poem of four stanzas, Whitman identifies his spirit with each of these gods in turn and makes claims that go beyond all of them. Only Satan receives his own stanza, which ends with these lines:

> Defiant, I, Satan, still live, still utter words, in new lands duly
>   appearing, (and old ones also,)
> Permanent here from my side, warlike, equal with any, real as any,
> Nor time nor change shall ever change me or my words.[26]

Both Melville and Whitman used satanic images to make claims for the Romantic individual, or what twentieth-century critic Quentin Anderson called the American "imperial self."[27] A gentler expansion of boundaries occurred in Henry Wadsworth Longfellow's *Sandalphon* (1857). Some Jewish traditions held that after Elijah the prophet was carried to Heaven in a fiery chariot, he became an angel named Sandalphon. Sandalphon, an enormously tall angel, was stationed at the ladder linking Earth and Heaven, and it was his duty to gather all the prayers of humanity. He transformed these prayers into flowers, then weaved them into a crown before presenting them to God. Apologizing for his subject ("It is but a legend, I know,— / A fable, a phantom, a show, / Of the ancient Rabbinical lore"), Longfellow still insisted on the human need for angels, which he saw as one result of the transgression in the garden.[28]

Longfellow had already brought the seven angels of the planets to Earth in *The Golden Legend* (1851). At the birth of Jesus in that long poem, each of the seven (among whom Longfellow lists Raphael, Michael, and Uriel, but not Gabriel) endows the baby Jesus with a different virtue, so that the child receives all three Christian virtues and four classical virtues. The angels of the sun, the moon, and Venus bring Faith, Hope, and Love (or Charity), respectively, while the angels of Jupiter, Mercury, Mars, and Saturn provide Justice, Prudence, Fortitude, and Temperance. Later in *The Golden Legend*, two nameless recording angels (one for good and one for evil deeds) reflect on the history of Christianity in Europe. The angel who records evil deeds questions the division of good and evil after noticing a "gigantic shadow . . . brightening / With sullen heat":

It is Lucifer,
The son of mystery;
And since God suffers him to be,
He, too, is God's minister,
And labors for some good
By us not understood![29]

Where Milton had made Satan a tragic hero, with a fatal flaw of pride
that cast the whole cosmos into doubt before the sacrifice of Jesus put
it right, the American Longfellow (like Emerson before him) wanted
to show that the Devil "labors for some good" in a practical way, and
that all the legends of angels had some practical connection with human needs.

Nearly a century after Longfellow, the American expatriate and im-
agist poet H.D., companion and lover of both Ezra Pound and D. H.
Lawrence, used angels to set forth nothing less than a new combination of religions in her *Tribute to the Angels* (1944). Beginning with an
invocation of Hermes Trismegistus, patron of medieval alchemists,
H. D. brought the angels of the planets one by one onto the stage, as-
sociating each of them not just with Jewish and Christian but also with
Greek and Roman, Babylonian, and Egyptian myths. Michael, the re-
gent of Mercury, was not just he who "casts the Old Dragon / into the
abyss" but also Thoth, an Egyptian god "with a feather / who weighed
the souls / of the dead." Uriel of the sun and fire also ruled the thunderbolts of Zeus, and Annael of Venus was also Aphrodite and Astarte, love
goddesses of Greece and Canaan. The poem ends with the marriage of
"Santa Sophia," or Holy Wisdom, who is designated "the Vestal / from
the days of Numa"—in other words, the virgin priest of an ancient Roman king—as well as Psyche the wife of Eros in ancient Greece. But
this goddess, in H.D.'s account, marries humanity: "The Lamb was not
with her, / either as Bridegroom or Child" and "we are her bridegroom
and lamb." Next, as the wedding proceeds, each of the six angels who
have been introduced is invoked by the sound of a bell: Gabriel, Azrael
(angel of death and Saturn), Raphael, Uriel, Annael, and Michael. After
these six, "another, deep, un-named, resurging bell" is heard, "sounding
through them all," for "*Zadkiel*, the righteousness of God," whom H.D.
also calls "Zeus-pater or Theus-pater, / *Theus*, God; God-the-father,

father-god / or the Angel god-father / himself." God the Father was the traditional husband of the goddess, but here H.D. reduces him to a kind of chief angel, come to bless a union of Wisdom with us humans and to celebrate our rebirth, for which H. D. thanks Zadkiel against the background of war and impending victory.[30]

From Emerson to H. D., some American writers used angels to develop what amounted to a new literary approach to religion. The writers saw many spiritual forces at work in the cosmos and in humanity. Among these forces, Jewish and Christian symbols still possessed the center, but angels provided a bridge to other gods who could be accepted as parts of a larger whole. The unity underlying all spirits could be just as well personified in the universal Self of Emerson or Whitman, or in the humanity of H.D., as by the God of a monotheistic system. The resulting faith was neither polytheistic nor monotheistic but transtheistic—a provisional acceptance of many gods, with acknowledgment of some oneness (possibly impersonal) beyond them all. Poets preceded scriptwriters and singers into this faith, but by the late twentieth century, American movies, television, and music would celebrate angels as part of a transtheistic culture.

Spiritualists and Skeptics

More on the level of screenwriter than prophet, Elizabeth Stuart Phelps helped to unify angels and humans with *The Gates Ajar* (1868), a fictional dialogue on the afterlife that sold more copies in the United States than any nineteenth-century novel other than *Uncle Tom's Cabin.* Sitting by the grave of her recently deceased, beloved brother Roy, the heroine of the book, Mary, says that she does not suppose her careful tending of the grave makes any difference to him. Mary is contradicted by her Aunt Winifred, who feels certain that God keeps the dead at work taking care of the living. "But I thought that God took care of us, and angels, like Gabriel and the rest," Mary says. "Why not use Roy as well as Gabriel?" answers Aunt Winifred. "What archangel could understand and reach the peculiarities of your nature as he could? . . . Will they send Roy to the planet Jupiter to take care of somebody else's sister?" Winifred teaches that all the places where angels appear in the Bible, from Abraham's guests in Genesis to the angels of Revelation, might testify to the continued life of the dead: "You see, if it could be proved that the Christian dead become angels, we could have all that we need, direct from God, about—to use the beautiful old phrase—the communion of saints." Recalling that the word "angel" translates the Greek *angelos* or "messenger," she claims that the word "applies to any servant of God, animate or inanimate." When Winifred concludes that "an east wind is as much an angel as Michael," the old, cosmic angels lose their relevance, perhaps even retreating into myth, just as they did when they were replaced by the vividly remembered human dead. Besides the title of "angel," Winifred appropriates other biblical titles for humanity, claiming that in the Bible, "the generic terms, 'spirits,' 'gods,' 'sons of God,' are used interchangeably for saints and for angels."[31]

The Gates Ajar has been ridiculed for making Heaven an exalted version of an American suburb, with family homes and gardens, but it also speculated in more daring ways. The special ire of Aunt Winifred is reserved for those who see Heaven as the pure contemplation of God, without personal love, conversation, or work. Instead, she is sure that the Jesus who lived thirty-three years on Earth would know what made people happy. Even the statement of Christ that a widow married to seven different brothers would have no competing husbands in the resurrection, because in the resurrection people are not married or given in marriage but live as the angels in Heaven, did not discourage Winifred's domestic hopes. "How do we know what heavenly unions of heart with heart exist among the angels? It [the statement of Jesus] leaves me margin enough to live and be happy with John [her dead husband] forever."[32] Something more than an apotheosis of middle-class ideals is involved in this hope, which parallels Swedenborgian and Mormon hopes for everlasting marriages and for the translation of humans to an angelic state. Although neither Elizabeth Stuart Phelps nor Swedenborg nor the Mormons used angels to express the transtheistic acceptance of Greek, Hindu, Egyptian, or other gods that appears in Whitman or H. D., Phelps and Swedenborg and the Mormons did shift the focus of faith dramatically from God to intermediary spirits. The Mormon and Spiritualist movements both gave people a chance to do practical things for and with angels, and both saw spectacular growth during the 1800s.

An explicit blurring of the human, angelic, and divine appeared in *Angels' Visits to My Farm in Florida* (1892), a Spiritualist book by W. W.

Hicks published under the pseudonym "Golden Light," with a dedication to the Rev. Dr. John Wesley Brown, rector of the prominent St. Thomas Episcopal Church in New York. Recounting a series of séances on his Florida farm, "Golden Light" quotes an entity called Celeste, "a very busy spirit" who denies that angels have wings but says that she loves "to wander far and wide" and "to visit human habitations," where "a baby's face is the prettiest thing I ever look upon." Celeste informs those gathered at the séance that she thinks that if she lived on Earth and could look at babies, "I should lose all desire to see the face of God." According to the spirit, "God is a great conceit—but the violet eyes, and primrose face (is it primrose?) of a human child, are realities, and mighty ones, too." Celeste adds that "children are indeed angels, but they become much deformed" while growing up. She speaks a bit petulantly about the lack of thanks she receives from people who cry to Heaven for help. Recalling an old man she encountered, groaning from the loneliness he felt because his loved ones were all dead, Celeste tells those at the séance that she caused the faces of his loved ones to appear to him and brought a smile to his face, after which he thanked Heaven. "That's gratitude for you!" Celeste complains. "It wasn't heaven at all, but I, Celeste, who provoked the trance and held the sunny mist in which the faces appeared." Then she consoles herself, expressing something like the doctrine of Swedenborg and the Mormons that angels continue to grow: "The food of angels is the good they do, and I am resolved to grow up large and powerful, perhaps beautiful, like the seven rayed star."[33] The reader is expected to leave the farm of "Golden Light" convinced that angels, humans, and God form a unified continuum, not separate realms or a strictly divided hierarchy. The angels who visited Florida in the 1890s were primarily interested in serving humanity, not in announcing messages or executing the judgments of God.

Of course, not all American writers who have dealt with angels have been transtheists. One of the greatest, Samuel Langhorne Clemens, or Mark Twain (1835–1910), wrote two late works using angels to satirize contemporary religion. In the first story, *Extract from Captain Stormfield's Visit to Heaven* (1909), a ship's captain describes his race with a comet and consequent arrival at the wrong gate of Heaven, a place where "a sky-blue man with seven heads and only one leg" hops in ahead of him.[34] Consultations with a map, on which our world is momentarily mistaken for a fly-speck, lead him to the right section, but even there Captain Stormfield finds that his expectations are entirely wrong. He is not surprised to be equipped with wings—the conflation between humans and angels that had occurred by the time Twain was writing makes this a given—but he did not expect the wings to cause such difficulty. He flies clumsily, enduring mid-air collisions with an Irishman and an elderly bishop, to the amusement of others. Then a veteran of Heaven informs him that the wings are just a uniform for official business, not a mode of transportation. When angels "appear in visions to dying children and good people," the veteran says, they wear wings so that they will be recognized, but the missions require travel over distances too great to fly.[35] The billions of miles of Heaven and greater distances to Earth demand instantaneous transport, which is available by wish.

Mark Twain did not entirely succumb to the modern tendency to identify angels with dead humans. As Captain Stormfield's old friend explains, Heaven was created as a kingdom, not a republic, and has a large and complex hierarchy. Its inhabitants, he says, are valued according to the work they do. Prophets are basically writers (including Shakespeare and others, who are nevertheless outranked by an Edgar Billings of Tennessee, whose poetry was great but never published), and they rank ahead of patriarchs like Abraham, but several prophets from Jupiter and from planets beyond our solar system rank ahead of all prophets from Earth. Besides prophets and patriarchs, there are "eighty Supreme Archangels" who never were human, about whom Twain says little.[36] At a climactic scene in which a repentant bartender is granted his wish for a grand reception into Heaven, Stormfield sees two archangels on the reviewing stand alongside Moses and Esau; they are described as "most glorious and gaudy giants, with platter halos and beautiful armor."[37] Ordinary inhabitants of Heaven never come any closer to such luminaries than ordinary humans on Earth come to Russian dukes, according to Stormfield's guide; ordinary people cannot sustain a conversation with great angels or with people like Moses who have lived thousands of years in Heaven. With regard to fundamentals like the existence of Heaven and even the role of Christ (one character says that countless worlds were saved by him),[38] Twain in this story supports the most conventional theology while using humor against sentimentalists and Spiritualists. Even as he skewers these opponents, however, Twain uses Captain Stormfield to support an emerging consensus that angels do practical work, rather than spending all of their time simply contemplating and praising God.

A far more bitter view of angels animates *The Mysterious Stranger*, a short novel that Twain's editor Arthur Bigelow Paine put together from two unfinished manuscripts and published six years after Twain's death. Scholars have decided that Twain tried three versions of the story, and that Paine took the ending of the third and combined it with the body of the first.[39] In all three manuscripts, an angel takes the form of a boy and visits a small town, where he befriends and plays with other boys; the first and third tales are set in Austria, in 1590 and 1702, respectively, while the second version includes Tom Sawyer and takes place in Missouri. All three stories hang on the angel doing strange and often cruel tricks, like leaving money on the ground to have those who find it condemned as thieves, or changing people into cats; at different points the visitor identifies himself as Satan's nephew (also named Satan), Satan's son, or a spirit called "Number 44." All versions include some consideration of how much responsibility Satan, God, and humanity bear for cosmic evil, but in one the young angel wishes to repair the damage his relative has done.

In the story that editor Paine published, young Satan tells his human friends that angels lack any moral sense and cannot love people: "An angel's love is sublime, adorable, divine. . . . If it fell upon one of your race for only an instant, it would consume its object to ashes."[40] The most chilling passage in all the manuscripts appears in the ending Paine selected for publication, in which the departing angel tells a human that he will never see him again, and that there is no afterlife and no God, but only his thoughts, which he should long ago have recognized as dreams, "because they are so frankly and hysterically insane—like all dreams." The absurdity of the world appears in "a God who could make good children as easily as bad, yet preferred to make bad ones; who could have made every one of them happy, yet never made a single happy one." The God of this dream "gave his angels painless lives, yet cursed his other children with biting miseries and maladies of mind and body"; he "created man without invitation, then tries to shuffle the responsibility for man's acts" away from himself, "and finally, with altogether divine obtuseness, invites this poor abused slave to worship him!" Before vanishing, the angel repeats that nothing exists but the boy: "And you are but a Thought—a vagrant Thought, a useless Thought, a homeless Thought, wandering forlorn among the empty eternities." The narrator confesses that he is left "appalled; for I knew, and realized, that all he had said was true."[41]

By imagining an angel on Earth, Mark Twain had dissolved the world. Perhaps Twain never published any version of the story because he knew how unwelcome its message would be to most Americans; or perhaps he never satisfied himself that any of the versions solved the problem of evil. Even if he did not succeed, the fact that Mark Twain, an agnostic or atheist who was arguably the most important writer of fiction in U.S. history, spent so much time and energy in his last years wrestling with angels shows how important a place angels have occupied at the intersection of American religion and culture. Other skeptical writers who have used angels and demons to challenge the pieties of Americans include Steven Vincent Benet in *The Devil and Daniel Webster* (1937); Ray Bradbury in *Something Wicked This Way Comes* (1962); Isaac Asimov in a short story, "The Last Trump" (1955); and Anne Rice in *Memnoch the Devil* (1994).

Images and Sculptures

Unlike the sometimes humorous angels and mocking demons of literature, the angels of nineteenth and early twentieth-century American art served people with solemn dignity. These militant or triumphant figures, usually female, represented a breakthrough of visual art among Protestants and a shift in the symbolic vocabulary of Catholics. Through paintings of angels, popular prints, and lithographs, and especially through statues, artists used angels to invoke spiritual power without dogma, contributing to a new realm of nondenominational religion. The spaces where this religion took hold included the cemetery, which was transformed from grim churchyard to beautiful park by the rural cemetery movement in the middle of the nineteenth century. With the application of steam to the printing press, the emergence of national magazines, and the development of lithography, especially by Currier and Ives, pictures of angels entered the homes of people who could not have afforded pictures of any kind in the past. Images of angels also broke the taboo on religious art among many Protestants. After the Civil War, angels proliferated in memorials on public squares and in murals on the walls of public buildings.

Both the classical revival in art and the Gothic revival in church architecture led artists to make more depictions of angels and to make them more solemn and chaste, as opposed to the colorful, personal, and playful angels of the Renaissance. By 1905, eleven stained-glass windows featuring massive and dignified angels surrounded the sanctuary of the First Presbyterian Church in Pittsburgh, where members of the American ruling class, whose ancestors had destroyed stained glass in English churches, now gathered to worship. Among Catholics, the shift was less dramatic but resulted in angels of the same type. Catholics in the Spanish colonies had painted and sculpted the three angels named in their Bible in Renaissance tunics and trousers, with traditional equipment: Michael with his sword and scales of judgment; Raphael with a fish, from his story in the book of Tobit; and Gabriel holding a staff.[42] As Irish and German Catholics built churches in American cities, they participated in the trend toward depicting angels without names who were more classically clothed and more ambiguously gendered. But before this trend took hold across the culture, one Protestant artist, who sculpted childlike angels drawn from the Renaissance master Raphael, created some scandal.

In 1829, the novelist James Fenimore Cooper was traveling in Italy, where he met Horatio Greenough (1805–1852), the man who is sometimes called "the first American sculptor." Cooper commissioned Greenough to carve statues in marble modeled on two cherubs from a painting by Raphael, the *Madonna del Baldacchino*, which hangs in the Pitti Palace in Florence. Problems arose from the fact that Raphael's cherubs, who sing together in the foreground of the painting, belonged to the type that Italians call *putti*—naked boys with visible genitals as well as childlike bodies and small wings. When Greenough and Cooper displayed their chanting cherubs in Boston in 1830, charging twenty-five cents per visit or fifty cents for a season pass, they planned for a run of six months. Receipts of $140 came in during the first week, but the naked penises caused such distress that in the third week, aprons were made for the angels. After this, the crowds diminished, and the statues were packed up and taken away three months early. The New York show met a similar fate. Cooper stored the statues until his death, after which they were lost.

Three years later, between November 1834 and February 1835, Greenough displayed a similar pair of figures, one an angel who grasped the wrist of a child emerging into the afterlife, at Armory Hall in Boston. This time there was no trouble, because the Boston merchant Samuel Cabot, who paid for the marble, "fought hard and carried the day" to keep them from appearing nude. Greenough made a device he described as "alabaster fig leaves which shall fall at a tap! of the hammer when the discerning public shall have *digested* the fruit of the knowledge of good and evil."[43] Later in the 1830s, the sculptor made other angels. One statue captures a moment in *Paradise Lost* when the angel Abdiel leaves the host of rebel spirits to return to the right side. Greenough depicts him as a youth with large wings wearing a tunic and breastplate, modeled on the Apollo Belvedere. He also did a bas-relief of the scene in Revelation 19:10 when an angel refuses to receive the worship of John of Patmos. This angel is also a male youth with large wings, but he wears a strangely draped toga. As he turns in profile to the right, the fabric flutters unattached along the left side of his body, covering his buttock only by chance and leaving the entire left thigh and leg exposed. One biographer remarked that the bas-relief had an "emotional restraint" worthy of its ancient Greek models and biblical subject but objected to the "effeminate details" of the angel's tunic and wings.[44] From the cherubs to the more adult young males, Greenough used angels to push American religious sensibilities into less Hebraic and more Greek, less divine and more human, directions.

Greenough's difficulties and the evolution of his work become more understandable against the background of American artistic poverty. Until photography and the lithographs of Currier and Ives made pictures popular and available, most Protestants in the United States saw little or no visual art. Puritan disapproval of idolatry kept paintings, statues, and stained-glass windows out of churches. Great painters like John Trumbull and Benjamin West were born in America but trained in England. In the 1830s, Samuel F. B. Morse, who later perfected the telegraph and Morse code, traveled up and down the Atlantic coast, hiring halls and charging admission for people to view an enormous canvas on which he had copied paintings from the Louvre. Though Morse and other Americans tried to justify art by claiming that paintings and sculptures of noble subjects could have good moral effects, depicting Jesus or the Virgin Mary would have come too close to Catholic practice. History and nature were safer subjects, and the safest way to suggest religious messages in art was to represent angels. Fully dressed female angels tended to supplant naked cherubs and male angels as the century progressed.

For example, the death of George Washington in 1799 led to many depictions of his apotheosis, or ascension to Heaven, and apotheosis usually involves angels to suggest the destination of the rising spirit. In an engraving by David Edwin from 1800, now in the National Portrait Gallery at the Smithsonian, two infant cherubs (one holding a laurel crown) float above the ascending president.[45] A version of 1802 has Washington's tomb surrounded by allegorical figures of the nation, including a mourning Indian, while one adult female angel and one elderly male angel carry Washington, who is seated on a cloud with his arms extended, into the skies. One of the more popular versions (painted by Samuel Moore and widely distributed as an engraving after 1860) has Washington wearing a toga that exposes his chest as he is borne aloft by seven markedly female, adult angels.[46] The most prominent public image of a Washington apotheosis, on the dome of the Capitol rotunda, was painted in 1865 by Constantino Brumidi, an Italian American who had to flee his country after fighting for freedom in the revolution of 1848. In Brumidi's dome, Washington, sitting amidst the angels of the thirteen original states and a winged female Victory, looks down from Heaven. The state angels, like Victory and so many other angels depicted in this era, are adult and female. The association of angels with "pagan" religious attitudes becomes explicit in the lower sections of the dome, where Roman goddesses and gods interact with famous Americans: Minerva is consulting with Benjamin Franklin, Robert Fulton, and Samuel F. B. Morse about science, Venus helps Neptune as he lays the Atlantic telegraph cable, and the god Vulcan and the goddess Ceres participate in industry and agriculture. Brumidi's murals deified the progress of American society in its practical achievements and its dominance of the world. By integrating angels, pagan gods, and legendary heroes, the paintings also brought a transtheistic religious vision into the Capitol of the United States.

A series of four paintings by the Hudson River artist Thomas Cole (1801–1848) called *Voyage of Life: Childhood, Youth, Manhood, Old Age* reflected a personalized dimension of the new religious attitude by featuring adult, female angels who surround the human voyager from the beginning to the end of life.[47] In the painting of childhood, a boat with a female angel carved at its prow carries an infant and his shining angelic guardian along a river. Next, the ambiguously sexed, but probably female, guardian stands on the shore as the youth continues in the boat. The youth takes an eager posture that echoes the angel of the prow. In manhood, the subject of the painting looks to Heaven for guidance as demons threaten the boat from the clouds. Cole ominously described the demons as "Suicide, Intemperance, and Murder." Lastly, in the painting depicting old age, the light of sunset fills one side of the canvas as the shining angel floats above a white-haired man, beckoning him to ascend from the boat. Many engravings were made of these paintings, but the originals hung in the childhood home of Julia Ward Howe, feminist and author of "The Battle Hymn of the Republic." For Cole and for his fellow Americans who bought reproductions of his paintings, pictures of angels appear to have served as ways to remember and perhaps to invoke the guidance of God in everyday life. They also taught Americans that angelic women, or divine female figures, were the normal mediums by which God offered such guidance to men.

By the early twenty-first century, dozens of American artists were specializing in angels. The first of these painters was Abbott Thayer (1849–1921), one of whose works appears at the beginning of chapter 2. The heir of a Boston family old and distinguished enough to have a dormitory in Harvard Yard named after it, Thayer painted his daughter Mary with wings and a grave expression in *Angel* (1889). Later, he transplanted the image into at least twelve different large paintings with various contexts and poses, including a scene in which she becomes the guardian angel of Mount Monadnock and one where she walks between her younger brother and sister, sheltering them while clouds form her wings.[48] Thayer's simple, calm, yet sentimental female angel became the ancestor of many guardian angel pins, pictures, and nightlights in the next century. Even the wings on Victoria's Secret lingerie models, as we have seen, owe a debt to Abbott Thayer.

Statues of angels made new sacred spaces in the parks, schools, and cemeteries of the United States. On one hand, unlike paintings and stained glass, a statue could serve as outdoor, public art, creating a location by itself. On the other hand, the vividness of statues made those who feared idolatry and those who objected to nudity particularly suspicious; even the Greek and Russian Orthodox, who make great use of painted icons and mosaics, allow no statues in their churches. At a time when statues of Jesus, Mary, or the saints would not have been acceptable in the Protestant churches of America, or even outdoors in a predominantly Protestant public square, the abstract yet biblical quality of angels made angel statues acceptable. Of course, as Horatio Greenough's difficulties with naked cherubs had shown, American sculpted angels were only acceptable if they were dignified and chaste. English and European artists of the nineteenth and early twentieth centuries produced pictures of angels that ranged from the fantastic to the sensual, moving from William Blake's engravings to the fantasies of Pre-Raphaelites like Edward Bourne-Jones, but American painters and sculptors gave their angels classical dignity without classical nudity.

The first, and one of the best-known, massive public angels came from Emma Stebbins (1815–1882), one of several American women who went to Italy to study sculpture in the nineteenth century. Stebbins's bronze *Angel of the Waters* was unveiled at Bethesda Terrace, at the heart of New York's Central Park, in 1873. With wings outstretched, this female angel still stands on a column above a fountain that is supported by four youths representing the classical virtues. The angel looks down at the waters and the people, holding a stick that she will use to stir the waters and to infuse them with healing power, as the angel did at the pool of Bethesda in Jerusalem according to the fifth chapter of John's Gospel (in the King James Version). The six-hour HBO version of Tony Kushner's *Angels in America* began and ended with this angel, who stirs to life in the opening sequence and is later used to embody the promise of healing from AIDS. The same angel and fountain also appeared in the opening scenes of the musical *Godspell* in 1973.

One of America's best-known sculptors, Augustus Saint-Gaudens (1848–1907), made several powerful female statues of angels. He sculpted Amor Caritas, or the Angel of Charity, originally intended for the tomb

*One of the first great statues of a female angel, and the creation of a female
sculptor, this figure of the healing angel from the Gospel of John furnished a
setting for the beginning of the movie* Godspell *and for the Broadway and
television versions of* Angels in America. *Emma Stebbins,* Angel of the Waters,
*1868 (placed in Central Park, New York, 1873). Bronze, stone basin at the base.
(Photograph by William Gardella)*

of New York governor Edwin Morgan near Boston, as well as a walking Victory who carries a palm before the mounted statue of General Sherman at Grand Army Plaza in New York. Saint-Gaudens created another dignified, winged female as a protective spirit to fly over the troops depicted in a bronze relief on the memorial for the Massachusetts Fifty-Fourth Regiment, a famed unit of black soldiers that fought in the Civil War. With each of these three works, Saint-Gaudens sent a message that angels protected Americans in the face of death and war.

The most important sculptor of angels in American history to this point has been Daniel Chester French (1850–1931), the sculptor of the Lincoln Memorial, the Minute Man of Concord, the Alma Mater of Columbia University, and John Harvard in Harvard Yard. French left at least ten major angels in cemeteries, museums, and public squares, and together they demonstrate the range of meaning that the American religion of angels had begun to command by the first decades of the twentieth century. Among those that celebrated Americans was *Victory*, an image of the Greek goddess Nike who spreads her powerful wings over the square near the White House and the Executive Office Building in Washington, D.C., serving as a memorial to the American army of World War I. Her helmeted head has been called the most beautiful in American sculpture.[49] A bronze angel by French celebrating the philanthropy of George Robert White has stood at the corner of Beacon and Arlington streets in Boston since 1924. Her wings dramatically curl to support her as she lands on her left foot; she holds a basket with her left arm and sweeps out her right hand, as though scattering seed. In a less triumphant mood, French's early works included an angel of death seizing the hand of a young sculptor. This is a bronze relief that he did for the grave of a colleague now buried at the Milmore Memorial in Boston's Forest Hills Cemetery.[50] French again paired the angel of death with a young man decades later, when he designed the brooding marble *Death and the Young Warrior* as a memorial to the graduates of St. Paul's School in New Hampshire who had lost their lives in World War I.[51] French's images of death cast angels less as comforters than as mourners or agents of tragedy, and at times they have inspired fear. When French did a memorial for a cemetery in Iowa City in 1911, the resulting 9-foot bronze turned black. It has since become a local legend, the subject of

The winged female who carries a laurel crown before General William Tecumseh Sherman is technically Nike, the Greek goddess of victory, but the figure of Nike has been assimilated by Christians to their angels for thousands of years. Augustus Saint-Gaudens, Sherman Monument, *1900 (placed in Grand Army Plaza, Central Park, New York, 1903). Bronze with gold leaf. (Photograph by William Gardella)*

tales about people who died after touching it disrespectfully or who were cursed after looking into its eyes.[52]

An heir of New Englanders who came to Massachusetts with John Winthrop in 1630, French did two statues that followed the Yankee tradition of Emerson, Whitman, and Longfellow in using angels to question religious orthodoxy. For the Panama-Pacific Exposition held at San Francisco in 1915, French made *The Genius of Creation*, a seated female angel with both wings and arms outspread; he placed Adam, Eve, and the serpent grouped around the column on which the angel sat. French here used an angel to cast a personal, female genius in the role of the creator God, perhaps representing the spirit (Hebrew *ruach*, feminine gender) that moved over the waters in Genesis 1.[53] An even more unorthodox angel appeared in 1924, when French unveiled a work with a title drawn from the story of the *bnai elohim* in Genesis 6, *The Sons of God Saw the Daughters of Men That They Were Fair*. Here a male angel and a woman, both nude and partly surrounded by his wings, begin to embrace; her left arm reaches partly around his back as she rises on one foot toward him, and his right hand grasps her shoulder. This statue violated the American rule in favor of chaste, dignified, and fully clothed angels; it merits further consideration in the chapter on "Angels, Love, and Sex."

Angels of Constancy and Change

In the era of Saint-Gaudens and French, and particularly from the Civil War through World War I, a trend in public art known as the City Beautiful movement led to the creation of neoclassical buildings and monuments in parks and park-like urban settings across the United States. This movement combined with the garden cemetery movement that first emerged in 1831 with the founding of Mt. Auburn Cemetery in Cambridge, Massachusetts, to generate a great demand for angel statues and murals. Because the buildings, monuments, and statues erected in this era evoke ancient Greece and Rome, they were criticized as out of place by progressive architects like Louis Sullivan and Frank Lloyd Wright, and they can be read as attempts to impose a changeless order on the world or as expressions of incipient American imperialism. The Lincoln Memorial, for example, has been said to express the triumphal spirit of the Spanish-American War more than the spirit of Lincoln, a man of the plains whom it turns into a god. There are angels in murals at either side of the Lincoln Memorial, on one hand setting free the slaves and on the other bringing together North and South, and these angels could be seen as proof that the memorial turns history into myth.

And yet, the era sometimes called the Gilded Age was also a time of serious doubt, spiritual exploration, and agnosticism, an era that included William James, the psychologist of religion, and Oliver Wendell Holmes, the jurist who never recovered from the deaths he saw in the Civil War. The Lincoln Memorial often inspires not simple reverence but unease, and it has been the site of massive demonstrations, such as the March on Washington led by Martin Luther King Jr. in 1963. The angels of cemeteries and monuments built in that time may convey complacency, but statues like Emma Stebbins's Angel of Bethesda also represented a broadening of the ways in which Americans imagined divine power. These predominantly female angels also stood for a basic change moving through the culture of that day, the growing recognition of women's rights.

The Women's Building of the 1893 World's Columbian Exposition in Chicago used the dignified, female angels of American art as symbols of the women's movement in society. On the roof of that 80,000-square-foot, two-story building, which was dismantled after the Exposition, stood bronze angels 12 feet high.[54] One of them, called Enlightenment, spread her wings upward while extending her arms down to two human women, one in academic cap and gown who looked up to the angel, and another who was looking down, but reaching up with one hand. In another group, a central angel, Innocence, took wing, her left hand on her breast and her face turned skyward, while at her feet the kneeling figure of a nun left her jewels on an altar and a woman sat nursing a child. These angels came from the hand of a nineteen-year-old student from the San Francisco School of Design, Alice Rideout (b. 1874). In the mural on the ceiling of the building's library, which held books by women from more than forty nations, a female angel, called Imagination by the artist, Dora Wheeler Keith, raised her gorgeous, multicolored wings above a man in academic garb who represented Science and a beautiful woman who stood for Literature.

All of these statues and paintings of female angels formed part of an age when Christianity was recovering its feminine side.[55] Although a few

Renaissance angels were female, the West had known centuries of predominantly male symbolism and male leadership. The Reformation had banished Mary, the female saints, and nuns in Protestant cultures, while Catholics responded with the all-male Jesuit order. In the nineteenth and early twentieth centuries, women and female symbols returned. The contexts of this recovery ranged from appearances of the Virgin Mary to young Catholic women, starting in 1830 in Paris and continuing at Lourdes in 1858 and Fatima in 1917, to the rise of female preachers among American Methodists. This return of the feminine surely included the art that convinced many twentieth-century Americans that angels were all women.

The angels of the 1893 Exposition, along with those who visited American farms in Florida and who settled on public squares at the end of the nineteenth century and the beginning of the twentieth, also expressed an optimism that became difficult even to imagine by the 1960s. Two world wars, a Great Depression, and fifty years living in fear of atomic devastation while fighting new wars in Korea and Vietnam took a toll. The Spiritualists derided by Mark Twain and the American artists who painted and sculpted angels in the early 1900s thought they stood on the edge of a millennium of peace, prosperity, justice, and spiritual power. To see death as the final end of life seemed shortsighted and foolish to them. Even World War I did not entirely banish this mood; the amendments to the Constitution prohibiting alcohol and enabling women to vote grew out of the same optimism. But many angels of that age departed before their time. Somehow, the teen sculptor Alice Rideout disappeared from history, and only photographs of her 12-foot bronzes remain. In the backlash against the women's movement that arose after the 1930s, artists like Rideout and Emma Stebbins were forgotten, and painting, sculpture, and literature became as much or more of a man's world than these realms had been in the Renaissance. Since the middle of the twentieth century, cemeteries have more often been filled with uniform stones and tablets flat to the ground than with glorious and protective angelic women. If angels had been suggested as part of the Vietnam War Memorial or the memorial to veterans of World War II on the Washington Mall, the idea would have seemed too sentimental, too religious, or (if the angels were female) even too sexist.

Still, many influences from the first angels of the United States have survived. Ralph Waldo Emerson's transtheistic angel Uriel continued through the poetry of H. D. in the 1940s and found his way into the pack of Angel Oracle Cards published by angel therapist Doreen Virtue in 2002. Abbott Thayer's *Angel* portrait from 1889 adorned the cover of *Ask Your Angels*, a best-selling manual on communicating with spirits, in 1992. By detaching angels from their roots in Judaism, the Bible, and traditional Christian doctrine, the writers and artists of the nineteenth and early twentieth centuries cleared an area of freedom in American culture where Hollywood could make angel movies and television shows. The angels of high art and public memorials were joined by angels of popular culture and mass consumption.

Founding a Cultural Religion

During the 1940s, three icons of popular culture entered the canon of the American religion of angels. First came a children's story, *The Littlest Angel* (written in 1939, performed on radio in 1940, and published as a book in 1946); then the *Night on Bald Mountain* sequence and other scenes from Walt Disney's *Fantasia* (1940; rereleased in 1946, 1956, and 1982; and redone in 2000); and then Frank Capra's last successful film, *It's a Wonderful Life* (1946, reshown every Christmas on television). These fictions embodied themes already associated with angels in America. *The Littlest Angel* celebrated angels in connection with gifts and with Christmas and as mediators between the realms of matter and spirit. In *Fantasia,* Disney raised the "satanic epic" of war between good and evil spirits to new levels of vividness and universality. *It's a Wonderful Life* underlined the homely role of angels as helpers in everyday life. Later in the twentieth century, many angel therapists employed variations on the strategy of the angel Clarence in that film.

The precious quality of common toys and the transformation of matter by spirit are central to *The Littlest Angel,* a Christmas story written by Charles Tazewell (the heir of a seventeenth-century colonial family transplanted to Des Moines, Iowa, and then to Hollywood) in 1939.[56] Conceived as a radio show and recorded by such luminaries as Helen Hayes and Loretta Young, the story deals with a boy who dies at four and a half. He cries and snuffles while being admitted to Heaven, making the

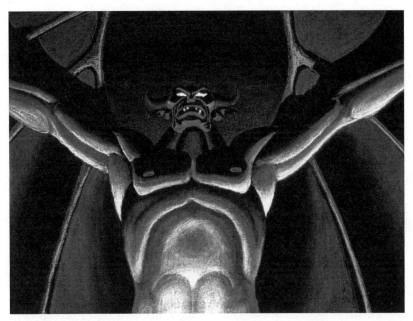

Chernobog (the Black God), the demon from the "Night on Bald Mountain" sequence in Walt Disney's Fantasia *(1940), one of the founding documents of the cultural religion of angels in the United States. (Walt Disney Pictures/Photofest)*

Gatekeeper blot the page of his record book, and soon becomes a problem in other ways. He tarnishes his halo by holding it with his hand, sings off key in the choir, and habitually arrives late to prayers, knocking everyone's wings askew as he rushes to his place. Called to account before the Understanding Angel, the boy ascribes his misbehavior to all that he misses on Earth. When the angel asks him whether anything can make him happy in Heaven, he recalls a box he kept under his bed in which he kept a dead butterfly, two white stones he found on a river bank, a robin's egg, and a leather collar that had belonged to his dog. After this box is fetched, the Littlest Angel becomes happy and well-behaved. Another crisis arises, however, when God announces that Jesus will be born on Earth. All the angels strive to make gifts for the baby, but the Littlest Angel finds he can do nothing. Finally he decides that he will give Jesus his box. When the day comes for the angels to present their gifts, he looks at the other glorious presents and feels ashamed. When God's hand picks out his box, he fears he has been "most blasphemous," feels "frantic terror," and tries to flee but falls "with a horrified wail and a clatter of halo," rolling "in a ball of misery to the very foot of the heavenly throne." God then declares that of all the gifts, "this small box pleases me most." Its contents are "of the earth and of men, and my Son is born to be king of both," he continues, predicting that Jesus also would come to love such things and leave them regretfully when his life was done. Then God causes the box to glow and rise from its place, and as the Littlest Angel watches, his box becomes the Star of Bethlehem.[57]

According to a 2002 edition of the book, various versions of *The Littlest Angel* have sold 5 million copies since it first appeared in book form in 1946. It was done as a Hallmark Hall of Fame television movie, with music by Cab Calloway and others, in 1969, and in animated versions, most recently in 1997. Although *The Littlest Angel* had a fairly negative view of the lives of angels and depicted Heaven as a dull place not fit for boys, it clearly struck an American nerve. It used angels to teach the lesson that ordinary people, and ordinary, material things, could have transcendent value.

According to an authorized Disney history of *Fantasia,* Walt Disney tackled the project of animating the world of classical music by keeping "the fairy tale, the legend, the myth" firmly in mind. He sought to create "elementally simple" images of eternal opposites. He understood that "good and evil, the antagonists of all great drama . . . must be believably personified. The moral ideas common to all humanity must be upheld."[58] To fulfill this purpose, Disney ended the movie with the remarkable juxtaposition of Modest Moussorgsky's *Night on Bald Mountain* with Franz Schubert's *Ave Maria.* The Moussorgsky sequence begins with the mountain of the title turning into an enormous Satan with huge horns and leathery wings, eyes glowing yellow against smooth black skin, with an enormously muscular, well-defined chest and abdomen. In a dramatization of the Ukrainian legend of Chernobog, literally the "Black God" who rises on Walpurgis Night and brings the damned back to life, this version of Satan exults in his power, looming over a sleeping town. He makes damned souls dance, crushes them into flames, and watches as they break apart and recombine with more and more frenzied dancing. It seems for a moment that the whole world must be damned, swallowed by the maw of Hell. Only the dawn, announced with the ringing of church bells, can bring the triumph of evil to a close. At each tolling of the bell, Satan (or Chernobog) flinches, holding his hand to his eyes to shield them from the increasing light, until he yields, folds his wings over his body, and turns again into the peak of Bald Mountain. Without a break, the last notes of Moussorgsky's piece blend into the opening of the *Ave Maria*. A predawn, bluish mist is punctuated by a line of lights held by indistinct figures, who may be human pilgrims, souls of the dead, or perhaps angels of the worshipful sort who appear in *The Littlest Angel*. The procession of lights enters a garden gate, then disappears into a golden sunrise. Good has finally triumphed over evil.

Walt Disney arose from Huguenot (French Protestant) stock and spent most of his first decades in the neighborhood of Kansas City, especially the city of Marceline, Missouri, which he recreated as the Main Streets of Disneyland and Disney World.[59] Having inherited the dualistic view of conflict between spirits of good and evil, he presented several versions of apocalypse in *Fantasia*. The *Sorcerer's Apprentice* sequence evokes a flood that nearly destroys the world of Mickey Mouse. To illustrate the music of Igor Stravinsky's *Rite of Spring*, the animation of *Fantasia* shows the Earth's surface being formed with great violence, dinosaurs arising and fighting each other and dying in a great drought, then another flood that destroys and renews the Earth. The world of Greek myth—complete with families of flying horses, male and female centaurs, cupids who resemble *putti* or cherubs, a slapstick Dionysus, and Zeus throwing thunderbolts—is brought to an end by another disastrous storm and flood, all to the music of Ludwig van Beethoven's *Sixth Symphony*. That sequence closes in peace, with Apollo riding his sun chariot to the West and the goddess Night drawing her curtain across the sky.

Amid all of this apocalyptic imagery, it seems fair to say that no single character (with the possible exception of Mickey Mouse) comes close to attaining the vivid power of the Satan from *Night on Bald Mountain*. All of the good winged spirits, gods, and holy figures seem insipid by comparison. Such a Satan was a worthy antagonist, but not of Zeus. The implicit power of good worked impersonally, bringing the dawn, standing behind the happy cherubs and the solemn light bearers, killing the terrifying dinosaurs, and cleansing the world. The cumulative effect of *Fantasia* contributed almost as strongly as *Star Wars* to the transtheism that underlies the religion of angels.

The most significant contribution of the 1940s to this emerging religion came from a Catholic immigrant from Sicily, Frank Capra, director of *It's a Wonderful Life* (1946). Based on a very short story, "The Greatest Gift," that was never accepted by magazines but privately printed as a Christmas card by its author, Philip Van Doren Stern (and then sold to RKO films by his agent), the movie concerns an angel who saves a man from suicide by showing him what his town would have turned into if he had never lived. In the original story, the angel was just a mysterious figure with the power to transport the near-suicide into a hypothetical world and then bring him back. What the suicidal man saw had little social resonance. If he had never lived, the bank where he was sick of working would have closed, because the man who did his job would have embezzled funds; his wife would have married the brother of the embezzler, an alcoholic; and his younger brother would have drowned as a teenager in an accident, because the suicidal man would not have been there to rescue him. The theme of recognizing life as a gift, not just to oneself but to others, was present, but the story evoked no social system.[60]

Though the story was developed into three different screenplays by three excellent writers (Marc Connelly, Dalton Trumbo, and Clifford Odets), none of these versions went beyond the personal. They made the suicidal man, George, into a frustrated businessman or politician, or even split him into two or three characters who argued about the meaning of his life. The angel was identified by numbers like "B-29" (the designation of a World War II bomber!) and "1163," and the angel had no stake in the outcome.[61] Only in the script that Capra developed did the full context of religion emerge as a network of relationships and commitments that holds life together, binding the human and whatever lies beyond the human, the rational and the nonrational (or, as Robert Orsi has said, Heaven and Earth).[62]

George Bailey (played by Jimmy Stewart), the hero of *It's a Wonderful Life*, is saved from suicide because angels hear eight different people praying for him. Angels named "Joseph" and "Franklin" (Stalin and Roosevelt?) assign Clarence, a "clockmaker" who has not won his wings in 200 years of trying, but who has "the faith of a child," to help George. Again adding to the original story, the final script made Clarence stop George from killing himself by falling first into the freezing river into which the man was about to leap, and so causing the human to rescue the angel rather than committing suicide. In the vision of life without the George Bailey character, the entire town, and not simply George's family and friends, has changed. The greed of a banker who triumphed because George did not stop him has turned a wholesome community into a den of vice and crime, abandoned homes, and slums. When George comes to his senses and asks to get his life back, even at the risk of facing bankruptcy and jail, his decision sets off a social chain reaction of small donations to save him, resulting in redemption not only for George but for the whole town. This result also gives Clarence his wings, which are not just a symbol of rank but an instrument of power to overcome time, seeing the human world at all moments in the past. Angels and humans belong to a single cosmos in which they work together for good—with the single exception of the banker, Mr. Potter (Lionel Barrymore).

With *It's a Wonderful Life*, the religion of angels was emerging as a form of religion specific to the United States. The sixteenth- and seventeenth-century epic of conflict with Satan had been shared with England and Spain, and English poets and artists dealt with angels through the nineteenth and early twentieth centuries. Often the English were more sexually daring (for example, the paintings of Edward Bourne-Jones) and less reverent than Americans, but they did consider angels nearly as much. With the 1930s and 1940s, however, Hollywood poured out angel films like *Gabriel over the White House* (1933), *The Green Pastures* (1936), *Here Comes Mr. Jordan* (1941), *Cabin in the Sky* (1943), *The Horn Blows at Midnight* (1945), *The Bishop's Wife* (1947), and *Heaven Only Knows* (1947), among many others. Often the angels in these films worked, as Clarence did in *It's a Wonderful Life*, as colleagues of humans rather than superior beings, and even the comedies tended to have serious moral lessons. English critics found the whole perspective baffling. Reviewing *It's a Wonderful Life*, one called it "an embarrassment to both flesh and spirit," and another wrote that it was "a very good film—for Americans." More remarkably, Capra had trouble in 1947 getting the movie past the English board of censors. Before *It's a Wonderful Life* could premiere in England, they demanded that all references to Jesus and Mary be removed, as well as discussion of first- and second-class angels and the word "wings," as when Clarence thanked George Bailey for his wings. It took a sustained argument on Capra's part to keep the line "Thanks for the wings" from being eliminated or changed to something else.[63]

Meanwhile, in America, *It's a Wonderful Life* has appeared on television every Christmas and has been remade in many variations. A 1977 ABC Sunday Night Movie, *It Happened One Christmas*, reversed genders by casting Marlo Thomas as Mary Bailey and Cloris Leachman as guardian angel Clara. An ABC After School Special from 1982, *Amy and the Angel*, transposed the story into adolescent terms, casting Meg Ryan as a high school villain who torments another teenaged girl until she almost commits suicide. Here James Earl Jones plays a chief angel who dispatches a former teenaged boy who had killed himself thirty years before to save Amy by showing her the value of her life. In an episode of *The Twilight Zone*, Carol Burnett played a single woman and secretary in Brooklyn who regrets her life until she meets a gruff angel who gives her a mansion on Sutton Place and a raft of wealthy friends, after which she finds that she already had what she wanted.[64] Another trope on the Capra theme came in an Albert Brooks comedy from 1991, *Defending Your Life*, in which angels show recently deceased people how they wasted their lives and what they should change the next time. Also in 1991, the Family Channel gave the angel Clarence from *It's a Wonderful Life* his own television movie, *Clarence*, which shows guardian angels growing younger with each good deed until they became cherubs. Far more important than any of these entertainments, however, was the model of angel as therapist, established by Frank Capra and Clarence in *It's a Wonderful Life*, which would dominate the angel religion of the 1990s, moving beyond the screen and into life.

As the American religion of angels flourished in the last decades of the twentieth century, people worked with angels in distinct but related contexts. Some wrote books about human contact with angels, drawing on their own experiences and collecting stories from others. Exorcists went to war with demons on a battlefield that alternated between fiction and lived experience, with each realm influencing the other. Television brought the model of angel therapy from the large scale of the movies into details of family life and individual psychology, and angel channelers sought to teach everyone how to speak with angels on a daily basis. To complete this part of the study, I attempted to practice this particular spiritual discipline, meeting with a group led by Trudy Griswold for an angel-channeling session.

Women Collecting Angel Stories

The angel craze that swept the United States in the 1990s was led by women who collected stories about angels in everyday life. In the work of Sophy Burnham, who wrote *A Book of Angels;* Martha Williamson, producer of the television series *Touched by an Angel;* and many other women, including Joan Wester Anderson, Eileen Elias Freeman, and Doreen Virtue, angels descended from the distant heavens, from the medieval past, and from war memorials and cemeteries to enter American streets and homes. As these women told their angel stories, taught people to pray through angels, and channeled the messages of angels, they brought Catholic, evangelical Protestant, and New Age constituencies together. This moment in popular culture affected religious belief across the nation. In March 2004, a Gallup poll showed that 78 percent of Americans (84 percent of women and 72 percent of men) believed in angels, up from 72 percent in 1994 and 64 percent in 1978. With regard to practice, fascination with angels made Americans more receptive to new kinds of prayer, to faith healing, and to direct experience of spirits.

The women who taught Americans about angels built upon the work of, and often opposed, a group of male writers and clergy concerned with demons. From Anton LaVey's Church of Satan, which flourished in the 1960s, to *The Exorcist* in 1973 and the panic over satanic ritual abuse in the 1980s, men led both the partisans of the Devil and those who warned against him. Often, exorcists denounced the cultivation of passive states of mind and other practices and theories taught by the female angel writers. By the early twenty-first century, a low-grade culture war had started over whether and how to speak with angels and demons.

The breakthrough book on angels did not express the values of a Protestant evangelist like Billy Graham (whose *Angels* urged people to accept Jesus at the end of several chapters), a Catholic novelist like William Peter Blatty (although *The Exorcist* helped to set the stage by getting people interested in demons), or a neutral scholar. *A Book of Angels* (1990), by Sophy Burnham, was steeped instead in the social world and spiritual ambitions of a woman raised an Episcopalian in an upper-middle-class Maryland family, a decade before the second wave of the women's movement began. Burnham began her account of angels by telling how she had met a good ghost (a male doctor) in the New York apartment, with its "walnut-paneled bedroom" and "bay window that gave onto the Statue of Liberty," that she had moved into with her husband when he wrote for the *New York Times.* Her stories of rescue by angels included one of her own yachting tales as well as a description of a black-clad angel who kept her from falling off a cliff while skiing in Val d'Isère, France.[1] The accounts framed a spiritual autobiography that moved from her childhood questions about God to her skeptical father (who was "brilliant, warm, witty, intellectual" and loved arguing in court—"Supreme Court being his favorite") to a deathbed reconciliation with her mother to a trance-like vision in which Burnham herself became an angel.

By reading *A Book of Angels,* millions of Americans took a vacation to a world of glamorous settings made more exciting by inexplicable coincidences and mysterious events. At the same time, Burnham assured the reader that she was a regular person. As a child she sat in "overheated classes, stupefied by the hissing radiators," until she went to boarding school and college (Smith). She then married, had children, and worked (at first as a typist, later as a freelance writer and author of books). Her sensibilities as a woman helped her to connect with life beyond the boundaries of social class. On the night when she first saw a ghost, she was sewing a dress for her daughter, which she specifically describes ("the softest cocoa color, with a square neck and ribbon bindings—adorable"). She observed with gently gendered humor that the Virgin Mary had an angel to tell her "news that every other woman gets by morning sickness or tender breasts or the absence of her monthly cycle"; this, she said, showed that the Bible made angels "as common as grapes."[2]

Sadness arising from personal relations cleared the space that angels filled in Burnham's life. "Loss and emptiness" were the words she used to describe her situation when she was saved by an angel at Val d'Isère: "For a week I have been grieving the separation and loss of people close to me—my divorce, my father's death, professional failures, the separation from a man I love."[3] Many of the stories in *A Book of Angels* came from women in similar positions. One, "married to a man of old family and a rigid, formal style of life," saw dark angels in the midst of a storm and felt threatened that they would come for her if she did not make changes in her life. "She never deserted or neglected her children, but her marriage eventually came to an end."[4] With rare exceptions, the angels described in Burnham's book came to women who were not only alone but lonely or afraid—in a new apartment, a strange city, walking alone on a Greek island at night. Almost all of those who reported angelic encounters were women; the last chapter consists of twenty letters Burnham had received from people who had met angels, and nineteen of them were from women. Although Burnham's sequel, *Angel Letters* (1991), included more male visionaries, the preponderance of reports continued to come from women, and this trend continued in other angel books.

Besides letters and stories, *A Book of Angels* offered more than a hundred pages of history and theory, moving lightly from Zoroaster, Hebrew prophets, and Catholic theologians to Emanuel Swedenborg. Reaching beyond the West, Burnham included Hindu gods with wings and Buddhist bodhisattvas in her search for evidence of angels. Her perspective in this survey sometimes lapses into that of the well-traveled white person who owns all cultures, as when she presents Native American visionaries as "simple nomads, innocent as children," who naturally "trust their own senses."[5] Still, the breadth of her account was impressive, genuinely informative without being too pedantic for a popular book.

Although Burnham undercut the significance of her survey by writing, "Look: we know nothing about angels . . . except that we are given brief, fleeting glimpses in our hearts,"[6] she actually drew many conclusions. Angels, wrote Burnham, are definitely not ghosts or spirits of dead people. Angels can be distinguished from ghosts in experience because ghosts are cold and angels are warm; ghosts are shadowy and dark while angels are brilliant, formed of light. While Burnham averred that she had some experience of demons, Satan, and the possibility of fallen angels or discarnate spirits possessing people (particularly beautiful people), she sympathized with Origen, the third-century Christian theologian who taught that Satan would eventually be saved, and she denied the eternity of Hell.[7]

Experience both broadened and challenged Burnham's theory during a past-life regression, induced with help from a friend acting as a guide, in which the author moved from past to future lives and found herself becoming an angel. During the first part of the transformation she giggled constantly, flying in a "whirling corkscrew motion . . . cutting the atmosphere." At the guide's request she landed on Earth, then hovered again and observed humanity, marveling at "how *dear* they were" and finding it absurd that people lived inside dark structures, but cut holes in them to let in air and light, and that they fought so hard with each other but then forgot what they were fighting about. "All appetite they were, and good intentions," she concluded. People were always going wrong, yet they went on because they "liked—they actually enjoyed!— the sensation of being smacked by fear and loss."[8] In her angel mode, Burnham was stunned by how much she loved the people she observed. She wanted to watch and help, but "could not do anything unless one asked for help," and so could not intervene "if two of them started a fight or war, since that was what they wanted to do." This confirmed what Burnham had thought after the angel on the ski slope in France had saved her, when she wondered why no spiritual beings had swept in "to save mothers in Vietnam or Palestine from bombs and napalm burns." Angels were unable to prevent the "blood of mankind shed by man."[9]

Now the guide asked the angelic Burnham whether any other spiritual creatures inhabited the Earth. In her trance she saw beings whom she called Big Ones, living at some distance from humans, who appeared to have "wider tasks to do." She swept beyond them to the realm of Sages, who lived alone, although there were many of them, sitting "in what is neither dark nor light" and giving off "a silent sound . . . a harmonious hum of pure being . . . that vibration on which the universe subsists." Seeing herself as a Sage, Burnham felt pure Compassion, in which there were no lesser or greater beings, only beings who thought of themselves as greater or lesser. Her guide asked whether she had become God, and she answered no, because there was "something greater," a Source, but also yes, because "Goodness lay everywhere." The task of the Sage was "to release the silent sound, compassion, which is God, into the spheres of God to fall as God on all else that is God, transmuting into God."[10]

Though unsympathetic readers might see Burnham's answer as gibberish, it also resembles some Hindu statements about yoga and the syllable *Om* or *Aum* used in meditation. Recently Diana Eck, founder of the Pluralism Project at Harvard University, has suggested that American culture is being transformed by Hindu perspectives in what some call New Age thinking.[11] Whether influenced by Hinduism or not, writers on angel therapy often blur the lines between humanity, angels, and God, modifying monotheism without becoming truly dualistic or polytheistic. They are, as I suggested when discussing Whitman and others in chapter 3, transtheistic—believers in many spiritual forces that come together in an underlying unity.

In any spiritual practice that seeks union with God, the prayer of simple petition to God may become problematic; asking God for something can be seen as reinforcing a false sense of division between self and God. In a later book, *The Path of Prayer* (2002), Burnham dealt with this question extensively, but *A Book of Angels* explained how to pray by analogy to the physical world: First, one must realize that "prayer is a law of the universe, like gravity." People who pray effectively don't have to believe in God, but they "must follow the rules," as in using gravity and aerodynamics to fly. "Imagine there is a giant radio station out in space . . . and all you have to do is to beam your thought, your longing to that station, and *if it is received clearly,* without static, the answer comes pouring down." People could rely on "an abundance of delight" in practicing such prayer, because "it is the pleasure of the universe to give us what we need." To avoid static, prayer should always be framed in positive terms and in the present tense, Burnham taught. A woman who prays "Don't let my baby die" gives off static in the form of two negatives; she is already imagining loss and grief, and so making the death of her baby "more possible." Instead she should pray "Let my baby live!" or, better, "Thank you that my baby lives," since "the universe has no concept of time." To pray in this way is "what Christ meant when he spoke of having faith," according to Sophy Burnham. After holding the image of the prayer being fulfilled in the mind for a moment, the next step is "to submit to the universe again," not allowing any doubt that the prayer will be answered, but recognizing that "Providence knows more of what is best for us than we ourselves." Finally, those who pray should notice how their prayer is answered and respond with gratitude.[12]

Burnham sees angels as a sign that spirit fills all of nature; here she touches themes that have resonated from as far back in American history as Jonathan Edwards and Ralph Waldo Emerson, and that would continue in many New Age angel therapies. In a later book, *The Ecstatic Journey* (1999), a chapter on "Angels and Visitations" again related angels to Burnham's pantheistic (or transtheistic) worldview. Her emphasis on positive thinking and confident prayer connects her with some evangelical Protestants and Pentecostals who have also said that believers should confidently claim God's blessings and visualize their prayers being answered.

Writing from a very different part of the religious and social spectrum, Joan Wester Anderson received more traditional messages from her angels. Anderson had been publishing articles, columns, and books of family-based humor, sometimes touching on religion, for seventeen years when Burnham's *A Book of Angels* became a best seller. A native of Chicago (not Maryland), raised Catholic (not Episcopalian), a graduate of Northeastern Illinois State University (not Smith), and a mother of five (not two), she represented a different social class, cultural milieu, and spiritual style from those of Sophy Burnham. Her book, *Where Angels Walk: True Stories of Heavenly Visitors* (1992), offered not spiritual autobiography, angelic theory, or instruction in prayer but simply testimonies to the acts of angels from across the Christian world, ranging from missionaries of the Assemblies of God and people with children at Southern Baptist daycare centers to famous Catholics like Mother Teresa of Calcutta, Mother Angelica of the Eternal Word Television Network, and Padre Pio of Italy. Many of Anderson's stories involved automobile accidents or near-accidents, especially during winter nights in Ohio, Indiana, and Illinois; she began the book with an account of how her own son was mysteriously rescued in a blizzard outside of Fort Wayne.

Attending to angels changed the focus of Anderson's career from family humor (involving book titles like *Love, Lollipops and Laundry* or *Stop the World—Our Gerbils Are Loose!*) to spiritual teaching. Not only did three more books on angels follow *Where Angels Walk,* but she also developed a website featuring an image of a dramatic female angel surrounded by three white doves. The site listed thirteen public appearances at churches and bookstores with various affiliations (Catholic, Greek Orthodox, Lutheran, Episcopalian, and nondenominational) over the last five months of 2005.[13] In 2007, Anderson remained active, with nine appearances in two months between April and June. The message she delivered in these settings and in her writing was very simple and practical: that angels were actively helping people and that people should emulate them by helping each other. "We can all be angels to each other," she said on the last page of *Where Angels Walk.* "The world will be a better place for it. And wherever they are, the angels will dance."[14]

Anderson's first book sold 400,000 copies by 1994, after being in print for less than two years. By then, sales of Sophy Burnham's *Book of Angels* stood at 566,000 after four years, and her sequel, *Angel Letters,* had reached sales of 200,000.[15] Others entering the lists with angel books included Eileen Elias Freeman, who wrote *Touched by Angels* and set up the AngelWatch network on the Internet, and several authors (most prominently, psychologist Doreen Virtue) who taught people how to contact angels and to channel communications from them. By 1995, when Philadelphia attorney and veteran Catholic author Janice T. Connell published *Angel Power,* it seemed plausible to begin a new book, as she did, by saying that "Humanity stands at the brink of the Era of Angels."[16]

Connell believed that the world was being transformed and that people could access spiritual power that pervaded the universe. Her approach merged these New Age convictions with deep commitments to Roman Catholicism and systematic theology. A Jesuit priest, Robert

Faricy, wrote a foreword for Connell, and the book was "consecrated to God in thanksgiving for the angels" by another priest, the Rev. Thomas King, "at the actual site of the visit of the Archangel Gabriel to the Blessed Virgin Mary at Nazareth" in Israel. Though *Angel Power* did not require an Imprimatur or a Nihil Obstat from a bishop, because it dealt with private revelations rather than dogma, a declaration above the copyright notice stated, "The author wishes to manifest her unconditional submission to the final and official judgment of the Magisterium of the Church in matters of faith and morals."

Despite all of these bows to Catholic authority, the claims that Connell made for angel power included statements about unity, immediacy, harmony, and almost magical effectiveness that echoed the most radical New Age thinkers. "Sweetness of life surrounds those who access Angel Power," Connell wrote. "Those who do not yet live in harmony with the angels in seeking solutions to the miseries of the earth suffer needlessly."[17] Natural disasters and moral evils were all part of God's plan. Because "Angel Power serves as a trumpet blast to the forces of nature," any natural disaster could be seen "as a message and an invitation."[18] As for evil, "the experience of evil and its ugliness is a great sign of God's unconditional love for us and His Trust in us" to overcome everything negative. "Those who confront the ugliness of evil surrounded with conscious awareness of Angel Power" would inevitably triumph.[19]

Among the stories of angels Connell told, some seemed to teach that angel power could do magic. A book that her colleague had left in the office 30 miles from his home and could not retrieve in time as he packed for a flight suddenly appeared on a hall table after he asked God to "grant Your angels permission to deliver the textbook I so urgently need."[20] A mother about to board a plane felt "an overwhelming desire to rush outside, hail a cab, and return to her home," where she found her six-year-old daughter saying, "Oh, Mama, I knew you would come! I sent my Guardian Angel to get you!" After kissing the child, giving "reassurances of the presence of angels," and putting her to bed, the mother returned to the airport, "certain that her plane would be waiting." Her confidence proved correct. "The angels are kind," Connell wrote. Not only was the flight just boarding when the mother arrived, but "her seat had been upgraded to first class."[21] Behind such stories, critics could easily see the mechanisms of psychological repression and social roles. The man mislaid the textbook because he wanted to and found it again when he decided he really needed it. The woman felt conflicted about working and guilty about leaving her child, and projected the action of angels to confirm that she had made the right choice. However much truth such explanations may hold, however, it is significant that these people (like all the others in these collections of angel stories) were attributing the help they received to angels rather than to God or the saints. They found the angels less intimidating and demanding than God and more ubiquitous and powerful than the saints.

Perhaps because Connell's work as a lawyer brought her into more contact with men than Burnham's or Anderson's work as writers, *Angel Power* had a few distinctively masculine stories of angels, though the majority still dealt with women. The five angels who visited Ben, whom Connell introduced as "better-looking than the average Washington power broker," were "huge warriors," at least 7 feet tall, "dressed in armor and carrying swords" as well as spears. As a former military man, Ben felt that he could tell that they were "high-ranking officers with large forces under their authority." The angels had come to him "at the request of my guardian angel" because Ben's business and financial circumstances had become "distorted." A large corporation had taken over a small company Ben had founded; the corporation was treating him and his former clients badly, the dispute was headed for the courts, and Ben felt desperate. Explaining the situation to his angelic visitors from about 3 A.M., when his anxiety had awakened him, until dawn, he asked that they take on "the formidable task of opening the minds of those who had become my enemies" so that he could "present my equitable claims to them with their minds receptive to truth."

The angels did not speak, but they appeared to understand the situation before they left on their mission. Several steps of negotiation followed, during which the president of the larger firm seemed "extremely uncomfortable" as he went through stages of acceptance and rejection of Ben's position, but the final agreement "included much more than [Ben] had asked for or expected." The experience taught Ben to appreciate that "everyone on earth, even my worst enemy, has a personal Guardian Angel who always sees the face of God," and that angels can communicate with each other instantly. He ascribed the intervention of the warrior angels to his own guardian, Michael, who "comes from the Choir of Angels that administrates [*sic*] countries," and whom he described not as a warrior but as a man appearing to be in his mid-thirties, "big, virile, with curly blond hair," given to wearing "white or sometimes blue robes."[22]

Once, when Ben was driving with Michael in the car and sought advice about "a policy issue that involved many lives and much money," the angel told him that he should speak to "the Blessed Mother" about it, and that she was "sitting in the backseat." Ben admitted that he had not yet found enough courage to address Mary directly. Since Mary has long been called the Queen of Angels by the Roman Catholic Church, it was natural for Connell to mix her stories of angels with stories of Mary.

Toward the end of *Angel Power,* Connell told a sixteen-page story of a woman raped and stabbed eight times who found no peace until Mary led her to forgive the assailant, and then a seven-page story of a boy who fought a desperate, cinematically physical battle with a demon in a dream and grew up to become "president of an international nonprofit organization that cares for the needs of people all over the world."[23] By emphasizing Mary, the need for forgiveness, charitable activity, and the physical dimensions of life, Connell linked her book on angels to Catholic spiritual tradition.

With regard to contacting angels or praying to God, Connell offered traditional Catholic methods rather than the positive thinking of Sophy Burnham or the visualization techniques taught by the angel channelers who came to prominence later in the 1990s. She advised fasting twice a week and renouncing all heightened passions in order to avoid "a sensual dullness that makes it difficult to hear the words of angels or to experience their presence."[24] She recommended a "habit of sacred silence" in which one asked other people for nothing but instead asked one's guardian angel "to communicate your needs and desires to the Guardian Angels of the other people in your life." Connell was seeking Heaven while fearing Hell, not hoping for new incarnations as an angel or Sage. She took the power of demons very seriously, writing that some places on Earth are inhabited by evil angels. According to Connell, some angels from the choir of Powers, the rank of angels that governs nations, were among the fallen followers of Lucifer.[25] She shared this conviction with evangelicals, who will be considered in the chapter on "Angels of War and Apocalypse."

The Rise of Exorcism

As more attention was paid to contacting and listening to angels, fear of demons also increased among Americans. Nothing contributed as much to this increase as *The Exorcist,* which was a best-selling novel in 1971 and opened as a movie on the day after Christmas in 1973, quickly surpassing *The Godfather* (1972) in gross receipts. Still the highest-grossing horror film of all time,[26] *The Exorcist* was redistributed to theaters in September 2000 with previously expurgated footage and renewed success. Scholar Michael Cuneo was thinking primarily of *The Exorcist* when he complained, in 2001, that "far more than the Roman Catholic Church or any other religious institution . . . it is the popular entertainment industry in America that has been responsible over the past thirty years for promoting the mystique of exorcism."[27] Cuneo found that *The Exorcist* had touched off a wave of exorcisms in the United States. The movie also formed part of a larger cultural shift in which transactions between humans and fallen angels, which had been the subject of ridicule and disbelief in the 1940s and 1950s, became widely accepted and sometimes viewed as positive from the 1960s onward.

Before *The Exorcist,* the number of priests with experience as exorcists in the United States could have been counted on one hand, and many Protestants discounted the existence of the Devil. By the turn of the millennium, Catholic bishops were appointing exorcists for their dioceses and hundreds of evangelical and Pentecostal churches had taken up exorcism. Exorcisms were also being performed by charismatic groups in more liberal denominations and by occasional psychotherapists, most notably psychiatrist and best-selling author M. Scott Peck. Peck described demonic possession in *People of the Lie* (1982) and detailed his own work as an exorcist during the 1980s and after in *Glimpses of the Devil* (2005). Positive American interest in Satan had manifested itself earlier, in small groups from Anton LaVey's Church of Satan to the murder cult of Charles Manson to the followings of some "heavy metal" musicians. In the horror film *Rosemary's Baby* (1968), which included sex between Satan and Mia Farrow (which merits consideration in chapter 5 on "Angels, Love, and Sex"), modern Satanism appeared both on and off screen. Not only did the plot of the film center on a coven of Satanists in Manhattan, but Anton LaVey himself played the demon who impregnated

Rosemary. Later in 1968, the filmmaker Roman Polanski lost his wife, Sharon Tate, to murder at the hands of Manson's Satanists.

The Satanism of the 1960s and 1970s inspired evangelical fears of a national Satanist conspiracy. These fears paralleled and reinforced a panic over accusations of satanic ritual abuse of children, which was often charged by adults claiming "recovered memory," in the 1980s. After those charges of abuse were largely discounted, interest in Satan fell again, only to return in the mid-1990s. Polls showed that 66 percent of Americans believed in Satan in 1981, but only 55 percent in 1990. Those claiming belief in Satan rose to 64 percent in 1994 and then up to a new high of 70 percent in 2004.[28]

Over these decades, exorcisms gradually became less concerned with dramatic scenes of possession and more focused on everyday problems. Exorcism became a specialized form of angelic therapy, the negative side of what Sophy Burnham and Joan Wester Anderson and others did with good angels. Evangelical pastors began to use exorcism (or the "ministry of deliverance," as some called it) to drive demons such as Perfectionism, Childish Self-Will, Rebellion, Rejection, Stubbornness, Hopelessness, Despair, and even Schizophrenia from members of their churches and from themselves.[29] As Cuneo noted, exorcism had become a Christian form of psychotherapy, perhaps "the crazy uncle of therapies," but similar to Alcoholics Anonymous and other branches of the recovery movement in promising "a new and redeemed self."[30]

Those who focused on evil spirits revealed clear patterns of gender difference. Just as the people who collected stories about angels and prayed with angels were almost all women, so the hunters of demons (whether in fiction or in fact) were almost all men. Within stories of possession, the most powerful demons were also male. Control of female sexuality, and by implication denial of leadership to women, were also inscribed in the stories of exorcism and the practices of exorcists that arose in the United States during the late twentieth century. The manner in which the male encounter with demons paralleled and countered the female spirituality of angels becomes apparent in the story of The Exorcist and its effects.

The fiction of The Exorcist began with a real case and became a national obsession because of a male writer's search for evidence to strengthen his faith. In 1949, William Peter Blatty was a college student at Georgetown University when the *Washington Post* covered the exorcism of a fourteen-year-old boy who lived in nearby Mount Rainier, Maryland. A priest involved in the case spoke at Georgetown, and Blatty became fascinated. As Blatty said in 1974, the paranormal events of the possession (which included the unassisted movement of the boy's bed and other heavy objects; his cursing in Latin, a language he did not know; and the appearance of words on his skin) seemed to offer "tangible evidence of transcendence." Demonic possession and successful exorcism could confirm the truth of Roman Catholic religion. Blatty reasoned, "If there were demons, there were angels and probably a God and a life everlasting."[31] As Blatty made a career as a writer in Hollywood, he continued to compile material on the case. He obtained a copy of a twenty-five-page diary by a priest who assisted the exorcist and eventually interviewed the exorcist himself (a Jesuit priest named Thomas S. Bowdern), but permission to publish a book about the case was always denied by the diocese and the family. Eventually, Blatty fictionalized the case, making the boy a girl and the daughter of a movie star who was a single mother. Blatty also moved the setting from Maryland to the posh Georgetown neighborhood of the District of Columbia. He made the priests both more glamorous and more troubled than the actual priests were, so that their intellectual power and spiritual struggles became the vehicle to express his conviction that the exorcism revealed eternal truths.

In a sense, *The Exorcist* brought the whole history of angels and demons from ancient Persia into the United States of the 1970s. The film begins when a minor god named Pazuzu is encountered by an elderly priest (who is also an archaeologist) in the ruins of Nineveh, the ancient capital of Assyria, near modern Mosul in Iraq. A small charm representing the grimacing face of Pazuzu, who was said to protect women in childbirth because of his enmity with a goddess who was jealous of human women, is unearthed. The priest brings the charm to a local dealer in antiquities, who explains its use as "evil against evil." Then the priest goes to Nineveh and sees a large statue of Pazuzu, which has four bat-like wings extending in the shape of an "X" from the god's back; he feels a malevolent force from the statue, which seems to cause nearby dogs to fight. The film next abruptly shifts to Georgetown, where a girl in her early teens is gradually becoming possessed. Besides telekinetically moving her bed and other objects, levitating, cursing in Latin, and having words appear on her body, the girl Blatty calls Regan MacNeil penetrates her own vagina with a crucifix and rubs her mother's face into her crotch. At this point, the mother convinces a young Jesuit priest (who is also a psychiatrist) from Georgetown to try an exorcism; he receives permission from the bishop, but only on condition that the elderly priest who had been digging in Iraq actually perform the ceremony while the younger priest assists.

In the film, as in the actual case, victory is not immediate for the exorcists. The girl in the movie vomits green liquid on the exorcists, swivels her head 360 degrees on her neck, makes vile accusations against the dead mother of one of the priests, and turns the atmosphere of the room intensely cold and foul-smelling. Just before the climactic expulsion of the demon, the old priest has a vision of Pazuzu with his bat-like wings superimposed on the girl.

Some readers of the novel and viewers of the film (including psychiatrist and exorcist M. Scott Peck[32]) have expressed dissatisfaction that Blatty gave no good explanation for why this particular girl should have been the object of demonic assault. A scene in which the priests discuss this question in a break during the exorcism was cut from the 1973 release and restored in 2000, but even that scene offered no more than generalities. The older priest suggests only that the demons use the disgusting and grotesque manifestations of possession to cause people to doubt that God could love them. A more specific reason would suggest itself to any Catholic or evangelical conversant with the literature on demonic action: Both the boy in the real Maryland case and the girl in *The Exorcist* had played with Ouija boards. In the real case, the boy was taught to use the Ouija board by an aunt who died before his symptoms began. In the film, Regan MacNeil finds a board in the cellar of the house her mother is renting and meets a spirit she calls "Captain Howdy" by this means. The notion that use of a Ouija board (and other forms of fortune-telling and astrology) could expose users to communication from demons had long appeared in Catholic catechisms.[33] In the years after *The Exorcist,* this idea also became a staple of evangelical Protestant practice. As Win Worley, pastor of the Hegewisch Baptist Church of Chicago and author of widely distributed tracts on deliverance (his tradition's term for exorcism), advised, people seeking freedom from demons should "take no chances and state this: '*I am closing any door I may have opened to you, Satan, through contact with the Ouija board, astrol-ogy, fortune telling, hypnosis, ESP, etc.'"*[34]

Such forbidden forms of spirituality, like the séances of Spiritualists, have traditionally been associated with women. Blatty's depiction of the possession of Regan MacNeil, and changes he made in the real case on which it was based, also fit cultural patterns concerning the sexual content of possession. In the real case from Maryland, the boy spoke about masturbation and contraception, had an arrow pointing to his genitals painted by demonic power on his stomach, and made accusations about sex between priests and nuns. Those seeking nondemonic explanations for the boy's condition wondered about the relationship between him and his deceased aunt. Both in reality and in the movie, the fear of possession gained force by building on adult fear of adolescent sexuality. In the imagery of *The Exorcist*, that fear looked more gender-specific as the two priests lashed a levitating, pubescent girl with holy water, their actions making unaccountable whipping sounds and the water leaving bloody marks on her flesh as they chanted, "The power of Christ compels you."

An association between the sexuality of women and demonic possession already existed at least as far back as the *Malleus Maleficarum* (Hammer of Evil-Doing Witches), which served as a textbook for inquisitors during the witch craze of the Renaissance. The *Malleus* said that women became witches by having sex with Satan, whose penis was cold. Inquisitors also asserted that witches gained power over the sex organs of men, sometimes keeping penises in a nest where they ate like birds, and that women were more likely than men to become witches because women were more driven by lust.[35]

In contrast to sexual demons and their victims, the heroes of *The Exorcist* and of the real stories of exorcism were usually men sworn to celibacy as Roman Catholic priests. The priests of the movie were tragic heroes. The old archaeologist, named Lankester Merrin by William Peter Blatty, was modeled on French Jesuit Pierre Teilhard de Chardin (1881–1955), who had made discoveries in evolution and who was temporarily silenced by the Vatican for espousing a philosophy of the evolving God. After Pazuzu the demon in effect kills Father Merrin (who dies of a heart attack during the confrontation) in the film, the young psychiatrist (Father Damien Karras) becomes enraged and challenges the demon to come out of the girl and attack him instead. When Father Karras becomes possessed, the demon within him nearly forces him to strangle the girl, but with a great effort of will the priest throws off its influence and jumps out the bedroom window, killing himself. Some viewers feared that this represented a triumph of evil, but others saw the ending in more positive terms: Regan MacNeil had been delivered from Pazuzu; and the priest retained enough consciousness to accept absolution before he died, presumably in a state of grace.

The exorcist as a self-sacrificing, male hero saving the female victim appeared in a milder form on the ABC prime-time news show 20/20. The show reported on a sixteen-year-old girl named Gina who was delivered from (among others) a spirit of Lust and an African female demon named Minga. Though the exorcist in this case, an anonymous "Father A," did not die or kill himself, he said in an interview that part of him died in each confrontation with the pure hatred of the demons.[36]

Perhaps because The Exorcist and 20/20 sought to magnify the priest as hero, neither mentioned the role of Michael the Archangel in casting out demons. In the Maryland case from 1949, the priests were actually unsuccessful. Only after nearly three months of their futile attempts did the boy himself finally sit up in bed and call out, "Satan! Satan! I am Saint Michael, and I command you, Satan, and the other evil spirits, to leave this body in the name of Dominus. Immediately! Now! Now! Now!" With this, all the boy's symptoms apparently ceased. Michael the Archangel's role in defeating Satan traditionally appeared in a prayer asking "Holy Michael Archangel" to "thrust down to Hell Satan and all wicked spirits, who wander through the world for the ruin of souls," which was said after most Catholic Masses from 1884, when Pope Leo XIII prescribed it, until the liturgical reforms of Vatican II in the 1960s. Certainly, Michael's battles with Satan had inspired many medieval and Renaissance artists, but media in the era of The Exorcist focused instead on human priests against fallen angels.

The most famous Catholic exorcist of the 1970s and 1980s was ex-Jesuit Malachi Martin (1921–1999), who published the best-selling Hostage to the Devil: The Possession and Exorcism of Five Living Americans in 1976. In 1987, Martin discussed exorcism on Oprah with a Lutheran exorcist, Pastor Erwin Prange.[37] All of the priests in Martin's accounts suffered greatly during the exorcisms; they were beaten, sexually assaulted, assailed by doubts, and forced into temporary retreat. Ironically, Martin's book made Father Pierre Teilhard de Chardin, the model for one of the heroes of *The Exorcist*, into a villain of sorts. One of Martin's five cases involved a man who became possessed because he began to see the world in the way that Teilhard de Chardin presented it, not as a collection of individual things but as a single evolving entity in which Christ was not a supernatural Savior but another product of evolution. The vision held great beauty and even enabled the possessed person to gain psychic powers like telekinesis and bilocation, but it was a false concept that deprived the victim of supernatural protection against supernatural enemies. In four of the five cases from *Hostage to the Devil*, modern thought was somehow to blame. All five of Martin's cases involved sexual sin; one of those who needed exorcism was a male-to-female transsexual who was possessed during her most fulfilling sexual encounter, as the main passive participant in an orgiastic Black Mass. In Martin's concluding chapters, he argued that Americans of the 1970s had become especially vulnerable to possession because they had lost a sense of integral "humanness." To be safe from possession, in Martin's view, people needed a conviction that they were not just the sum of their parts or the results of natural forces, but also spiritual beings redeemed by the Spirit of God in Jesus and threatened by the fallen spirit of Lucifer.[38]

Whether Malachi Martin's elaborately detailed accounts were real or imagined is difficult to determine. Michael Cuneo expressed serious doubts after interviewing Martin and others involved in exorcisms during the 1970s, but Martin's argument that he was working under confidentiality agreements, with maverick priests who did exorcisms without church approval as a Christian duty to the afflicted, made his stories both unverifiable and relatively unassailable. In a realm of documentation where the largest comparable public source is one priest's twenty-five-page diary of the case on which *The Exorcist* was based, Martin's closely printed, eighty-page accounts of each of five cases look very anomalous.

Psychiatrist M. Scott Peck believed Martin's book, calling it "a brilliant work of both scholarship and leadership." Peck accepted referrals for exorcism from Martin, and in *Glimpses of the Devil* (2005) he published two accounts of exorcisms comparable in length and detail to the five in *Hostage to the Devil*. Peck's confrontations with evil also led him to share something of Malachi Martin's religious conservatism. Even though Peck began as a skeptic from a Protestant background and was not baptized until adulthood, when he chose a Methodist minister, who did a "deliberately nondenominational" ceremony in an Episcopal church, he wrote in *Glimpses of the Devil* that "the Roman Catholic Church, by virtue of its tight hierarchical and authoritarian structure, plays a role for the entire Christian church as a guardian of 'correct' theology and practice." He hoped that Roman Catholic authorities would take his findings about possession into account and enlarge the list of acceptable signs of supernatural evil that justify an exorcism.

By the 1990s, American popular culture had left behind both Malachi Martin and M. Scott Peck in the struggle for spiritual healing. The cases Peck described in 2005 took place between 1976 and 1982, after Peck had met Martin and before he published *People of the Lie*. They were epic struggles extending over months, with many unsuccessful rituals; the second victim appeared to be delivered but was not, and died in a state of "perfect possession," apparently lost to the Devil. In contrast, the fifty exorcisms that Michael Cuneo witnessed in researching his *American Exorcism: Expelling Demons in the Land of Plenty* were quickly done in evangelical churches or in the offices of priests who were handling four or five cases a day. M. Scott Peck wrote that Cuneo had actually seen no exorcisms at all, but rather "deliverance procedures." However exorcism and deliverance are defined, there is no question that Americans were looking for convenience and quick results in handling demons, as in other forms of therapy. Even within evangelical churches, the newer thinking about deliverance in the 1990s ceased to permit possessed people to howl and foam at the mouth for hours, as they had in the 1970s. By the simple expedient of binding the demons before throwing them out, Protestant exorcists obtained quicker and quieter results.

Angel Therapists on TV

Cultural depictions of angelic therapy underwent a transformation from the sensational model of *The Exorcist* in the 1970s to the television series *Highway to Heaven* in the 1980s and *Touched by an Angel* in the 1990s. Each of these shows attained great success and great influence, reaching audiences of between 16 million and 20 million each week for a total of fourteen years (nine for *Touched by an Angel* and five for *Highway to Heaven*). In comparison, *The Exorcist* was seen once or perhaps twice by about 60 million people in the United States and another 100 million abroad, and the most popular angel books reached 2 million to 3 million Americans. Although books and movies may communicate more complex messages and have more potential to convince people of their point of view than commercial television dramas, television delivers numbers and the power of repetition, with characters who become part of the families of viewers. When people encountered angels and demons on television in their homes, rather than in churches, on film, or directly in exorcisms, the encounter was mediated by the domestic setting. Therapy was the explicit intention of those who created the angel shows, but the effects of this kind of therapy were indirect. The masculine powers of Satan and the exorcists, Michael the Archangel, and Jesus and God retreated, leaving women and nurturing men in the foreground. The gender dynamics of these therapies resembled those of the female angel therapists who wrote books. On television, supernatural power and spectacular effects like levitation also retreated in favor of human psychology and ethics.

When *Touched by an Angel* handled possession, the female angels who starred on the show went undercover as people and used human friendship and faith (supported by the power of God), not dramatic rituals or heroic sacrifice, to vanquish the demon. One such episode aired on Halloween of 1999 and was set in a fictional Mercy Hospital in Salt Lake City. It began with a character named Lonnie, a homeless man who was also suicidal, being brought to the emergency room with various injuries. The head of the ER is an old friend of Lonnie's from childhood, Duncan, who believes that Lonnie suffers from Multiple Personality Disorder; however, as a personality calling himself "Gregory" claims more and more to have power over Lonnie's soul, the angels Tess and Monica realize that he is possessed. Tess knew both Duncan and Lonnie as children, because she taught them Sunday school. Unfortunately, even an angel in the classroom could not overcome the effects of Lonnie's abusive family and an accident in which he burned down a house performing a Halloween prank. Racked by guilt, Lonnie had begun to do drugs and then dabbled in occult religious practices (as victims had in *The Exorcist* and many other stories), and so he had become possessed.

The cast of Touched by an Angel, *the CBS hit show of 1994 to 2003. From left, Della Reese as Angel Tess, Roma Downey as her subordinate, Angel Monica, and John Dye as Andrew, the Angel of Death. (Monty Brinton/Photofest)*

In a moment of lucidity, Lonnie asks Duncan for help and shows him a mustard seed representing faith. Both men had received such seeds as boys from Tess to remind them of the promise ascribed to Jesus in Matthew 17:20: "If you have faith as a grain of mustard seed, you will say to this mountain, 'Move from here to there,' and it will move; and nothing will be impossible to you." But Lonnie's seed is accidentally crushed by an orderly. Lonnie cries out in despair, "Gregory" takes full possession, and the possessed man flees to the boiler room of the hospital seeking to kill himself. The angels and Duncan follow him. When Monica calls out to Lonnie, urging him to ask God for help, "Gregory" shouts back and frightens Duncan, who flees. Tess catches up with the doctor, reveals herself as an angel, and tells him not to fear helping Lonnie, who needs a human with strong faith to stand beside him. Duncan then searches his office and finds his own old mustard seed. He brings it to Lonnie and tells him that the seed is only a symbol, because real faith lives in the heart. Encouraged by his friend, Lonnie calls on God, causing the demon "Gregory" to scream in pain and depart.

Healing by angels who acted less through supernatural power than by causing people to do the right thing typified both *Touched by an Angel* and *Highway to Heaven*. The angels in these shows acted as counselors and therapists, dealing with traumas from the past and mending broken relationships, and sometimes also as social workers, mobilizing communities against racism, poverty, or injustice. Each of these shows grew from an individual sense of mission on the part of its creator. As Martha Williamson, the creator of *Touched by an Angel*, said, the show aimed to put stories representing the "simple, but absolute truth" that God exists and loves us and wants to be part of our lives on television every week.[39]

Williamson did not really invent *Touched by an Angel*, but she did transform it. When CBS first hired her to produce the show, as someone with a background as writer and assistant producer with several comedy and variety series, the network had already made a pilot. In this pilot show, stars Della Reese and Roma Downey (a veteran black singer and minister and a young, beautiful actress of Irish descent) played angels wearing special-effects wings who disliked each other but had to work together. Both were former humans who had died, and both scorned and feared the Angel of Death, who was played for laughs as an arrogant and stupid spirit. The angel played by Della Reese still smoked cigars, and the heroes often disobeyed their orders from God and criticized God's decisions in conversation. In the pilot they resurrected a dog, just as John Travolta would later when he played Michael the Archangel in a comedy/fantasy film in 1996 and as the half-angel Aaron would in the ABC/Family movie *Fallen* in 2006.

Williamson was a born-again Christian in the Methodist tradition, and most aspects of the concept and the plot distressed her even though she admitted that the pilot succeeded in being funny. She turned down the offer to produce the show and applied to produce another. Something about the angel series would not let her go, however, and she went back to CBS with a critique of the pilot and an offer to change the concept while keeping the cast. In Williamson's vision, angels were not dead people but spirits created to be angels; angels could laugh, but they loved each other and loved the people they helped; and above all, angels obeyed God. The dramatic conflict and the humor in the show would have to come from special situations and from relationships other than that between angels and God. Williamson proposed to pitch *Touched by an Angel* to people who believed in real angels, rather than to an audience interested in what she called "cops with wings." She made the Angel of Death (named Andrew, played by John Dye) into a sympathetic, caring character. Finally, she ditched the wings, which apparently looked too silly even for comedy.[40]

Angelic therapy on *Touched by an Angel* dealt with a broad range of people and issues, from AIDS sufferers and their families to neo-Nazis in America, slaves in Sudan, a talk-show host who destroys her guests, and the ordinary challenges of marriage and parenting. Always the angels urged people to reconcile with each other, to work together with courage, and to forgive themselves for the past, remembering that God loved them whatever they had done. Angels also learned and made progress in their own lives: When the series began, young Monica was being transferred from the "search and rescue" division to "caseworker," a promotion that excited her greatly; as the series ended, Tess, Monica's supervisor, joined the singers in the Heavenly Choir, while Monica became a supervisor of other caseworkers. In the first episode, Tess had to remind Monica to wear shoes when she took human form. Later in the first season, Tess stripped Monica of her beautiful coat and her angelic powers so that she could understand the plight of a homeless man whom Monica found distasteful. By the end of that show, Monica had learned enough compassion to wash the man's feet (echoing the action of Jesus in John 13) while also enabling him to get a ticket to visit his sister.

Without going as far into theology or using as many Christian symbols as *Touched by an Angel, Highway to Heaven* made many points about social justice. The series aired only because of the proven ratings clout of Michael Landon, who had played the youngest brother (Little Joe) on *Bonanza*, one of the most popular shows on television from 1959 to 1973. Landon then had a hit of his own on *Little House on the Prairie* from 1974 until 1982. According to Landon, the idea for a show about an angel came to him when he was in a traffic jam near Los Angeles, as he wondered why people couldn't learn to be nicer to one another. The premise of the show was that Landon's character, Jonathan Smith, an honest lawyer, had died young and was sent back to Earth for a time to help those in need, and by these deeds to earn his wings and become a permanent angel. Although Jonathan Smith had special powers, he was supposed to use them sparingly, relying on kindness and ordinary good deeds to help people learn to help themselves.

In *Highway to Heaven*'s first episode, for example, Jonathan is assigned to work as a handyman at a nursing home that has been sold to a developer; the developer intends to close the home and scatter the residents to various fates. The home has been neglected; its residents watch television in the lobby or sit listlessly in their rooms. When Jonathan arrives, he organizes them to tend a garden, conjuring up plants for this purpose and saying that a florist friend of his had given them to him. He brings the seniors out of the dining hall for a barbecue. But just as they are becoming a community, the word comes out that the home will close in a week. Jonathan then takes the elderly people to a racetrack and has them put their combined savings on a horse that seems to signal him before the race. Though the horse appears at first to have lost (perhaps as a reprimand to Jonathan not to abuse his powers), the loss is reversed because of a foul on the winner's jockey, and the residents pool the money from their winnings to buy the home for themselves. During a party to celebrate the victory, Jonathan Smith steals away to the next assignment, but not alone: He takes with him a very human, bearded, and burly retired policeman who had suspected that Smith was a criminal when he first arrived on the scene.

Together over the next five years, Landon and costar Victor French had many adventures, most of which involved teaching people to face the truth about themselves and their society. Rather than washing the feet of a single homeless man, for example, angel Jonathan Smith inspires a lawyer to organize the homeless to demonstrate during a hearing at City Hall, where they chant "We will be heard" to protest a redevelopment plan that will displace them. Of course, gritty realism and social consciousness do not entirely triumph: These "homeless" are all very well-spoken and clean, marked as homeless only by tattered coats and little smudges of dirt on their faces.

The exploits and lessons of Michael Landon's angel—many of which were scripted by Landon himself, even as many episodes of *Touched by an Angel* were written by Martha Williamson and her husband Jon Anderson—were simultaneously more jocular and more heavy-handed in their preaching than the stories of Tess and Monica. Williamson's angels would never try to use their powers to pick a horse on which to bet the life savings of elders, and they never called God "the Boss" as Jonathan Smith did. In *Highway to Heaven,* comedian Bob Hope had a continuing role as the angel giving Smith his assignments. Even the struggle with demons could be played for laughs. In "The Devil and Jonathan Smith" episode, Landon had to deal not with possession or occult practices but with a contract signed by his sidekick to turn over his soul in exchange for the life of a child he had injured in an automobile accident. The dilemma of the contract resembled that of a Steven Vincent Benet short story, "The Devil and Daniel Webster." Unable to use supernatural power on a supernatural foe, Jonathan Smith turns to simple theft and fails, but then hires a human con man to trick the demon. The failure of the demon is punished, in turn, by Satan, who turns him into a mouse pursued by his own former pet cat.

On the heavy side, Dick Van Dyke starred in an episode of *Highway to Heaven* as a street entertainer who lives in an abandoned railroad car and goes around the city doing good all day. Without disclosing himself as an angel, Landon follows Van Dyke's character as he pays visits to a dying child and to seniors in a nursing home, puts on puppet shows to teach people to respect those who beg on the street, sets the broken leg of a stray dog, offers a fervent grace before sharing his bread with the visiting undercover angel, prays that God will take his own life rather than that of the dying child, and finally, takes a bullet to save the life of a thief in a liquor store robbery. In the ambulance, angel Smith is able to tell him that the child will now live, but the EMS technician dismisses Van Dyke's character as "just a bum who wasted his life."

Because the people on *Touched by an Angel* and *Highway to Heaven* were always making decisions about their redemption, they tended to become caricatures, ending up all good or all bad. The mischievous thirteen-year-old who finds a pack of Tarot cards and uses them to fasci-nate some adults on a Halloween episode of *Touched* turns out to be Sa-tan in disguise. A female prosecutor who refuses Jonathan Smith's plea not to seek felony charges against a Navajo alcoholic jailed for stealing a bottle sinks into alcoholism herself and ends the episode out of a job and on the street, in a pink jumpsuit and with a bit of dirt on her face. Though Michael Landon had a complex religious background—he was born to a Jewish father and a Catholic mother and became unattached to religion through two divorces and depression—he eventually reached a Christian rebirth that informed this series, at least according to his son and *Christianity Today* magazine.[41]

When describing and assessing these television angels, it is easy to become cynical. In the 1980s, when homelessness plagued American cit-ies for the first time since the Depression and the Reagan administra-tion eliminated the budget for building new subsidized housing, angel Jonathan Smith helped us to pretend that something could be done by the homeless themselves. *Highway to Heaven* was in this sense a formu-laic fulfillment of the dictum of Karl Marx that religion is "the opiate of the people" and "the heart of a heartless world."[42] In the 1990s, when Clintonian neoliberalism accepted the Reagan legacy but made multi-cultural tolerance into a moral crusade, *Touched by an Angel* and its mul-ticultural angels Tess, Monica, and Andrew (black woman, Irish woman, and white male American) arrived to tell us we were on the right path, only to disappear, along with the multicultural ideal, after the shock of 9/11. And yet, such interpretations do not stop the tears from well-ing in my eyes as Jonathan gets into the car with his human buddy, or when Monica tells another desperate soul that "God loves you more than you can possibly know." Although uncritical consumption of angel television may inhibit the growth of social consciousness, surely there is also something healthy about two shows that attempted to interject the message that God sides with those who are poor and suffering into this normally commercial, materialistic, and sexually obsessed medium.

Channeling Angels

As the flights of angels on television and in film receded during the first years of the new millennium, a more practical set of teachers, who had first come to prominence in the 1990s, remained active. These were angel channelers, who not only sold books and instructional discs and tapes but traveled the country holding workshops and retreat weekends. They taught their followers how to summon angels, how to speak with them, and how to locate both angels and themselves within a whole cosmology, developing elaborate forms of angel therapy.

"Channeling," or automatic speaking or writing on behalf of another entity, is known to have existed as far back as the oracle at Delphi, who sat above a crack in the Earth from which strange vapors rose and channeled Apollo. Ever since, people have been entering trance states and claiming to speak for others. The mediums at séances who became so popular among Spiritualists and curious observers in the nineteenth and early twentieth centuries believed, or at least claimed to believe, that they channeled the dead.

Americans have been channeling more celestial spirits for more than half a century. The influential practice of *A Course in Miracles* was led by Helen Schucman, who claimed to channel the spirit of Jesus, and later by Marianne Williamson. Ancient and powerful beings named Michael and Seth were channeled by other leaders, who gained followings rivaling that of churches in the 1960s and 1970s. But it was only in the 1980s and 1990s that the specific practice of channeling angels, with all of the theological consequences that it implied, really took hold. Among the first leaders were two sisters from Iowa named Trudy Griswold and Barbara Mark. Born into an Episcopal background, Griswold and Mark were led by family circumstances to Connecticut and San Diego, respectively, where angels began on the same day to speak with them. After calling each other in shock, they started to write books filled with messages from angels, to run a website called *Angelspeake.com,* and to tour the nation and run angel workshops. Griswold now continues this work alone, following her sister's death in July 2006.

Together, Griswold and Mark published their first book, *Angelspeake: How to Talk with Your Angels,* in 1995; they followed this up with a video-tape called *Speaking with Your Angels,* which was broadcast on Connecticut Public Television in 1996. In the video, after gathering about a dozen casually dressed people, evenly divided between women and men, into a parlor, Griswold explains that she was "living in misery" when she first heard her angels in 1988; she had moved to Florida from Connecticut with her family, and the move had not worked out as they expected. Her sister, meanwhile, who was recovering from a divorce, moved from Wyoming to San Diego, where she became a "church shopper" in search of meaning, doing jobs she hated such as data entry at a burglar-alarm factory. While the sisters prayed for help and talked with each other constantly on the phone, both women began to be awakened by voices in their heads that insisted they write things down. They introduce these beings to those attending the workshop in the show under four titles: three groups of angels, called Angels, Archangels, and Guardians, and a group of people who have lived on Earth called Masters (Mahatma Gandhi and Martin Luther King Jr. are mentioned as examples of the last category). Griswold and Mark then teach a simple method for questioning these beings, while insisting that their practice does not eliminate or bypass God and that it is compatible with any religious commitment.

What Griswold and Mark call "The Four Fundamentals" of their method paralleled the steps of prayer taught by Sophy Burnham in *A Book of Angels:* First ask, second believe, third let it happen (or "Let go"), and fourth, say "thank you." Asking is necessary because angels will not violate free will, according to Griswold, who receives a large response from the group on the video when she asks how many had prayed for a parking space. If you can ask for a parking space, why not ask for a BMW to put in the space, she wonders, trying to teach that people ask for too little. Help and messages may have already been coming without being recognized: She cites mysterious playmates from childhood, or words or images that may have suddenly become meaningful, as examples of angelic help. Through the workshop, participants might come to realize that angels have always been present and helping in their lives.

Now the group on the show is ready for the seven steps of communication: (1) Pray for the gift of spiritual hearing; (2) breathe, sitting in a relaxed position, not meditating but maintaining serenity; (3) listen, because angels "come as a whisper," but do not meditate or enter trance; (4) write without worrying about making sense; (5) accept that these are really angelic words and not your own, realizing that the angels are speaking with our language because they are using us; (6) follow your inner knowing, because when you reread these angel writings, they will always seem fresh; and (7) trust that this guidance will work out, even if you cannot see the pattern—sometimes guidance resembles ocean currents, working deep below the surface. Several participants in the televised session raise their hands when asked whether they had ever practiced meditation, and Griswold says that meditation involves a much deeper and less conscious state than they should aim for in this exercise. She wants them not to meditate here, but to remain more "connected."

Having been instructed in what to expect, the participants prepare the way for their angels with both New Age and traditional methods. With all of the frustrations of the day, the leaders tell them, human energy fields, or auras, become very jagged and spiky. This condition of the auras makes it difficult for angels to approach, so everyone must "unruffle" their energy fields by running their hands a few inches above their bodies. They help each other to unruffle the fields in back. The group then joins in prayer, reading from a handout: "Dear God, please help me to hear you clearly, through your loving angels. Allow me to be healed in my areas of greatest need and to learn more about your truth, love, and joy."

Everyone then takes a deep breath, takes out a piece of paper, and writes across the top, "Dearest child, we love you and . . ." after which they continue as their angels bid. Most initial responses are very general and encouraging. A thirtyish woman with long, straight blonde hair says that "it was really wild" but that she was told simply that she was doing well and should continue to "walk the spiritual path." A heavy man in his thirties was told he was "a son of God" and reports that his handwriting grew much larger than usual. When Griswold asks whether anyone felt his or her angel was male or female, no one has any sense of gender. A participant asks how they can know that the words are not just coming from them. Barbara Mark points out that the angels say "we," which people would not normally do as individuals, and that the messages simply have an alien feeling to those who get them. Trudy

Griswold urges them to save what they received and read it again later, to see how the words always seem fresh. A participant adds that she could tell it was not her because she could not possibly write so fast and remain coherent. Some members of the group had clearly done automatic writing before.

For those who might fear that cultivating receptivity to spirits could provide an opening to the demonic, Barbara Mark says that if they receive anything "less than loving," they should simply send it "right back, like an uninvited guest." A man reports a printed message from archangel Michael, and Barbara responds that Michael is around a great deal lately, defending Earth from environmental dangers. Finally, Trudy Griswold channels a message for the group, thanking them for coming and reminding them that "God blesses you and loves you." The group disperses with the assurance that their lives will never be the same now that they have put their keys in the lock, but also a friendly warning not to be surprised if the angels "start waking you up at 4:30 in the morning."

More dramatic events initiated the career of Doreen Virtue, whose byline always includes her degree (a Ph.D.) and whose picture on books projects long-haired blonde glamour, though no public listings reveal her age. Virtue has produced an inventory of angel products that by 2007 included twenty-six books, fifteen audio/CD programs, and ten sets of Oracle Cards; she also runs the website *Angeltherapy.com* and trains Certified Angel Therapists. She began with unhappiness, like many of the women who have pioneered angel therapy. Virtue has described herself as "an uneducated housewife who was unhappy because I wanted to make a contribution to the world but didn't feel qualified to do anything meaningful."[43] Eventually she obtained qualifications, which all of her publications emphasize: bachelor's, master's, and doctoral degrees in psychological counseling from Chapman University in Orange, California. She began a career in standard psychotherapy but found her true calling through spiritual experience. On July 15, 1995, by her own account in *Angel Therapy*, she was already giving talks in churches, though she was not yet listening to angels. As she dressed for and drove to an appointment at a church in Anaheim, California, she heard an "angel's voice outside and above my right ear" warning her to put up her convertible top to keep her car from being stolen. She did not take the time to stop and put up the top, and as she parked she was nearly carjacked.

Screaming, she got enough attention to thwart the robber, and she decided to listen to her angels.

After this experience, Virtue's approach to therapy changed completely. Through automatic writing at her computer, she compiled short homilies from her angels on fifty-eight topics running the gamut alphabetically from Addiction and Anger through Dreams and Jealousy to Pregnancy and Stress, Weight, Worry, and Writing. Besides recommending these to her clients, she would channel their angels for them and help them hear their angels for themselves. Sometimes she used the cards she developed to get a reading from the angels.

Virtue added a new dimension to angel therapy when she decided that she was counseling "many people whose origins are not of this Earth."[44] She came to believe that some of her clients were extraterrestrials who had chosen incarnation on Earth to help humans. Others were incarnated angels, or "walk-ins," angels who had taken the place of a human who had wanted to leave in the midst of life, so that these patients had not gone through the processes of conception, birth, and maturation. Others had lives rooted on Earth but had entered humanity from the "elemental" realm, "which consists of the leprechauns, fairies, brownies, and elves."[45] For readers who suspected that their problems might result from their forgetting such nonhuman origins, Virtue offers lists of characteristics that identify such people. For example, incarnated angels have sweet faces but tend to be fat; elementals "often have reddish hair, fair skin, and light eyes," while incarnated fairies tend to be "slender and willowy females."[46] As a last resort for those confused about their identities, she suggests asking one's "spiritual group" for a dream.

For Virtue, working with angels meant that "the world is a 100 percent safe place to live." Danger comes only when people "miscreate" with their thoughts and forget to ask the angels to protect them from their mistakes. Often she seems to regard angels as servants, as when she advises readers who want "the telephone to be quiet" to "ask your angels to screen your calls." The heavenly spirits will influence those who might call to wait, "unless the news is really important."[47] Unlike Griswold and Mark, who said to "send back" any hostile messages, Virtue tells new channelers to use the archangel Michael as a gatekeeper: Since they "may not be able to readily distinguish an earthbound spirit [Virtue's term for a ghost] from an angel," they should know that, on request,

"Michael will act as a doorman who only allows invited guests to enter your territory."[48] Angels, she says, could function as secretaries, security guards, and even "loving nursemaids and nannies" like Mary Poppins.[49] Such images suggested that angels were ideal servants for a harried American woman trying to succeed as wife, mother, and professional.

A more elaborate method for contacting angels appeared in *Ask Your Angels* (1992), which was written by three humans and an angel. This celestial/earthly collaboration included humans Alma Daniel, Timothy Wyllie, and Andrew Ramer and a recording angel they called Abigrael, with some notes from the "companion" (not guardian) angels of each author. The authorship of *Ask Your Angels* itself represented a New Age community spanning generations and continents. Alma Daniel was already a veteran entrepreneur in religion and self-help—a minister licensed to perform marriages and willing to work across denominations, a psychotherapist, and the owner of an "isolation tank" therapy business—when she met Timothy Wyllie in 1988 and began to talk with him about angels. Wyllie and Ramer are among only a few males who have written on the subject of angel therapy. Wyllie, an artist, was born in England in 1940 and raised as an atheist, but he became a believer in angels after nearly dying in 1973. His companion angel, Joy, directed him to settle in the United States, first in New York and later in the Southwest. Ramer, a child of the baby boom, an activist in gay rights, and a writer of fiction, met his angel, Sargolais, at age three. He learned the angel's name in 1987 at the age of thirty-six. Perhaps because these human authors collaborated in New York City and none of them had families, their book does not feature the intensely domestic concerns of other angel literature; yet it was practical enough. The book begins with a few standard stories of rescue; later, it mixes advice about attracting the attention of a waitress—and about showering with your wings before going to work the early shift at McDonald's—with information on meditation techniques and cosmic speculations.

In what *Ask Your Angels* calls "the GRACE method," readers are told how to proceed through steps of Grounding, Releasing, Aligning, Conversing, and Enjoying, gradually learning to perceive and to expand "an intricate tracery of fibers" composed of "flowing energy."[50] The authors relate these fibers to the acupuncture meridians of Chinese theory and to the chakras of Hindu medicine. After mentally extending some fibers from the root chakra deep into the earth and letting fear, anger, and other negative emotions flow out of the self, those practicing the GRACE method are then supposed to spread fibers from their heads up and out into the universe to receive and send energy. The perception of such networks of fibers has led many people to see angels as beings with wings, the authors report, and the light given off by the networks has been interpreted as halos; through GRACE, people will grow their own wings. Once people perceive their wings, they can use them "to broadcast love into the world" no matter where they are, "sitting on a bus or standing on line in the supermarket." One practitioner is said to have opened his wings to get the attention of a waitress in a restaurant; she came immediately to his table, and her nametag read "Angela." A woman who was conscious of her wings used the shower to "clean and open" her wing fibers in the morning, then used her wings "to help brush away the residue" of any emotional issues from the day before.[51]

For Alma Daniel, the primary human author of *Ask Your Angels*, it was not entirely clear or really important whether her companion angel was really a separate being or an inner or spiritual aspect of herself. Daniel worked as a therapist and gave her patients readings from her angel, which she wrote as though someone else was saying the words, but she also questioned her companion about whether these ideas came from some part of her own mind. The answer was ambiguous. Although her companion said that she was only connecting her with "the divine spark, the God That Is" within her, Daniel communicated best by relating to her as a separate entity with her own name. Besides, Daniel knew "many other celestials who assist in different ways—facilitating my travel through the city [New York], directing my actions in a tax audit, and so forth," so she concluded that angels in general were definitely not just aspects of humanity.

Beyond calling waitresses and influencing IRS auditors, angels were bringing humanity into a new age in which people would begin to communicate with the other intelligences on the planet (including whales, dolphins, and trees, which also have angels) and with the extraterrestrials, who would make themselves known as humanity became "more fully part of the galactic community." *Ask Your Angels* gave readers a ritual to open contact with Eularia, an angel from the rank of the Principalities who has charge of the entire Earth and especially the United Nations.[52]

According to Andrew Ramer's companion angel, whom he addresses as a male named Sargolais, angels "are the social workers of the universe," each with a large caseload. "For example," Sargolais is quoted as saying in *Ask Your Angels*, "Andrew shares me with 118 other entities, each of them in a different galaxy . . . all of whom are sentient, but not all of whom are human." Sargolais assures readers that the numbers do not diminish his attention, "because we angels are not focused in space/time in quite the way that you are."[53]

Like the books of Trudy Griswold, Barbara Mark, and Doreen Virtue, *Ask Your Angels* presents the world as a safe place, and like them it dismisses fears of demons and possession. Lucifer exists, the authors admit, but he has not fallen; rather, he is "one of the seven great archangels of our solar system, serving as the guardian of the planet Venus." He volunteered when God asked for an angel to "help strengthen humanity's spiritual resolve by offering constant temptation," but people misunderstand him.[54] If, while channeling, one encounters a "negative voice," including the fear of channeling a bad angel, it comes from doubts and fears within that need only to be recognized and released.[55]

Not all angel channelers are so sanguine. Eileen Elias Freeman, author of *Touched by Angels* (1993) and founder of the AngelWatch network, which collects angel stories, had more traditional training in religion than any of the others (a bachelor's degree in comparative religion from Barnard College and a master's in theology from Notre Dame), and she warned against trying to control angels or using them for tasks like contacting dead people or getting lucky numbers for gambling. "The only angels such people will 'conjure' are fallen spirits, the absolute zeros on the love scale," she wrote, "and it is far better to have nothing to do with them under any circumstances."[56] Later, Freeman urged readers not to believe anyone with a "foolproof method" for contacting angels. Trying meditation with such teachers would lead to union "with the mind of the other person" at best, or "at the worst you will encounter a dark spirit masquerading as your angel." She laid out a cautious, indirect approach that involved asking "the highest Source you acknowledge . . . for help and enlightenment," then making an honest statement about who you are ("I am the girl who went to Carteret Grammar School in Bloomfield, New Jersey"), saying why we would like to know our guardian angels, and then trusting the result to God and the angels.

Freeman herself needed no techniques. She first saw her guardian angel at five years of age, when her grandmother had recently died and left her terrified of death and unable to sleep. A silvery mist lit from within ("If a diamond were made of silver") formed in her room and partly materialized as a male, "tall and quite strong of physique," without wings but with "very long and fine hair that seemed to flow and blow around him." His face was "angular rather than smooth or rounded," and his eyes were large, dark, "and full of compassion for me and my fears."[57] He told the child Freeman that her grandmother was happy in Heaven with God, that he was her guardian angel, and that she had nothing to fear. Never forgetting the vision, Freeman asked six years later to be confirmed as a Roman Catholic rather than in her parents' Episcopal church because "Catholic tradition has always accepted supernatural intervention as a normal part of life . . . and such supernatural help included angels."[58] Another encounter with her guardian occurred during 1970, while Freeman was attending college at Barnard, when she felt a hand on her shoulder and heard the voice from her childhood telling her not to go into an apartment house. Moments later, a drug dealer killed a woman in the building. Seeking answers, Freeman decided to take a master's and work toward a doctorate at Notre Dame, where she "began to see more clearly the different ways that our angels have worked" both with individuals and groups. She wrote on angels for Catholic and academic journals, but she did not yet write or speak about her own experiences.

The decisive event occurred on a night in September 1979, when Freeman was employed by a church publishing company, living in Glendale, Arizona, and sitting at home working on her stamp collection. Overwhelmed by a feeling of sensory deprivation, inward focus, and tranquility, she heard a voice that said, "I am Enniss, servant of God, and your guardian by divine grace; and you are my ward in this world." Then came other beings with the same voice, yet distinguishable. One was Asendar, the head of guardian angels and the superior of Enniss; another was called Kennisha, "who serves the Most High as a protector of your race"; also present was the recording angel Tallithia. Freeman spent the next two hours dancing to angelic music and following heavenly colors around the room. Over the next few years, as she returned to New Jersey and helped her father through his death from lung cancer, the angels gradually imparted enough about their activities and plans for working with humanity to fill a 1,200-page manuscript, which has not yet been published, though Freeman remains confident that it will be at the right time.

Besides writing, Freeman began attending angel workshops run by Sophy Burnham and Joan Wester Anderson and spread the word of a nonprofit corporation, the AngelWatch Foundation, that she hoped would overcome the isolation of those who had encountered angels and did not know what to make of the experience. In *Touched by Angels*, she spends her last chapter advertising a journal of the foundation. In the chapter before that, she answers a letter from a woman who saw an angel in a dream. Because the angel warned her not to drive for three days, the woman had inconvenienced her neighbor, who had driven her on errands. The woman with the dream had also missed her usual visit with her mother and deprived her children of some activities. No good had come of the dream, so Freeman concludes that it was not a real angel, or at least not a good one.

Freeman's warnings were child's play compared to the terrors of Sharon Beekman. In *Enticed by the Light* (1997), Beekman describes her odyssey from an introduction to channeling in 1976 through infestation by various spirits. The principals of this demonic action were named Egglog, Starlight, and Seth, and included a false Jesus and a false angel of light. She reached deliverance in 1992 by giving up trying to speak with spirits, converting to Jesus, and renouncing any practice of prayer that involved release of her own will. The key difference between the approach to prayer that Beekman developed and the practices recommended by the other writers (besides the invocation of Jesus alone) was the avoidance of passive states of mind. Being "filled with the Holy Spirit" was "so different from channeling demon spirits," Beekman wrote. "With them I vacated myself, detached as in a trance," she said, but in the Holy Spirit, "I remained fully myself, alert, in control, yet willingly yielded to the power of his Spirit."[59] Before gaining freedom from demons and attaining such blessedness, Beekman had to confront horrors like the wrath of Starlight, who came to her mind "dressed in white with light beams streaming from her gown" then turned into "a gargoyle, baring razor-sharp teeth" and "spit streams of fire" at her. King Egglog's voice remained "kind" and "authoritative" in tone, but his face "appeared as an ever-changing, amoebic-like mass, spitting venom and bile."

My Search for Angels

While reviewing the material for this chapter, suspicions stirred in me that had been instilled during my Catholic childhood and intensi-fied in my Protestant adolescence. It seemed to me that angels might be sent to people if God deemed it necessary, but that people should not seek out or invoke angels. Nevertheless, my sense that I should do some fieldwork bothered me enough to cause me to invest both time and money to sit with a group that sought to channel angels. After all, I reasoned, I had done a spiral dance with the Covenant of the God-dess at the World's Parliament of Religions in 1993. Taking students to Hindu temples and Buddhist meditation halls, I had often prostrated myself before idols of wood and stone, and then sat in the purely passive state that evangelicals warned against. Yet I feared angel channeling, because the biblical prohibitions against having familiar spirits and/or praying to angels were so specific. In Asian settings, unfamiliar exercises could be understood as relating to some aspect of God and/or the Self, as many Hindus and Buddhists themselves understood them, but I was not sure the angels (some of whom could be demons, after all) were amenable to this translation. Accustomed as I am to being able to pray with a sense of connection, I felt uneasy about taking the risk of losing that capacity. And yet, describing a session of angel channeling seemed a likely way to introduce a book on angels in American culture, and I felt that my research would not be complete without working directly with an angel channeler.

My first choice was Doreen Virtue, and her schedule for 2005 in-cluded an all-day, 9-to-5 session in a New York hotel on Sunday, April 10. Without entering into personal stories that might embarrass others, I can say that this plan was thwarted by a series of hesitations and ac-cidents ending in a case of misappropriated car keys that would gratify any believers in Freudian theory regarding parapraxis. Some have sug-gested that my angels prevented me from attending.

Another chance came on August 1, 2005, when Trudy Griswold came to a New Age healing and recreation center called the Rituals Spa in Guilford, Connecticut. When I called to sign up, there were no seats, but I was placed on a waiting list and allowed in the next day. Thirty people turned out on that Monday evening, with only four men, including myself. The ages of those in the group appeared to range from thirty to seventy, with a median at about my own age, fifty-four. This reminded me that the angel therapy movement of the 1980s and 1990s was started by members of the generation that preceded the baby boom, people like Sophy Burnham and Michael Landon and Trudy Griswold who began their public careers as spiritual leaders relatively late in life. Even for such younger leaders as Martha Williamson of *Touched by an Angel* and Doreen Virtue, interest in angels came after a substantial career in more secular work.

After assuring us that many angels were present, having come with us to the meeting, Griswold drew a firm distinction between spirituality, which was her concern, and religion. She said that we could retain any religious commitment we had while exploring our angels, and elicited from the group the idea that spirituality dealt with connections to the supernatural and with all that is neither body nor mind. Through a story about her daughter noticing the difference between her family and others, Griswold taught that spiritual people think that everything will come out all right, and other people don't. The most basic message of the meeting was to be more positive and more specific. "We came here with a purpose and a mission that we agreed to have," and the angels could help us to remember and to fulfill it, just as they helped Griswold and her sister to run seminars and to write books. The same specificity applied to material things. Don't frustrate your angels by asking for a new car without saying what make and model and color. When you finish such a specific prayer, Griswold recommended, always add "or better," because the angels know better than you what you could receive. Griswold quoted Marianne Williamson (of *A Course in Miracles*) for the point that "many are called, but few choose to listen." She also cited the Prayer of Jabez (an evangelical prosperity prayer based on 1 Chron. 4:9) with approval, telling a story from the Jabez tradition about a man who entered Heaven and was disappointed to see a warehouse filled with blessings he could have received in life if he had asked. But before we could ask our angels for help, we would have to make contact with them. Angels would not violate our free will, so we would have to ask.

The emotional climax of the meeting began with a prayer found in Catholic catechisms of the twentieth century: "Angel of God, my guardian dear, to whom God's love commits me here, ever this day be at my side, to light and guard, to rule and guide." Then we all wrote "Dearest [our names], we love you and . . ." at the tops of our papers and waited to write what our angels would say. The recommended attitude was attentiveness, like that of someone composing a list for grocery shopping, waiting to see what would come to mind.

All but one of us wrote something, and most read what they received; five people refused to share. One said that her angels missed her and looked forward to her return, which led Griswold to reflect that the angels knew us before we were born and sometimes said that. Another saw an "imaginary" friend, an old woman named Polly, whom she had last seen when very sick as a child. People were told that the angels wanted them to get a beautiful house, to succeed at writing books for children, to move to the Southwest. When the messages ended, we were told to ask our angel's name, and some found their messages signed by well-known angels like Uriel, Michael, Gabriel, and even Clarence (the angel from *It's a Wonderful Life*), whose name drew a large laugh and the comment, "We all know Clarence!" from Griswold. My own message reflected my resistance (and/or the angels' persistence): "Dearest Peter, we love you and want to know what you want of us. Help us to see what you need at this time of life and remember that we are with you always. Try not to shut down the lines of communication, but trust in our goodness and in your own. We can make a great team if you let us." Asking for a name worked less well for me than writing, but the name "Granby," which belongs to a town in Connecticut, eventually impressed itself on me. Reading the message in public made me feel slightly choked with embarrassment and emotion.

Next we were asked to choose words printed on tiny cards which also included angel figures; mine read "expectation." Then each of us exchanged words with a neighbor and tried to ask the angels what they wished to teach that neighbor about the word. My neighbor's word was "efficiency," and the writing I performed for her said something about efficiency being a joyful tidal wave, not just responsibility. I felt inspired by some force—no more intense than in moments of personal inspiration, but real—in writing out her message. My partner disappointed me by misunderstanding the exercise and providing no word from the angels, but she did pray to them for me to expect more. The session concluded with prayer in a circle, holding hands, thanking the angels, sending healing out to those we named who needed it as we raised our joined hands, then raising our hands again to receive healing in return. Before I left, I bought Trudy Griswold's first book and lined up with many others from the group to have her sign it, which gave me a chance to ask her about her religious background and to tell her that I was writing this book. She said to remember that it would be God's book, and that if God wanted people to read it they would. In this encounter, as during the class, it was clear that Griswold was a person of unusual clarity and charisma, vaguely reminiscent of the mystery writer played by Angela Lansbury on *Murder She Wrote.*

Reflecting on that night left me with a mixed assessment of angel therapy. Applying the pragmatic tests of reasonableness and helpfulness for life that William James suggested more than a century ago, in *The Varieties of Religious Experience,* it could almost certainly be said that some good was derived from these few hours for at least some of those who attended. They did not leave believing that they should give all their money to Trudy Griswold or that they were little messiahs, and they felt confirmed and supported in trying to find their mission in life, recover from sickness or divorce, or adjust to retirement.

And yet, Griswold's claim that her practice was a spiritual method independent of religion seemed doubtful to me. Doctrines like reincarnation and preexistence were implied by what she said and by what some of our messages from the angels revealed, and a definite celestial hierarchy involving God, archangels, angels, guardian angels, ascended masters, and deceased loved ones was described. The group in fact became a temporary congregation that included some more permanent members—people who had been to other seminars and who had corresponded with Griswold. Judged as a sociologist of religion might judge a church, Griswold's congregation looked a bit unhealthy in its concern for each member in isolation, rather than for people in greater need or for social justice. This need not mean that angel channeling is harmful or that Trudy Griswold was running a scam on that night in Connecticut, however. As a professor of world religions at an expensive, private liberal arts college, I can claim little immunity from charges similar to those that Griswold's critics might raise against her.

 Romance between angels and humans was regarded as evil or impossible for thousands of years, but Americans have been putting such relations into visual art, plays, movies, novels, and love songs since the 1920s. In a few works of art, angels (or demons) and humans have had explicit sex. Often, unconsummated romances between angels and humans, or transformations from angel to human, have been used as devices to illustrate or to criticize sexual inhibitions and social boundaries. As one reviewer of this project wrote, "No wonder Americans want to have sex with angels." Sex with angels would be "heavenly" and include no fears of pregnancy, disease, or "commitment issues." Angels also offer "a transgendered sexuality" that can appeal to both women and men, whether straight or gay.[1] And yet, some mystery is suggested by the breach of a taboo that has remained in force since the book of Genesis began to shape human morality. Because angels combine animal wings, spiritual innocence, and the potential to fall from grace, they have been caught up in the American effort to unify love and sex, to redeem sex, to find redemption in sex, and even to redeem the world through sex. With regard to sex and love, Americans have used angels not just as objects of pleasure but also as symbols of cosmic change.

Repression and Recovery of the Forbidden

The Bible says that male angels once married human women. "When people began to multiply on the face of the ground, and daughters were born to them," according to the sixth chapter of Genesis (in the Revised Standard Version), "the sons of God saw that they were fair; and they took wives for themselves of all that they chose." Offspring of these unions are called "fallen ones," or "Nephilim," two verses later. The wickedness of these Nephilim has often been blamed for Noah's Flood.

Scholars now commonly understand the "sons of God" (Hebrew *bnai elohim*) as a reference to angels.[2] The same Hebrew words designate the heavenly beings who rule nations in Deuteronomy 32:8 and the spirits (including Satan) who gather around God in the first chapter of Job. Job 38:7 says that the "sons of God shouted for joy" at the creation of the world. When Jews translated their Scriptures into Greek, they often used the Greek word *angelos*, meaning messengers, the root of the English "angel," to translate *bnai elohim*. The book of Enoch, a Jewish text dating from between 300 and 100 B.C.E. that never was recognized as part of the Jewish or Christian Bible, still contributed strongly to Jewish and Christian speculative traditions by telling how 200 angels had children with human women before the Flood. According to Enoch, these spirits were rebuked for their deeds by the archangels Michael, Gabriel, and Raphael.[3] In the New Testament, the epistle of Jude quoted Enoch and referred to angels who "abandoned their proper home" and "committed fornication and followed unnatural lusts" (Jude 6–7). Paul told the Christians of Corinth that women should always cover their hair at worship "because of the angels" (1 Cor. 11:10), probably referring both to the notion that angels attended Christian worship and to the fear that the uncovered hair of women might offend or tempt those angels.

Comparing the angels of Jews and Christians to the Persian spirits on which they were based brings out the fact that any sexual differentiation among angels seems to have been repressed in the transition. All names for angels in Hebrew are masculine, even though the Seven Immortals of Zoroastrian Persia included four sons and three daughters of God.[4] In Persia, the male Vohu Manah, or Good Mind, sat at the right hand of God, and the female Armaiti, or Devotion, sat at God's left. Ranked below the seven were many male spirits, such as Vayu and Mithra, but also an occasional female, such as Anahita, the spirit of water and wisdom, and the demoness Jahi, who personified impurity.[5] Before Persia, the Mesopotamian gods of the seven planets included Ishtar, who was the wife of Marduk and goddess of Venus. Ironically, the Hebrew attempt to repress divine sexuality by insisting that angels were all male might have encouraged the development of stories about angels taking human wives in Hebrew tradition. Male Hebrew angels also became the targets of attempted homosexual rape by the human males of Sodom in Genesis 19.

Although the earliest Christian thinkers held to the view that angels had married human women, a reaction against myths about spirits and in favor of philosophy set in during the fourth century, and the idea of angels having sex with humans began to seem absurd. Augustine (354–430) knew the old story of Genesis 6 but read those marriages as an illicit mixture between a human "city of God" (the children of Adam's good son Seth) and a city of godless humans descended from Cain. Thomas Aquinas (1225–1274) was led by Aristotle to insist that angels had no bodies and no sexual functions, even in bodies they assumed.[6] Moses Maimonides (1135–1204) pushed Jewish thought in the same direction, and as late as 1937 the standard Jewish commentary on the Torah in English rejected angelic sex in its reading of Genesis 6.[7] Among Reformed thinkers who influenced early American Protestants, John Calvin (1509–1564) and Jonathan Edwards (1703–1758) both taught that the "sons of God" meant sons of Seth and that the "daughters of men" referred to daughters of Cain.[8] Only with historical research on the Bible, supported by the twentieth century's renewed willingness to believe in wicked spirits, did the most obvious meaning of Genesis 6 again find acceptance among scholars and religious authorities.

Like other taboos, the ban on images of angel-human sex arose to restrain a powerful and dangerous desire. Stories of gods or other winged, heavenly beings making love with people abounded in the ancient world. The myths of Eros and Psyche and Leda and the Swan from Greece showed a double tendency of such stories: on one hand to elevate people to the gods (as the human woman Psyche was elevated), and on the other to subject them to the level of animals (as when Zeus, in the form of a swan, raped Leda). Most of the winged, heavenly lovers of the ancient world were male, but there were exceptions, such as Eos, goddess of dawn, and Tithonus, her male human lover who disastrously asked for eternal life without eternal youth, and therefore aged and shrunk into a cricket. Artists of the Renaissance, artists of the classical revival of the nineteenth century, and especially the Pre-Raphaelites of the late nineteenth century in England made the leap from depicting gods and goddesses to imagining sexualized angels, yet sexual relations between angels and people remained surprisingly rare in Western art. Female angels did not appear in the art of Christian cultures until the

Renaissance, and angels were not normally female in Christian art until the 1800s.[9]

American author Edgar Allan Poe (1809–1849) offered a new perspective on angels and sex. In what may have been Poe's last work, the posthumously published poem "Annabel Lee," the writer reflected on his marriage at twenty-seven to a thirteen-year-old cousin (he had lived with her for six years before she suffered an aneurysm, and she then lived as an invalid until her death, five years later, of tuberculosis). Poe attributes these disasters to angelic envy: "We loved with a love that was more than love—I and my Annabel Lee; / With a love that winged seraphs of heaven / Coveted her and me." He then describes an angelic murder:

> The angels, not half so happy in heaven,
> Went envying her and me—
> Yes!—that was the reason (as all men know,
> In this kingdom by the sea)
> That the wind came out of the cloud by night,
> Chilling and killing my Annabel Lee.

Yet the angels did not succeed in parting the lovers, for, as Poe wrote, "Neither the angels in heaven above, / Nor the demons down under the sea, / Can ever dissever my soul from the soul / Of the beautiful Annabel Lee." The moon brought him dreams of her, the stars became her eyes, and the Night in which he slept became his bride. Though many later American writers, artists, and moviemakers depicted angelic influence on love in more positive terms than Poe, some continued Poe's theme that angels envied human love.

In 1923, the American Daniel Chester French, sculptor of the Lincoln Memorial, demonstrated the power of a winged angel seizing a human woman in a marble group he named for Genesis 6, *The Sons of God Saw the Daughters of Men That They Were Fair*. The statue stood out as the only allusion to sex among all of French's numerous and prominent works, which included the Minuteman statue at Concord, John Harvard in Harvard Yard, and the Alma Mater on the campus of Columbia University. Though French deflected attention from the subject of his statue by claiming it was inspired by a photograph of the geyser Old Faithful, and

The sculptor of the Lincoln Memorial, the Minuteman at Concord, and John Harvard in Harvard Yard, Daniel Chester French, also produced this dramatic image of sexual love between an angel and a human. The Sons of God Saw the Daughters of Men That They Were Fair *(1923), marble, 79 1/2 x 42 in. (In the Collection of the Corcoran Gallery of Art, Washington, D.C., Museum Purchase)*

at least one critic said that *The Sons of God* lacked passion in comparison to Auguste Rodin's *The Kiss*,[10] French's depiction of the angel and the woman did show both naked, his wings curving, as she rises on one foot to meet his grasp. The angel has a definite, though roughly sculpted, male organ.

French's design may have proved too explicit for Americans. The inclusion of a brown patch in the marble of the woman's buttocks may also have detracted from its fame. No patron had commissioned the statue, but French sold it to the Corcoran Gallery in Washington, where it remains a very powerful presence today.

Movies about Angels in Love

The theme of angels falling in love with people came to Broadway in 1938 with the musical *I Married an Angel* by Richard Rogers and Lorenz Hart. Nelson Eddy and Jeannette MacDonald made the story into a movie in 1942, and Hollywood continued the theme with *The Bishop's Wife*, starring Cary Grant, in 1947. That same year, the heavenly muse Terpsichore, played by Rita Hayworth, enlisted an angel to help her come to Earth, where she fell for a human man, in *Down to Earth*. Twenty years later, Jane Fonda took the innocence of a blind, winged young man in *Barbarella* (1968).

Each of these movies uses some device to avoid completely breaking the taboo. *I Married an Angel* has the marriage take place in a dream. *The Bishop's Wife* leaves the love between Cary Grant and Loretta Young unconsummated, and Grant's angel departs while expressing envy for her husband with the line, "Kiss her for me, you lucky Henry." *Down to Earth* uses an angel to bring the goddess Terpsichore and her human lover together, but Terpsichore herself is the pagan muse of dance rather than a biblical angel. In *Barbarella*, sex with Jane Fonda restores the power of flight to her lover Pygar, but that angel-like creature is really an extraterrestrial.

Despite such plot devices, romances involving angels still managed to challenge social-class restrictions and to offer gentle critiques of moral standards. In *I Married an Angel*, for example, the angel wife in the dream (who is really a stenographer that the dreaming bank director saw dressed as an angel at a costume party) loses her wings after she marries the man, but she retains enough of her angelic morality to refuse to wear the furs her human husband has given her, since animals were killed to make them. At a dinner party, she insists on telling the truth to her guests, which nearly results in a run on the husband's bank. The final transgression of social boundaries occurs when the banker wakes up from his dream. Though at first he is relieved that it was a dream, he is convinced that he should ask the stenographer to marry him.[11] Presumably, he would not feel this way unless the dream had conveyed a message giving him a new outlook on life.

The Bishop's Wife permits no consummation between the wife and her angel and offers an even gentler social critique. This film has become a Christmas standard on television because the crisis of the story occurs around Christmas, when the harried Episcopal bishop, played by David Niven, receives help from angel Dudley, played by Cary Grant, in answer to his prayer. As in *It's a Wonderful Life* and other Christmas stories, the special time of the holiday helps viewers to accept the presence of an angel and the temporary suspension of social norms. The bishop of this movie is trying to build a cathedral, which the wealthy donor, Mrs. Hamilton, wants to design as a memorial to her deceased husband, and the pressures of the project lead the bishop to neglect his wife and daughter. Posing as a new assistant to the bishop, the angel takes the wife out skating and shopping, and the obvious mutual attraction of angel and wife makes the bishop jealous and helps to rekindle his interest. By meeting with the wealthy donor and playing her husband's favorite hymn on a harp, Dudley the angel redirects her motives from family aggrandizement to genuine charity, so that she abandons all plans for the cathedral and decides to give her money to the poor. Dudley has now irked the bishop enough so that he prays that the angel will depart, but in reality the whole situation has been greatly improved. As the angel leaves, he expresses regret over not being likely to return. According to the script, angels are rarely sent to the same place twice, lest they form attachments like that of Dudley to the wife. "When an immortal finds himself envying a mortal, it's a danger signal," he reflects.[12] Despite Dudley's undeniable charm and influence, the cosmic order of *The Bishop's Wife* puts people firmly in charge of their servants, the angels, who must avoid succumbing to human beauty. Meanwhile, the movie confirms the (slightly improved) social status quo: Mrs. Hamilton is now both rich and good; the bishop and his family are in order; and none of them remember that they ever needed help from an angel.

Fifty years after *The Bishop's Wife* appeared, *The Preacher's Wife* (1997) remade the story in a black church setting, with Denzel Washington playing the Cary Grant role and Whitney Houston playing the wife. The wealthy donor is replaced by a black developer who offers to move the preacher of the title from his inner-city Baptist church to a megachurch (complete with child-care facilities and an adult activity center) in the suburbs, incidentally destroying the old neighborhood. The angel and the wife again go shopping, skating, and even dancing in a nightclub without consummating their romance, though they come closer to kissing than in the 1947 film.

Angelic envy of humanity and angelic desire for the human wife is expanded in the remake; instead of being concentrated in a few lines, it becomes a major theme. When the angel first appears, he is surprised to find himself lying in the snow between two boys (the preacher's son and his best friend), who are making snow angels by flapping their arms; he rises to his knees and rapturously thanks God to be back on Earth (the earlier Dudley never seemed to have lived on Earth as a human). Eating a piece of pizza, the Dudley of the 1990s mentions waiting a long time for this chance, saying he stood in line with other spirits for thirty years. Out dancing with the preacher's wife, he makes himself conspicuous by doing moves like the Popeye and the Swim dating from the 1960s. Then, as Whitney Houston sings as a guest in the club where she had often sung before her marriage, the angel gazes at her and falls in love. He never transgresses, but he does use the threat of losing the wife's love to influence the preacher, arguing that if the old church is lost, "Julia will never look at you the same." Finally, the Christmas sermon that rouses the congregation to save the old church turns the desire of angels to return to Earth into a virtue by mentioning angels who wait in long lines just to help humanity. *The Preacher's Wife* did not meet with the critical success of *The Bishop's Wife* or attain the enduring popularity of the earlier movie, but it did show that the purveyors of American popular culture were somewhat more willing to bring humans and angels together in 1997 than they had been in 1947.

Envy of people by heavenly beings was also the theme of a musical number, "People Have More Fun Than Anyone," in which Rita Hayworth danced while lip-synching in *Down to Earth*, another heavenly romance of 1947. Though the lyrics of that particular song celebrated electric light, cigarette lighters, and drinking fountains as human equivalents of divine power over the sun, the stars, and the rivers, the movie left no doubt that romance was the main reason why people have more fun. Here angels—particularly the calm and dignified Mr. Jordan, angel in charge of shepherding souls between Earth and Heaven, a character who first appeared in *Here Comes Mr. Jordan* (1941) and later in Warren Beatty's *Heaven Can Wait* (1978) and Chris Rock's *Down to Earth* (2000)— supervise even the ancient gods and run the universe. The main protagonist, Terpsichore, muse of dance and daughter of Zeus or Dionysus (depending on which myth is read), begs Mr. Jordan to let her descend from Mount Parnassus, a neighborhood of Heaven where she lives with the other muses, in order to "help" a struggling theatrical producer. Her real motive, which she fruitlessly tries to conceal from the angel, is to stop the producer from putting on a show called *Swinging the Muses*, in which American soldiers parachute onto Mount Parnassus and have romances with the muses (particularly a fictional Terpsichore), who respond with unseemly enthusiasm.

After capturing the lead in the musical as well as the heart of the producer, the real Terpsichore remakes the plot, the musical numbers, and the costumes into a very dignified show; as a result, it nearly folds in Philadelphia. Angry and about to return to Heaven, she is convinced to remain by the angelic Mr. Jordan, who informs her that the producer owes gambling debts to the gangster financing the show and that he will be killed if it does not succeed. But after she agrees to perform in the original, undignified show, saving the New York opening, Mr. Jordan returns and demands that she go back to Heaven with him. "You saved his life—that's all we had for you to do," the angel explains to the muse. She wants to renounce divinity and live as a human, and she wants to cry, fulfilling the gender role of a human woman, but she cannot. "Tears are only for mortals," says the angel; "It's an advantage they have over us." This point is reminiscent of Thomas Aquinas's description of the damned, who cry in Hell without producing any tears, since they cannot lose matter from their bodies.[13] Fortunately for Terpsichore, Mr. Jordan has a consoling vision of the future to share: When her producer dies and arrives in Heaven, she will meet him again. Though *Down to Earth* was little more than a star showcase for Rita Hayworth, it shows the increasing willingness of the American public to accept the idea of love between earthy and heavenly beings, at least if the ultimate marriage is to happen in Heaven.

Angels in Love Songs

The next stage in the progress of angelic romance toward the explicit sex of the 1990s came not in film but in popular music. Although every age writes love songs, people do not always think of angels when they want to evoke romance. In recent American history, there have been two periods when angels appeared in many Top 40 hits—the late 1950s and early 1960s and the late 1990s. The songs of both eras pushed the limits of traditional gender roles while advancing toward breakthroughs in sexual explicitness. Angel imagery added a transcendent dimension, enabling the songs to affirm the happiness of love while implying an urge to get beyond barriers.

The first "angel" Top 40 song of the 1950s was "Earth Angel" ("Earth angel, earth angel, will you be mine?"), originally recorded by a black group, the Penguins, in 1954 and then by a white group, called the Crew Cuts, in 1955. The white version reached number three on the charts. Though the song referred to prayer and visions, it clearly focused on a human lover and used the angel concept to convey worshipful admiration. Remade in 1986 by the band New Edition and returning to the Top 40 as part of the soundtrack from the movie *Karate Kid II*, it has remained popular as a slow-dance song at weddings.[14]

Far more explicitly angelic, even at times theological, content appeared in "My Special Angel" by Jimmy Duncan, recorded by Bobby Helms (famed for "Jingle Bell Rock") in 1957, when it reached number seven on the charts. The beloved in this song was said to have been "sent from up above" when "the Lord smiled down on me / And sent an angel to love." The angel was associated with cosmic events: "The smile on your lips brings the summer sunshine / Tears from your eyes bring the rain." This love had everlasting resonance and participated in the guardian angel motif: "You are my special angel / Through eternity / I'll have my special angel / Here to watch over me." In 1968, a group called the Vogues remade the song, and it again reached number seven on the pop charts. Bobby Vinton recorded a popular version, and this song also gained a lasting role at weddings.[15]

On February 8, 1960, "Teen Angel" became the first angel song to reach number one on the pop chart.[16] The song used the concept of dead people becoming angels to invoke love that surpassed limits. The "Teen Angel" of the title had been a passenger in a car "stalled upon the railroad track," who is now remembered after her death by a boyfriend who recalled pulling her out. "We were safe, but you went running back," he croons, and she runs to a death that seems inexplicable. After the accident, "they found my high school ring / Clutched in your fingers tight," a testament to the seriousness of going steady in those days. Unlike "My Special Angel," this song made no claims that the girl had been sent by God or that she caused the sun and the rain, but it did seek communion with her despite death. The chorus invoked an eternal love: "Teen angel, can you hear me / Teen angel, can you see me / Are you somewhere up above / And am I still your own true love?"[17] The inimitable, adolescent voice of singer Mark Dinning and the idiocy of the girl dying for a class ring have made "Teen Angel" impervious to remakes, but it remains an iconic memory for millions who were teens and preteens in 1960. According to "Teen Angel," going steady could extend to Heaven.

Less spectacular in its success but reaching number thirty-two for the whole year of 1960 was a song in the nightclub swing style, "Devil or Angel," by Bobby Vee: "Devil or angel dear, whichever you are / I need you, I need you, I need you."[18] There was no theology or eternity invoked here, but the metaphor of the angel again seemed appropriate for the lover. A stronger association of sex appeal and angels came in the rhythm and blues song "Pretty Little Angel Eyes" by Curtis Lee, produced by recording pioneer Phil Spector, which reached number seven on the charts in 1961 and stood at number twenty-one for that year. Though Lee's lyrics did affirm that his darling was sent "from heaven above" and that they would be "happy for eternity," the power of the song arose from its driving repetition of the title, or part of the title, in a vaguely sexual frenzy.[19]

A more ethereal, lyrical evocation of angels as objects of love came from teen singer Shelley Fabares, whose "Johnny Angel" reached number one for two weeks in 1962 and finished nineteenth in sales among popular songs of that year. In a record marked by echo effects, Fabares longed for an angel: "Johnny Angel, how I want him / How I tingle when he passes by." Her voice rose in the chorus, "I'm in heaven, I get carried away," and descended to the hope that "together we will see how lovely heaven will be."[20] Lyrics and production combined to cast Fabares as an American Psyche, longing to be carried to Olympus by her angelic Johnny.

In October of the same year, doowop singer Neil Sedaka reached the top ten with "Next Door to an Angel," which on one level was nothing more than a tribute to a girl growing up ("She used to be such a skinny little girl / But all of a sudden she's out of this world") but on another used relentless biblical rhetoric to express sexual attraction. Sedaka said that he had "found a garden of Eden at the house next door to mine" and "a little bit of heaven right on my block"; he watched the girl walk on Main Street and exclaimed, "It used to be such a plain street but now it's paradise." He identified with the fallen angels: "I'm feelin' happy, I'm feelin' so good / I'm the luckiest devil in the neighborhood." In building its climax, the song repeats "I'm livin' right next door to an angel" three times, setting up the statement of sexual intent: "And I'm gonna make that angel mine." Such a confident, positive use of the concept of an angel seemed playful and harmless in 1962, but it might not have been acceptable before the 1950s and would not have held anyone's interest a few years later.

Between the early 1960s and the 1990s, love songs about angels appeared only sporadically. An era dealing with the effects of the birth-control pill and a second wave of feminism led by Betty Friedan and Gloria Steinem did not want to idealize lovers of either sex. Bob Dylan, the Beatles, the Rolling Stones, and the Who did not sing to women as angels, and the few female artists who had hits in this intensely masculine era in popular music did not see their men as angels either.

In 1968, a disillusioned form of the angel metaphor made number twenty-eight on the charts for the year, just behind "Love Child" by Diana Ross and the Supremes and ahead of "Born to be Wild," the theme song from *Easy Rider*. "Angel of the Morning" was written by a man named Chip Taylor but always sung by women, first by Merilee Rush, who had the hit in 1968, and later by Olivia Newton-John, Chrissie Hynde and the Pretenders, Nina Simone, Juice Newton, and Bonnie Tyler. Its theme is a promise, by a woman agreeing to have sex—probably for the first time with the man in the song, and possibly with the loss of her virginity—that she will hold the man to no obligations: "Just call me angel of the morning (ANGEL) / Just touch my cheek before you leave me (BABY)." Of course, the singer is not claiming that she is an angel in any literal sense, but again, the angel metaphor brings sex and religion together quite explicitly: "If morning's echo says we've sinned," she promises not to be "blinded by the light."[21] This woman wants to be regarded as innocent no matter what she has done. "Angel of the Morning" was a sad, late anthem of the sexual revolution that had enduring appeal to women over the next few decades—until the culture gained more hope for women and for real angels.

A somewhat anachronistic but commercially successful account of angelic interference in human love appeared in the summer of 1970, when a sister and brother act called the Carpenters had their first number-one hit, "Close to You." As Karen Carpenter's sweet voice sang this Burt Bacharach/Hal David song, "On the day that you were born the angels got together / And decided to create a dream come true, / So they sprinkled moondust in your hair / Of gold and stardust in your eyes of blue."[22] In contrast with the envious angels of Edgar Allan Poe's *Annabel Lee*, angels here encourage human love. Their actions create a cosmically attractive boy, for whom birds "suddenly appear" and stars "fall down from the sky," while "all the girls in town" follow him "all around." The song suggested a gender shift, both because angels and cosmic beauty were usually associated with women and because the singer declared an unusually frank desire of females to be "close to" a male. Girls did not usually follow boys around in 1970, but they would in ensuing decades. Angelic imagery accompanied a shift in romantic practice.

A rare breakthrough to full affirmation of angel-human marriage (or at least mating), and the first such scene to involve a male human and female angel, came in the song "Angel" by Jimi Hendrix, which was released on an album called *The Cry of Love* in September 1971, almost exactly a year after Hendrix died. A ballad with deep echo effects in the vocal, and signature Hendrix guitar work that carried the lyrics toward Heaven, "Angel" evoked all of the pagan power of being carried off by the winged mate. Although male humans later had sex with angels in Tony Kushner's *Angels in America* and in Andrew Greeley's *Angel Fire*, those encounters happened in the human settings of apartments and hotel rooms. Only Hendrix wrote as a male rescued from this world and taken "high over yonder," into the sky, by his angelic female. After seeing him for the first time, for "just long enough to rescue" him, the angel tells him about the love of the moon and the sea, then promises to return. She comes back in the morning and says that it is time for him "to rise" and be her man. He agrees, repeating the chorus of "Fly on my sweet angel" and ending with the promise to stay by her side.

However melancholy this song may seem in the light of Hendrix's early death, it struck an unusual note of beauty, optimism, and redemption from traditional gender roles when it was recorded. Hope for transformation through angelic sex would not long survive the end of the 1960s, when it crashed in the forms of parody with *Barbarella* and horror with *Rosemary's Baby*. It would rise again in the 1990s.

Consummations with Angels and Devils

Barbarella (1968) was directed by Frenchman Roger Vadim and took aim at the American market through Vadim's wife and star, Jane Fonda, who in those days personified the ethic of innocent ecstasy[23] as the utterly healthy, unselfconsciously sexy American girl. In a scene still resented by some feminists, Fonda opens the movie in a bulky spacesuit that she gradually strips away while floating in simulated zero gravity. She then spends much of the film wearing uniforms like knee-high boots and one-piece swimsuits with semi-transparent plastic bubbles over her breasts. The plot centers on an evil scientist who dispatches his foes with an Orgasmatron, which shorts out when matched against Barbarella's sexual capacity. Before this climax, the heroine meets a beautiful and innocent young man with wings, called Pygar, who lives in a nest. Barbarella shares the nest with him, introducing him to sex, which restores his power of flight. Pygar later carries Barbarella aloft, where she shoots down enemy aircraft with her futuristic rifle, playing havoc with 1960s gender roles. The movie became an icon of the sexual revolution, a highlight of the moment when *Playboy* was cool. Though its "angel" was actually an alien, he refers to himself as an angel. When Barbarella asks him if he has ever made love, he answers that "an angel doesn't make love, an angel *is* love." His winged innocence and redemption through sex is central to the movie's theme of regaining Eden.

In Barbarella: Queen of the Galaxy *(1968), sex with Jane Fonda restored the power of flight to an angel. From left, Jane Fonda as Barbarella and John Philip Law as Pygar. (Paramount Pictures/Photofest)*

If *Barbarella* exemplified the naïve energy of the 1960s, *Rosemary's Baby* (1968) belonged to the descent toward nihilism that marked the late years of the Vietnam War. The director was another European, Roman Polanski, and the star another American icon of innocent sex appeal, Mia Farrow, who had just finished starring in the television series *Peyton Place* and marrying Frank Sinatra. As in *The Exorcist*, which came five years later and for which it prepared the way, *Rosemary's Baby* derived much of its impact from the contrast between beautiful young people living in bright urban settings and a demonic underworld.

The plot involves newlyweds Rosemary and Guy Woodhouse, played by Farrow and John Cassavetes—he an aspiring actor and she a young wife working at nothing but getting pregnant. They find an apartment in a beautiful old building, the Dakota on New York's Upper West Side, and are virtually adopted by an elderly neighbor couple. The young people plan to have sex on a night when Farrow ends up ingesting some of her neighbor's special chocolate mousse, which leaves her in a trance that turns into a sex scene that has become almost as famous as Barbarella's striptease. During this trance, the act of the husband stripping his semiconscious wife and putting her to bed turns into a Black Mass under Michelangelo's frescoes in the Sistine Chapel. Surrounded by her naked elderly neighbors, friends, and husband, Rosemary is tied naked to an altar by a woman portraying Jacqueline Kennedy (an explicit identification in the novel, but only implied in the movie). Before sex begins, a figure with red eyes and a scaly black body—a costume actually worn in the movie by Anton LaVey, leader of the Church of Satan—is briefly seen. Enormous black paws covered with scales and ending in claws rake over Farrow's very white body—an inescapable, even if unintended, reminder of race at the time—and lift her hips. The camera focuses tightly on Farrow's face as a dark head fills the place where her partner's head would be in sex. A figure dressed as the pope approaches from the right, and Farrow kisses his ring. Suddenly she screams, "This is no dream! This is really happening!" The movie then returns to the bright reality of the New York apartment, where she awakens to find long scratches on her body and her husband apologizing for not wanting to miss "baby night" and for failing to clip his nails. Pregnancy ensues, with much attention (including potions and talismans) from the neighbors and from the doctor they recommend. The birth involves another scene of understated horror. Viewers are never shown the baby, but Rosemary's revulsion ("What have you done with his eyes?"), which is followed by her eventual agreement to care for the child.

Critics have noted that *Rosemary's Baby* left open the option of interpreting the plot as a metaphor, rather than as a literal story of sex between Mia Farrow's character and Satan. Few in the audiences of 1968 actually took the metaphoric view, however, and the images of the Black Mass and of those massive, black, scaly hands and claws moving over the woman's white and waiflike body would retain their power whether one interpreted the scene as fantasy or fact. Another signature image of demonic sex came in 1973, when *The Exorcist* showed the fallen angel Pazuzu forcing an adolescent girl to stab her vagina repeatedly with a crucifix and then to rub her mother's face into her bloody crotch. The theme of the Devil having a human child would also inspire *The Omen* (1976) and its sequel, *Damien* (1978), but these films focused on the child rather than on sex between demons and humans. In *Angel Heart* (1987) and *The Devil's Advocate* (1997), fairly noteworthy films that cast Robert De Niro and Al Pacino as Satan, the Devil manipulates human sexuality and sometimes has sex with humans, but the main emphasis is on his human pawns.

Two movies of 1987, *The Last Temptation of Christ* and *The Witches of Eastwick*, expressed strong suspicions that ordinary sex with women might belong to the realm of the demonic. Both films were based on novels by important male writers. Both used demons to imply that for humans to transcend gender roles, or even to obtain salvation from sin and death, required that they give up sex.

Nikos Kazantzakis, a Greek novelist and Nobel Prize winner, attained fame in the United States as the author of *Zorba the Greek* decades before director Martin Scorsese decided to film his novel *The Last Temptation of Christ*. Only after the sexual revolution, the demise of Hollywood's Production Code, and the explicit blasphemies of *The Exorcist* did it become conceivable to make an American film that depicted Jesus succumbing to sexual desire, even if the ultimate context framed the event as a fantasy. The story makes Jesus a reluctant Messiah driven by headaches and an inexorable sense of destiny until the end, when he confronts a trick of Satan's that nearly derails the crucifixion and so the redemption of humanity. The "last temptation" of the title (following the three temptations in the desert, which are mentioned in the Bible) is the temptation to live a normal life as the husband of Mary Magdalene.

The controversial, sexual part of this movie begins with an angel coming to Jesus on the cross and rescuing him, removing each nail and kissing each wound, and telling him that God has sent the angel in order to lead him to his wedding. Only after Jesus marries three women and fathers children by two of them, and is lying on his deathbed while the Romans sack Jerusalem, is the secret revealed: The guardian angel, who is played in the film by a beautiful adolescent girl, was actually Satan, and he has apparently won. Jesus then drags his dying body back to Golgotha, begs God's forgiveness, asks to be crucified, and gets his wish, restoring the redemption. Whether this works because God can reverse time or because the whole sequence of events is only a fantasy is immaterial; the point is that Jesus longed for human life, and especially for sex and marriage, but could not have them. Repeatedly, in the novel and in the film, Satan (disguised as the guardian angel) assures Jesus that sex is the vehicle that is to bring the Kingdom of Heaven, which "comes from embrace to embrace," to Earth. When the first wife, Mary Magdalene, dies, Satan leads Jesus to marry both sisters of Lazarus at once, assuring him that "there is only one woman in the world" as far as the power of life is concerned.

The Catholics who picketed *The Last Temptation of Christ*, warning those who entered the theater that they could lose their souls, did not seem to appreciate that the film unequivocally supported two Christian ideas: that Jesus had to be celibate, and that the death of Jesus was essential to human salvation. Conservatives were offended by people watching as Jesus made love to women. In the storm of controversy, it was little remarked that the fallen angel Satan had been transformed from the powerful forms in which the movie depicted him tempting Jesus in the desert (a pillar of fire, a lion) into a feminine form with a seductive message about salvation through sex. A similarly feminine, subtle Satan appeared in Mel Gibson's *The Passion of the Christ* (2004) to tempt Jesus in the Garden of Gethsemane and lurk in the crowds in the scenes preceding the crucifixion.

While Kazantzakis published his novel in 1951, with an English translation in 1960, John Updike published *The Witches of Eastwick* in 1984, and Updike's association of sex with Satan was much more explicit and masculine. The Devil in this novel and film comes to Long Island in response to three women who are practicing magic. Arriving in disguise as Daryl Van Horne, a rich man who has bought an old mansion, Satan lures the women to a kind of perpetual party which includes great sex. One of the women (played by Cher) exclaims with glee that Van Horne's penis bends upward; the demure cellist played by Susan Sarandon learns to release such passion that her playing sets her strings on fire. The demon (played by Jack Nicholson) shows his darker side, and his powers, when a fourth local woman suspects his real identity. After Van Horne enables his three witches to kill this neighbor with a spell, the women become frightened of him and make a voodoo doll, which they attempt to use to drive him away. While they torment him at long distance with the doll, Satan takes refuge in a white New England church, interrupting services with an impromptu sermon against women. In one sense, he has the last laugh, because each of the women bears a child of his, but in another way the women win. The final scene shows Nicholson managing to contact his children for a moment by appearing on a television screen and talking to them, but the blonde witch, played by Michelle Pfeiffer, cuts him off with the remote.

The reigning metaphor of *The Witches of Eastwick* is marriage, divorce, and custody from a male and misogynist point of view: The women end up with the mansion and the children. With regard to the sexual role of angels in American culture, the story represents an increased emphasis on sexual pleasure in comparison to medieval and Puritan doctrines on Satan and witchcraft. The fifteenth-century Catholic handbook on witches, the *Malleus Maleficarum*, and the Puritans both said that women became witches by having intercourse with the Devil, but traditional wisdom held that his penis was cold; the transaction had more to do with power than with pleasure. The suspicion that women were sexually insatiable and therefore more susceptible than men to seduction by the Devil did appear in the Catholic handbook,[24] and this notion seems to have continued unchanged from the Renaissance through John Updike. In fact, modern male suspicions of women have infused a new sympathy for Satan into the whole concept of witchcraft.

Meanwhile, both fiction and movies have also gingerly approached sex between good angels and people. A Catholic priest, Andrew Greeley, wrote a novel called *Angel Fire* (1988) in which a female angel, Gabriella, tells a human that "Most High was greatly displeased" about the marriages of Genesis 6, and that angels made rules to govern their interactions with humans afterward. Despite this statement of the taboo, Gabriella herself later nearly kills the human hero of the book with her lovemaking, which the other angels had agreed to allow.[25] The shift of gender from the story of Genesis 6 was probably essential to making Greeley's story acceptable in an American context. By 1988, the image of a male angel Gabriel making love with a human woman would have had an unavoidable connotation of rape or sexual harassment, but the angelic "Gabriella" receiving a human male (however dangerously) could be contextualized as sexual therapy.

Greeley's novel features fictional biologist John James (or in the Irish form that Greeley loved, Sean Seamus) Desmond, who expounds theories predicting intelligent evolution toward forms of life higher than humanity. Because such evolved beings already exist in the world of the novel—their visits to Earth are already known by Greeley's espionage agencies (with the Cold War still raging) and private criminal organizations—the novel's hero scientist (Desmond) is in danger as he journeys from Chicago to Stockholm for his Nobel Prize. The danger is met by a guardian energy being named Gabriella Light, who turns out to be the biblical Gabriel in person. As Gabriella tells Desmond, she is not immortal but very long-lived, though susceptible to death by extreme magnetic and electrical attack. Lucifer was not a demon, but a very pious angel and Gabriella's former husband, who died centuries ago; the story of war in Heaven from Revelation 12 represents a human misunderstanding of a large argument that was typical of life among the angels—who love, she says, to argue. Their disputes are playful but arise from real uncertainty. Although angels dedicate their lives to patterns of beauty and work to see these patterns grow, they do not "act as messengers for Anyone, at least not regularly." In fact, they are "as ultimately uncertain about the existence of Anyone" as any human.[26] They are "pattern-obsessed creatures," Gabriella explains: "There are some patterns that almost demand our intervention," she says. "In that sense we might be called messengers of God. Heralds of the pattern anyway." She recalls Nazareth as a moment when a new pattern succeeded, and she bitterly regrets World War I as the result of a failed attempt by her species to foster an emerging pattern of international order.[27]

Staying in hotel rooms adjoining those of Professor Desmond, Gabriella has many opportunities to become intimate with her human ward. She is naturally female, and she explains to the professor that angels "do join our energy fields as part of the reproductive process and we enjoy it far more than you do. . . . We do it for weeks and weeks of your time too."[28] Gabriella assumes an analog body and reproduces clothing from magazines to keep the professor interested, and the first time she touches his cheek affectionately he feels that he is "filled with all the peace and goodness and beauty of the universe," a sensation that he says transcends sex. Eventually she shows him her real self in a demonstration that begins with "intricate and exquisite light patterns" and culminates in "a massive waterfall of gold and silver that seems to fill the whole of creation," leaving him "sobbing in his guardian angel's arms" and emotionally bound to her forever. After Gabriella destroys the last of the enemies (East Germans) who had sought to kill Professor

Desmond and harness the power of the energy beings for their own purposes, she permits him to make love with her analog body. As she draws him into her "raging blast furnace," he finds that he wants "nothing but timeless union" even though "his own existence would end." Recalling Genesis 6, Desmond reflects that "maybe the scripture was afraid to even hint at the daughters of God and the sons of man." Gabriella stops the angel-human intercourse just short of killing him, but her plans for his sex life are not finished. She insists that he accept the invitation of the Irish government to visit Ireland. As the novel ends, Desmond meets and quickly proposes marriage to a woman in Ireland whose body and face almost exactly resemble the analogs that Gabriella had assumed.

Like most stories of angelic love, Greeley's novel uses the angels to provide critical perspectives on human inhibitions and social mores. Gabriella notes that Professor Desmond avoids women who are emotionally available to him and pursues those who are not; the angel therefore designs her human body to guide him to an emotionally open woman with the correct cultural background for him. Gabriella also expresses hope that human sexuality might evolve in the direction of angelic matings, which, she says, are permanent, unlike Desmond's first marriage, which had ended in divorce and annulment. She thinks that to accomplish this, humans will have to learn to select more compatible mates. At the same time, Greeley also depicts Gabriella learning from her human: Just before she departs, Professor Desmond makes her promise to take a new companion in place of the long-deceased Lucifer. A later novel of Greeley's, *Angel Light* (1995), assures readers that Gabriella has remarried, as it tells the tale of Raphaella, another female seraph, who leads another male character to marry an Irish woman.[29]

A trend in the direction of more and more human, physically present angels was visible in Greeley's novels and in *The Witches of Eastwick*. The same trend went back through *The Last Temptation of Christ* to *Down to Earth* and *The Bishop's Wife*. In Greeley's *Angel Fire*, the angel becomes so physical that she kills several people directly, picking one up by the feet and swinging his head into the wall of a shower.[30] The Raphaella of *Angel Light* never has sex with a human, but she does let the male character go to sleep while resting his head on her breasts; she doesn't kill anyone, but she does direct the villains' guns so that they injure each other.[31] The trend toward physical angels reached one of its peaks in a minor film comedy called *Date with an Angel* (1987).[32] Here the targets of social criticism are venerable Hollywood clichés like the greed of businessmen and the subordination of love to wealth. An original touch appears in that the human character spends most of the movie protecting the angel, who must lose her power, at least temporarily, to have a fling with him.

In the opening scene of *Date with an Angel*, a female angel (Emmanuelle Beart, a blonde French actress of some note) collides with a satellite in orbit miles above the Earth. Meanwhile, a California man (a soap-opera actor named Michael Knight) is celebrating his impending marriage with his friends at a bachelor party when it is interrupted by the sound of a body crashing into the backyard pool. Investigating, the groom-to-be finds a beautiful blonde angel lying unconscious. As he does mouth-to-mouth resuscitation, she wakes up and embraces him, then winces with pain from her broken right wing. She kisses him despite her pain, and the kiss knocks him unconscious. When he wakes up, he finds that the angel cannot communicate in words but can only make high-pitched sounds that are unintelligible to him. Conflict arises from several sources, especially his fiancée (Phoebe Cates, the biggest American star in the film), who becomes more and more jealous as he appears everywhere with the angel, and her father, a businessman who wants to use the angel to advertise an "Ethereal Beauty" line of beauty products. Seeking information about how to get medical treatment for an angel, the hero goes to a Catholic priest who tells him to "try the Baptists." Worst of all are the friends from the bachelor party, who try to kidnap the angel and put her on display for money.

Meanwhile, angel and human fall in love as he tends her. He sets the broken bone in her wing and offers her a hamburger, which repels her, but she loves French fries and stuffs her mouth with them. Often she tries to kiss him, but he avoids this, trying to retain consciousness and to preserve his engagement. He dances and cuddles with her instead. Finally, all the bad humans pursue the angel and the man in a slapstick chase scene. Having recovered her power to fly, the angel hovers above them all and attacks the fiancée and her father with focused lightning and rain. All of the pursuers then give up, but in the process of this ordeal the hero has been knocked unconscious and needs to be hospitalized.

The angel who fell to Earth now comes to the hospital to take the hero into the afterlife. She had been sent to do this on the night of his bachelor party, when the accident with the satellite interrupted the plan. He asks whether she guides everyone who has died, and she says no. When he confesses to jealousy, they finally kiss and then dissolve in light. The next scene shows him awake, surrounded by his friends visiting the hospital, when a woman who appears to be a nurse comes into the room. The nurse (who is played by the same actress who played the angel) says that she's there because of "an answer to an angel's prayer." She has received "a leave of absence for good behavior" from her angelic duties, and she wants to know whether the man feels "good enough to take [her] out for some French fries."

Although *Date with an Angel* was no masterpiece, or even a memorable film on a par with *Barbarella* or *Rosemary's Baby*, it picked up on two trends in the United States having to do with angels: the tradition of angelic romance as an occasion to criticize social conventions, and the descent of angels from messengers of God to servants of humanity. As she descends from angel to nurse, the angel of this movie also confirms traditional gender roles and brings another modern theme into focus: that angels envy humanity. Of course, this angel was not a bodiless spirit or a supernatural being even before she became a nurse. She more closely resembled an intelligent animal incapable of human speech. Disabled by collision with a physical satellite, and capable of being kidnapped with the bait of French fries, she also had a strong rapport with animals—turning, for example, the raging Dobermans guarding a rich family's home into loving pets with nothing more than a glance of her eyes. This theme of angelic affinity with animals occurred in another film as well—*Michael* (1996), with John Travolta. In this movie, the angel has sex with a human (off-camera) while remaining an angel.

Written by Nora Ephron, *Michael* offers a contrast to the male perspectives on angelic love that have dominated most movies and songs. It centers on Michael the Archangel, who "smites" a bank in a small town in Iowa, demolishing the bank building with a windstorm, in answer to the prayers of a woman named Pansy (played by Jean Stapleton of *All in the Family* fame), who owns a rural motel. He then takes up residence at Pansy's Milk Bottle Motel, which uses a giant milk bottle as its sign, for what he calls his "last blast"—or last visit to Earth (angels are apparently allowed twenty-six such appearances).

When viewers of the movie are introduced to Michael, through the eyes of reporters (William Hurt and Andie MacDowell) who have been sent to write about him, the angel is coming down to the kitchen in boxer shorts and wings, slightly potbellied, unshaven, and smoking a cigarette. For breakfast, he enjoys cereal with pounds of sugar, pouring enormous heaps that rise above the bowl. Then he walks into a field and, just for fun, challenges a bull to butt heads (Michael wins). At night, he goes into town with a coat over his wings and dances in a bar, where every woman present is drawn to him by a mysterious scent they describe as combining caramel, cotton candy, and cookies. A bar fight ensues when the men in the bar become jealous, but Michael proves invulnerable. He brings a woman back to his motel room, and her cries of pleasure (along with a shout of "Wings, far out!") and utterly satisfied expression in the morning testify to his sexual prowess. Taken to court because of the fight in the bar, he is acquitted when the judge smells him approaching the bench.

After all of this fun and sex, *Michael* reaches, less successfully, for sentiment and love. When a little dog belonging to the motel owner is hit by a truck and killed, Michael, at the insistence of one of the reporters, uses his last miracle to resurrect the dog, and then disappears in a cloud of feathers. Pansy also dies, and the reporters, who had been romantically involved, quarrel and separate. One night in Chicago, however, the male reporter thinks he sees Michael in the street. Pursuing him for blocks, he runs into the woman reporter and they are reunited. The faintly glowing, translucent figures of Michael and Pansy are seen dancing in the streets, stopping traffic.

Michael generated little controversy, although one evangelical complained that the real archangel Michael must have been very angry to see himself portrayed in this manner.[33] The movie was another step in the humanizing of angels and in their subordination to humanity, another portrayal of angelic envy of people and of visits to Earth as the highlights of angelic life. Whether Michael the Archangel was really offended cannot be investigated, but it can reasonably be said that human audiences of the 1950s or even the 1970s would have been far more scandalized than those of 1996.

Sentimentality and Freedom

In 1998, Hollywood put two of its most marketable stars, Meg Ryan and Nicholas Cage, into a movie about an angel and a human in love. *City of Angels* (1998) may have seemed a sure thing because it began as a remake of a hit German film from 1987, two years before the fall of the Berlin Wall, called *Wings of Desire.* Where the German film affirmed freedom by celebrating the choice of an angel to become human out of love for a woman, however, the American film affirmed sentimentality; supported traditional roles for angels, men, and women; and emphasized the goodness of the physical world.

In *Wings,* young German filmmaker (and Christian believer) Wim Wenders presented a simple and powerful romance. Angels observe Berlin in the opening scenes: Dressed in long black raincoats, they are sitting on top of buildings and walking among humans through streets, libraries, and bus stations, but the humans cannot see them. As they slip past people or look at people on the bus, they overhear thoughts, including many internal monologues of hopelessness and despair. The film makes exquisite use of the landscape of a city divided not only by the Wall between East and West but also by blocks of barren neighborhoods cleared for security, or simply not rebuilt since World War II. In contrast to all of this gray bleakness, filmed in black and white, Wenders focuses on a circus and a female acrobat, a symbol of hope who wears angel wings in her performance. One of the observing angels becomes enamored of her and wants to join her in mortal life. He throws himself down from a building and finds himself bruised but alive, with only his angelic armor as an object to pawn for money, and now living in a world of color. Peter Falk of the television series *Columbo,* playing himself as an actor filming a movie in Berlin, tells this newly fallen angel that he did the same thing years ago and advises him about what to do next. In the end, the angel-turned-human sets up housekeeping with the acrobat, happily assuring his former angelic colleague, Cassiel, that he will learn to live as a mortal: "She will teach me everything," he says.

City of Angels keeps the long overcoats from the Berlin of *Wings of Desire,* but they look strangely out of place in California and therefore have a very different emotional impact. Three key scenes, at the beginning, middle, and end of the movie, show dozens of angels standing on a beach at dawn and sunset in their black trench coats, listening to the music of the universe. The effect of these scenes is to make the angels appear to be members of some bizarre cult of the sun.

In contrast to the melancholy and somewhat listless angels, a cardiac surgeon named Maggie Rice (played by Meg Ryan, who is first seen from above, through the eyes of an angel), rides to her hospital on a bicycle and saves lives, and she is devastated whenever she fails. When an operation she performs does not save one patient, an angel named Seth (played by Nicholas Cage) leads the person's ghost away, and Dr. Rice sinks toward despair. The angel becomes smitten with the strangely sensitive surgeon and begins to stalk her. He receives advice from Nathaniel Messinger (played by Dennis Franz), a former heart patient and former angel who now lives as a human, who fills the role of Peter Falk from the German movie. When Maggie and angel Seth both attend a party hosted by Messinger, Maggie sees that there is something different about Seth, especially when he cuts through his thumb with no effect. One night when she cannot sleep, Maggie senses the angel's presence in the room and asks him, although he is invisible, to lie down with her until she goes to sleep. The film allows viewers to see this chaste embrace. Maggie nevertheless plans to marry a fellow surgeon, but Seth now plunges from a building, renouncing his life as an angel, and pursues her to a cabin at Lake Tahoe. Without money or a sense of how to survive in the world, he arrives at her vacation home bloodied and bruised. Maggie cleans his wounds, playing a scene that suggests the image of the Virgin Mary from Leonardo's *Pieta* and, more directly, Mary Magdalene cleaning the wounds of Jesus in *The Last Temptation of Christ*.

The surgeon and the angel have one night of bliss, after which Maggie goes for a ride on her bicycle and raises her arms with her eyes closed in a gesture of flying, just before she collides with a truck full of logs, sustaining fatal (but not disfiguring) injuries. She dies in the arms of her former angel of death. Asked by an angelic friend whether he thinks this single day was worth giving up immortality, Seth answers that he would trade Heaven for the scent of Maggie's hair. As the angels again stand on the beach in their trench coats listening to the music of the universe, Seth can no longer hear, but as he plunges into the surf that the angels cannot feel, his angel friend watches and seems pleased.

The changes that *City of Angels* made in *Wings of Desire* showed, among other things, that the taboo on angel-human sex was reasserting itself as American culture took biblical religion more seriously. The American movie punished the couple that German Wim Wenders had allowed to live happily ever after. The concept of an angel having sex with a human had to be pushed in the direction of broad comedy, as in *Date with an Angel* and *Michael,* or sentimental tragedy, as in *City of Angels;* it could not be left on the uncomfortably human, magical-realist plane inhabited by Wenders's *Wings of Desire.*

Meanwhile, the social dimensions of the German movie were lost in translation. The American romance made angelic envy of people and affirmation of gender roles its primary concerns. The male angel had to become human so that he could have sex with the woman; the female doctor had to stop worrying so much about her work and find the right man. In contrast, *Wings of Desire* ended with the female acrobat giving a speech straight into the camera, with the audience seeing her face through the eyes of the former angel, and her words were filled with hope not just for the couple but for the world: "We two are more than we two . . . we're incarnating the people now." With this affirmation, the movie made the descent of an angel to marry a human into a metaphor for the healing of Berlin and the reunion of East and West that would begin at the end of 1989, two years after *Wings* was released. The landscape and the people of Berlin were characters in *Wings of Desire,* while *City of Angels* used Los Angeles and Lake Tahoe only as backgrounds or scenery for the story of two individuals.

City of Angels pushed the love of angels and humans even further into the private sphere through the lyrics of several songs about angels that were played on its soundtrack, including "Iris" by the Goo Goo Dolls (which was released with a music video featuring clips from the movie), Sarah McLachlan's "Angel," and U2's "If God Will Send His Angels." Each of these songs took angels more seriously than the love songs of the 1950s and 1960s, but none of them addressed the beloved as an angel. The words of "Iris," by the lead singer of the Goo Goo Dolls, Johnny Reznik, could have been written as an angel's song to a human lover. "And I'd give up forever to touch you," the song begins, "'Cause I know that you'd feel me somehow." It continues by saying that the human woman is "the closest to Heaven that I'll ever be" and that the angel doesn't "want to go home right now." The theme of giving up eternity for time appears in the assertions that "all I can taste is this moment" and "all I can breathe is your life," and that, although "sooner or later it's over," the singer doesn't "want to miss you tonight."[34] Later, by repeating a line about not wanting the world to see him three times and then repeating "I just want you to know who I am" three more times, Reznik made the song an anthem for those who feel invisible and who try to connect with life through a single other person. Such a pattern is basic both to love in adolescence and to the idea of a personal guardian angel. The single became the ninth-ranked song of 1998.[35]

Though Sarah McLachlan's "Angel" had a less direct message than "Iris," its refrain of "You're in the arms of the angel / May you find some comfort there" also pointed to a guardian angel's love, which in the case of this song had less to do with sex than with escape or relief. "In the arms of an angel / Fly away from here," McLachlan twice urges. But to whom is the song addressed? Sometimes she seems to be singing to some dysfunctional individual, someone who spends all his or her time "waiting for that second chance" and who needs to be "pulled from the wreckage" of a "silent reverie." Then again, there are moments when the singer seems to be speaking for and about herself: "I need some distraction / Oh beautiful release. . . . Let me be empty / And weightless and maybe / I'll find some peace tonight."[36] The angel of McLachlan's title stands for peace but never becomes a person in his own right. Love between angel and human in this song does not demand that the human come to know the angel, as in "Iris," but only that the human find rest in the angel's arms. The angel stands for human longing for love without limits.

The first song on the *City of Angels* soundtrack, U2's "If God Will Send His Angels," was again (as with Reznik's and McLachlan's songs) more explicitly theological than any angel songs of the 1950s or 1960s, but U2's lyrics pull back even further from personal relationships with angels to general commentary and concern for humanity. "God has got his phone off the hook, babe / Would he even pick it up if he could?" asks Bono, the lead singer and writer of this Irish (but very transatlantic) group. The singer complains that he used to count on Jesus, but "then they put Jesus in show business / Now it's hard to get in the door."[37] Angels appear in the refrain, repeated three times, as a last hope that the song is not really counting on: "If God will send his angels / I sure could use them here right now."

Taken as a whole, the message of the soundtrack songs from *City of Angels* are as individualistic, sentimental, earnest, and emblematic of American culture as the message of the movie itself. Robin Taylor, a critic from the *National Catholic Reporter* (an independent, liberal Catholic weekly based in Kansas City) extolled both the movie and the soundtrack as cultural expressions that real angels probably would like because they could bring people closer to God. In contrast to the characters of the television series *Touched by an Angel,* whom she dismissed as "oversize, celestial Beanie Babies" who "comfort and protect us, reminding us in weekly television episodes that God loves us in spite of ourselves," Taylor wrote that the spirits revealed by the movie and songs from *City of Angels* "know we are broken but love us anyway with a brilliant passion and fierce embrace."[38] Though Taylor correctly sensed the intentions of the movie and the songs, she did not seem to notice how narrowly focused those intentions were.

City of Angels met with only moderate success in the marketplace (number nineteen in gross receipts among the year's movies, well behind *Armageddon* and just ahead of *You've Got Mail*) and with even less success among critics, which must have been a disappointment to Warner executives hoping for a blockbuster from Meg Ryan and Nicholas Cage executing a proven concept from Europe. Somehow, the revelations of angelic life that seemed magical in *Wings of Desire* lost their charm in the context of so much personal obsession. The denial of happiness to the couple may have kept the movie from violating the biblical norms that remain so powerful in American religion, but it also kept people from leaving the movie with any sense of having enjoyed themselves. Finally, the good conscience that American believers in "innocent ecstasy" have cultivated about orgasm as a spiritual good, not simply a goal of sex (a message reinforced every month in magazines like *Glamour* and *Redbook*), has never extended to feeling good about bodies and sensuality in general. The concept of a spirit taking a real body, eating a peach, as Ryan's character had taught him, and splashing in the surf offered small consolation for the loss of ecstatic love.

Many Americans wanted their angels to remain chaste and to remain angels, as in the episode of *Touched by an Angel* that first aired on May

6, 2001. There the young angel Monica, played by Irish actress Roma Downey, has her faith in humanity shaken by the bombing of a building by terrorists. She is tempted by Satan to stop worrying about people in general and to take her own happiness as a human being with a husband and children. A man played by Mandy Patinkin kisses Monica and leads her to the edge of a precipice, from which she could throw herself down to become human, emulating the angels who became incarnate in *City of Angels* or *Wings of Desire*. Instead, she asks God's forgiveness and goes back to work.[39]

Cosmic Sex and Change

Writers of fantasy can often get away with transgressive perspectives that are unacceptable in other genres, and this is true of the fantasy literature involving angels. The same conservatism about angel-human sex and human gender roles that has restricted TV shows, movies, and mainstream fiction could be reversed in fantasy stories presenting angel-human sex as an essential ingredient of cosmic order. For example, Anne Rice went through a transition from fantasy writer to fantasy theologian that culminated in *Memnoch the Devil* (1995). Fifth in a series of novels chronicling the life of the Vampire Lestat, *Memnoch* concerned itself less with vampires than with angels and demons.

When Rice's vampire hero is recruited by Satan (who prefers the name of Memnoch), he is subjected to a long explanation of good and evil in the universe that hinges on sex between angels and humans. According to Memnoch, God made angels first, then humans, but as the humans died their souls entered a state of confusion called "Sheol." In Sheol, some of the stronger spirits of the dead managed to communicate with the living and present themselves as gods, demanding sacrifice. Some of the angels accepted this as a sign of God's genius in creating spirits that could surpass their limitations, but others (including Memnoch) thought that both Sheol and the human religions developed by these spirits were appalling. In punishment, God had exiled Memnoch and some other angels to live as humans. Memnoch found that his "essence went . . . into the scrotum and the penis"; he "knew maleness" and "was very surprised at how powerful" he felt.[40] According to Memnoch, sex had "always fascinated" angels; he himself had often observed human couples, but when he had sex himself and "felt the passion," he "knew then what no angel could possibly know!"

As Memnoch and his human lover lay spent, the light of God found them out. He cried out his joy to God in "a great anthem" that dissolved his material body and revealed him at full angelic height, with wings, so that the woman fled in terror. God condemned him, asking, "What is an Angel, a Son of God, doing with a Daughter of Men!" Caught up to Heaven for judgment, Memnoch was flung down again. The woman saw him, "visible, falling—winged and enormous—smashing towards earth," until he lay in the dust, "wingless, and in the flesh once more and the size of a man."[41] She brought him to her people and there he lived, teaching them how to find metal in the earth, how to tell the seasons by the stars, and how to write.

Addressing the era of innocent ecstasy, Rice updated the ancient story of angels marrying human women and teaching the arts of civilization, but she went beyond any ancient source in ascribing meaning to sex itself. "In the orgasm, as my seed had gone into the woman, I had felt an ecstasy that was like the joy of Heaven," Memnoch told God and his fellow angels at his trial in the heavenly court. He argued that this joy had taught him "that men were not part of Nature, no, they were better, they belonged with God and with us!"[42] Later he expanded the case for humanity from sex to the love of family, asking that humans be granted "eternity because their love demands it."[43] Still, Memnoch always returned to the experience of orgasm: "In the moment when . . . we knew that pleasure together, that small flame did roar with a sound very like the songs of the Most High!"[44]

When Memnoch's argument was done, he seemed to have lost the case, and God cast him again out of Heaven; but then on Earth he saw a man in whom he felt the presence of God. Memnoch had convinced God to enter humanity as the angel had. In Rice's fictional version of the temptation of Jesus in the desert, Jesus says that he, too, had "lain with women and . . . known that ecstasy" of which Memnoch spoke.[45] He came to bring people to eternity by means of their love, but not directly by the love of sex; instead of Memnoch's "paltry little discoveries made in the arms of the Daughters of Men," Jesus would make people perfect through the love shown in suffering and self-sacrifice. He would take the sacrificial religions that humans had developed and make them true. Memnoch found the idea abhorrent and wanted to deliver people from death directly, without suffering, through love, and for this God placed him in charge of Sheol, where he would have to teach people to accept the consequences of their actions and learn to forgive all, including themselves and God. At the end of this theological argument, Memnoch asks Rice's hero, the vampire Lestat, to help him in Sheol; then Jesus makes his appeal, but Lestat refuses both. The story of the vampire would continue in Rice's other novels about life on Earth. She had used angels and sex to give her readers an alternative view of history that closely resembled Roman Catholic orthodoxy, with Sheol functioning in the role of Purgatory and Christianity fulfilling all of the pagan religions that preceded it. By focusing on angels, Rice provided more room for free will exercised by beings other than God.

A more influential fantasy about angels, sex, and history hit both stage and screen when Tony Kushner's *Angels in America* (1991 on stage, 2003 HBO) brought a hermaphrodite angel crashing through the roof of a New York apartment building (quoting a story by Franz Kafka). Kushner's angel, the Continental Principality of America, has sexual relations with two humans, a gay man who seemed to be dying from AIDS and the Mormon mother of a closeted gay male son. The Continental Principality has eight vaginas and a "bouquet of phalli"[46] that it is willing to use with humans, but no love or sentiment to share. On the contrary, the angel blames humanity for driving God into leaving Heaven. (Its mission will be considered further in chapter 6 on "Angels of War and Apocalypse.")

According to Kushner, the reason for God's departure grew out of sex. "Angelic orgasm makes protomatter, which fuels the Engine of Creation," the gay prophet of the play and miniseries, Prior Walter, learns. These angels had used their multiple and balanced genitals "to copulate *ceaselessly*" before the creation of the world.[47] Then God made humanity—to quote words that the angel played by Emma Thompson pronounces with some distaste in the HBO version—in two sexes: "Unigenitaled. Female. Male." That unbalanced sexuality set loose "Sleeping Creation's Potential for Change," also known as "the Virus of TIME."[48] Unsatisfied and partial, women and men migrated and invented. God grew bored with his angels and left Heaven for parts unknown on the day of the San Francisco earthquake (April 18, 1906). Through all the traumas of the twentieth century he did not return, and the angel had come to Prior Walter to give him a new scripture, a book that would tell humanity to stop changing, stop moving, stop migrating, so that God might come back to Heaven and the angels. Transmitting the book would involve sex. The angel says, "Open me Prophet. I I I I am the Book." People had to learn from experience with angels (not the other way around, as in Anne Rice) that "Not Physics But Ecstatics Makes the Engine [of creation] Run." While on Earth, Kushner's angel tells people that "the body is the garden of the soul." This is what the angel says both to Prior Walter after having sex with him and to Hannah Pitt, the Mormon mother, who tells the prophet that he should wrestle with the angel, and who in turn has an enormous orgasm after receiving the angel's kiss.

With *Angels in America*, gay males moved into the center of American political discourse as never before, and they have not departed. Meeting with two male friends and the Mormon woman near Emma Stebbins's Angel of Bethesda statue and fountain in Central Park, the gay prophet declares, "We will not die secret deaths anymore. We will be citizens. The time has come."[49] The symbolic power of angels, and especially their indeterminate gender and transgressive sex, had furnished the metaphoric bridge between Salt Lake City and New York for Kushner's "Gay Fantasia on National Themes." Kushner's triumph meant that the angels did not get their wish, however: Human history did not stop, and angels remained servants of humanity.

Most strangely, the world had not changed very much after all, despite the relations between angels and humans in the two parts and six hours of *Angels in America*. The spectacular sex scenes, Prior Walter's climb up the fiery ladder to Heaven, his refusal to accept the angels' Gospel of Stasis, and his wrestling with the Continental Principality for the blessing of "More Life!" all made little difference. Gay men entered the center of American culture and made no more difference than the first openly gay representative, Gerry Studds of Massachusetts, made in Congress. The title of the play's Part Two, "Perestroika," perfectly expressed what happened in the course of the plot. Like Gorbachev's "restructuring" of the Soviet Union, which apparently changed everything but left the same bureaucrats to become oligarchs in Vladimir Putin's Russia, *Angels in America* actually had conservative consequences. By having sex with the angel, the sometime drag queen Prior Walter regains a masculine role, both emitting seed for the first time in "months" and later fighting, so that his friend (the black drag queen and nurse Belize) asks, "You turning straight on me?"[50] The character of Roy Cohn, the lawyer for Senator Joe McCarthy and the power broker of the Ronald Reagan years, is portrayed as a gay man in denial who died of AIDS, but the play does not then plunge Cohn into Hell. Instead, Cohn finds his calling in an afterlife where he serves as defense attorney for God in a suit for child abandonment. At the Angel of Bethesda statue in Central Park, the same characters have the same arguments in the epilogue that they have been having throughout both plays, but now these New York radicals are also hearing instruction on the New Testament from a Mormon mother.

Angels in America resembled other angelic romances in transforming perspectives rather than provoking revolution. Something about the combination of angels and sex and romance seemed especially suited to conveying the assurance that "it's a wonderful life" just as it is, and that what people want is more life as we know it, not any fundamental change. Angels in love appear at first to be radically disruptive and transgressive, taboo-breaking and gender-bending agents of change, but they turn out to be mediators who help gender roles to stay as they are no matter who occupies them.

Among all the examples of American culture examined here, only five artifacts—Daniel Chester French's obscure statue of 1923, the lyrics of Jimi Hendrix for "Angel" (1970), Andrew Greeley's novel *Angel Fire* (1988), Tony Kushner's play and HBO television special *Angels in America* (1991, 2003), and Nora Ephron's movie *Michael* (1996)—have presented angels who remained angels while they had sex with humans. Although few in number, these were five more such relations than had been acceptable to the Western imagination for thousands of years.[51] Of the five, only *Angels in America* qualified as a major cultural event, but this did not mean that the idea of sex with angels had little importance in American culture. All the romantic near-misses, from *I Married an Angel* and *The Bishop's Wife* through *City of Angels*, testified to the continuing power of the idea; nor should the satanic sex of *Rosemary's Baby*, *The Witches of Eastwick*, and *Memnoch the Devil* be forgotten. As popular music from the 1950s through the 1990s showed, what Americans primarily wanted from angels was not sex but love. Americans also preferred that angels not change our world out of love, but rather love humans so much that they would trade their world for the chance to help us appreciate ours.

Since angels are messengers, it seems fitting that the simple message that angels could fall in love with people proved more important than any action of the angels in any of the love stories or songs. This chapter includes no modern evangelicals, because evangelicals rarely connect angels with sex, and never unless the angels are fallen. As we saw at the beginning of the chapter, the great evangelist Jonathan Edwards (1703–1758) even denied that the "sons of God" who took human wives in Genesis 6 were fallen angels. Today, evangelical theologians have been moved by biblical scholarship to admit that the sexual transgressors of Genesis 6 were probably angels, but this has not led them to speculate further on angelic sex or gender.[52] They have actually become more insistent that angels are always male, sometimes criticizing art or literature that implies anything else.

New Life Community Church of Stafford, Virginia, for example, might be considered a typical evangelical church. With a membership of seventy households and a weekly attendance of about 220 people, it resembles hundreds of other small evangelical churches across the nation. According to an article on the church's website in 2007, angels take offense at being depicted as anything other than adult males. "I have seen some of your paintings of angels," the website quotes an anonymous angel as saying. He is pictured in armor on one knee, holding a helmet with his left hand and a sword in his right. "Not very accurate," he complains. "Why do some of your artists try to make us look like lovely, soft women or cute, chubby babies? Let's correct that idea right now. . . . Angels are terrible warriors. . . . Every time a human actually sees one of us, he collapses in terror." And yet, unlike some armies, as the New Life website continues, the angelic host is motivated not by a sense of "grim, unquestioning duty," but by love. This is love not of humans but of "the Commander," Jesus. "You can hear our love for Him in the songs we sing when we are on the march." Again, the imagery is purely masculine: "Have you ever heard a really big men's choir?" the angel asks. "Start with that idea, but imagine them not in choir robes, but girded for battle. Not grim draftees, but soldiers terrible in joy." He recalls that this was the sort of singing that happened on the night when "the Commander" planned a "birth action" (known in less militaristic circles as

Christmas or the Nativity) at Bethlehem. Because no enemy opposed them, the army of angels was told to sing, and they sang not "peace to men of good will," but "Glory to God in the highest, and on earth peace to men on whom the Commander's grace rests."[53]

At the New Life Church of Colorado Springs, Colorado, the 14,000-member church where Pastor Ted Haggard served as president of the National Association of Evangelicals until he fell in a scandal regarding his relationship with a male escort in the fall of 2006, a statue of a very macho angel with a sword still dominates the lobby. The topics of love, sex, and gender among the angels provide some of the clearest divisions between evangelical and New Age angel believers. In one sense, even the frothiest movies, plays, and songs about angels in love or angels having sex with people have contributed to the New Age movement. Without posing any formal theological questions, such fictions have undermined the cultural presumptions of divine exclusivity and human sin. They have brought humans and angels together on a basis other than what the angel of New Life Community Church calls the "rescue mission" of "the Commander." As the next chapter indicates, what New Age angel believers found in love and sex, evangelicals found in war.

CHAPTER 6

Angels of War and Apocalypse

Lieutenant General William Boykin, director of the U.S. Army's Delta Force, took time from the search for Osama bin Laden to speak to 2,000 people at the First Baptist Church in Broken Arrow, Oklahoma, on June 30, 2002. In full dress uniform, Boykin showed an aerial photograph he had taken over Somalia in 1993, during a battle between Delta Force and local warlords. Pointing to black marks in the sky, Boykin said, "Ladies and gentlemen, this is your enemy. It is the principalities of darkness. It is a demonic presence in that city that God revealed to me as the enemy."[1] In the War on Terror, he said, "Our enemy is a spiritual enemy. . . . His name is Satan."[2] Boykin received a letter of concern from the secretary of the army in the fall of 2004, but it was only a warning to be more discreet.[3] His beliefs did not isolate him from the American mainstream. Conflict with demons appeared on television in *Touched by an Angel* and *Charmed*, in movies like *The Prophecy* (1995) and *Dogma* (1999), and in the *Left Behind* series of novels that topped best-seller lists through 2004. Like Boykin's photos, the card game "Magic: the Gathering," and the practice of "spiritual mapping" by Pentecostal Christians also featured good and evil spirits fighting for territory. Boykin expressed a worldview that Americans found in the Bible, where they saw a pattern of aggressive defense by angels.

Biblical Angels and Aggressive Defense

When ancient Jerusalem was surrounded by an Assyrian army that had already taken ten tribes of Israelites into exile, according to the Hebrew Bible, "the angel of the Lord went forth, and slew a hundred and eighty-five thousand in the camp of the Assyrians" (2 Kings 19:35). The Torah also hints at angelic warfare, as when the angels who visited Lot in Sodom said that "the Lord has sent us to destroy it" (Gen. 19:13), or when an angel went before Israel in the wilderness. According to one reading of Deuteronomy 32:8, every war between nations involves angels because God assigns every nation an angel, fixing national borders "according to the number of the sons of God" (*bnai elohim*). The concept that God's people in this world are always embattled, and even surrounded, but then delivered by angelic intervention is a common biblical theme. Though it arose from the situation of the ancient Hebrew nomads, it remained relevant for Jews of different eras caught between clashing empires and for later believers in the Bible.

Extending this pattern of biblical history, both the Gulf War of 1991 and the Iraq invasion of 2003 formed part of a great conflict with fallen angels, according to many Americans besides General Boykin. The world of "strategic spiritual warfare" and "spiritual mapping" develops the idea of national angels attached to certain territories and holds that some of these angels are fallen angels. The most important biblical text for this theory is the tenth chapter of Daniel, where the angel Gabriel tells the prophet that he had met opposition when he tried to answer Daniel's prayer for a vision. According to Gabriel, "the prince of the kingdom of Persia withstood me twenty-one days," until "Michael, one of the chief princes, came to help me" (Dan. 10:13). The angel also says that when he finishes visiting with Daniel, he "will return to fight against the prince of Persia; and when I am through with him, lo, the prince of Greece will come." In these battles, "there is none who contends by my side against those except Michael, your prince" (Dan. 10:20–21). The angel then gives Daniel two chapters describing the end of the world, which conclude with another association of angels with nations. He says that Israel will be oppressed by a king who will claim to be God, but the nation will be delivered by "Michael, the great prince who has charge of your people" (Dan. 12:1). The idea that nations had spirits must have seemed plausible in the time when Daniel was written, which was probably about 165 B.C.E., in the midst of wars among and between Jews and Greeks who championed different visions of truth and different hopes for the world's religions within the former Persian Empire. Similar conditions have made the idea of national spirits seem plausible to believers today.

War with and between spirits may seem heretical or exotic to those who have been exposed only to moderate or liberal views of religion, but the idea of such warfare has deep resonances with traditional Christian worldviews. As Paul warned the Christians of Ephesus, "we are not contending against flesh and blood, but against the principalities, against the powers, against the world rulers of this present darkness, against the spiritual hosts of wickedness in the heavenly places" (Eph. 6:12). In John's gospel, Jesus refers to Satan as the ruler of the world who will be cast out and judged (John 12:31, 16:11). Matthew depicts Jesus tempted three times by Satan, then helped by good angels (4:11); and the letter of Jude refers to Michael and Satan fighting for possession of the dead body of Moses (Jude 9). Finally, Revelation shows armies of angels and devils in conflict. In Revelation 5:11, "myriads of myriads and thousands of thousands" praise the Lamb. Later, in Revelation 8:15–18, four angels lead 200 million cavalry who kill a third of all human beings on Earth. Revelation ends with chapter after chapter of destruction at the hands of angels, culminating with an angel who swings "his sickle on the earth" and gathers the wicked into "the great wine press of the wrath of God," from which blood flows to the depth of a horse's bridle for about 200 square miles (Rev. 14:19–20). "Demonic spirits, performing signs," draw the kings of the Earth to Armageddon in Revelation 16:14. At the place of battle, they meet "the Word of God" riding a white horse and "the armies of heaven, arrayed in fine linen, white and pure," also riding white horses (Rev. 19:13–14). Perhaps the influence of such images, which express the Christian sense that life is spiritual warfare, help to explain the paradox that Christianity includes both an absolute prohibition of violence and the most violent history of any religion.

American Warrior Angels

This concept of a surrounded people of God perfectly suited the self-image of outnumbered Europeans in colonial America. Both Spanish and English colonists could identify with the children of Israel in Exodus, to whom God sent an angel "to guard you on the way" (Exod. 23:20). As chapter 3 has already noted, the conquest of the Americas by Spanish soldiers resulted in many books about conflict with Satan, who, according to the Spanish, ruled the Aztecs or Mayans or Incas or Hopi. Often these books were translated into English, and the English Puritans also saw themselves as fighting Satan in the wilderness, particularly after the native revolution known as King Philip's War (1675–1676).[4] So in America, Christians from the Conquistadors of the Southwest to the Puritans of Massachusetts Bay waged many wars in which they found religious meaning, often ascribing demonic influence to the Native Americans they were fighting. Later, as the English and French colonists fought intermittent wars for seventy years over the land that would become the United States, and as the English colonists fought a seven-year war for independence from the British Empire, Americans integrated angelic warfare into powerful worldviews. For example, Samuel Hopkins (1721–1803), who succeeded Jonathan Edwards as the intellectual leader of New England's Calvinist pastors, wrote in *A Treatise on the Millennium* (1793) that the battle of Armageddon was described over several chapters of Revelation because it would be a series of wars lasting for a century and a half, and that would end, he predicted, by about 2016, or at the latest by the 2040s. Hopkins also chillingly predicted that this extended Armageddon would kill most of the Jews but allow the survivors to reclaim the land of Israel. He taught that "the holy angels" would fight in that war against Satan and his demons.[5]

After the English colonies became the United States, the usefulness of the biblical precedents were not lost but heightened. A new nation whose capital city was burned by the British in 1814, the United States could not afford to feel secure. As settlers moved west, the pattern of aggressive defense became clear. Indians attacked the settlers, and later the wagon trains, so the Indians had to be attacked and a fort built for the cavalry. Then came more settlement, another Indian attack, another war, and another fort. In the traveling Wild West shows of Buffalo Bill Cody, in which the Lakota Chief Sitting Bull made a living after the final defeat of his people, the mock battles followed this pattern. The Cody show represented a wagon train, an attack by the Indians, and a rescue by Buffalo Bill. Then it showed a village, an attack by the Indians, and another rescue, followed by a stagecoach, an attack, a rescue. Finally, General Custer and his men, riding through the Black Hills, were attacked—and on that one occasion, Buffalo Bill would arrive too late.[6] A similar pattern of justifying any intervention by the pretext that "we were attacked"—whether in Charleston harbor to start the Civil War, in the port of Havana ("Remember the Maine!"), at Pearl Harbor, in the Tonkin Gulf of Vietnam, or on 9/11—still operated in our War on Terror through 2007. President George W. Bush and many other Americans said we were fighting in Iraq and Afghanistan because we were attacked.

Mormonism and Seventh-Day Adventism, both relatively new American religions, also feature angelic warfare. According to Heber C. Kimball, counselor to Brigham Young and grandfather of Mormon President Spencer W. Kimball, he and several other Mormons saw an army of angels that "moved in platoons" with visible "muskets, bayonets and knapsacks," and heard the clash of these angels with an army of demons, on the night of September 22, 1827, when the angel Moroni brought the records of the Book of Mormon to Joseph Smith.[7] Ellen Gould White, who is regarded as a prophet by Seventh-Day Adventists, made the war between good and evil angels the central subject of her book *The Great Controversy between Christ and Satan* (1888).

As the Civil War broke out, the Evangelical Tract Society (a southern version of the American Tract Society) set the politeness of the archangel Michael, even in battle, as an example to the Confederacy. Citing the letter of Jude on Michael and Satan fighting to possess the body of Moses, the southern evangelicals wrote that "it was a sharp conflict, no doubt, a sort of Manassas struggle [recalling the Battle of Bull Run]." Yet Michael allowed himself "no passionate railing, no biting slang, no struggle for words of aggravated denunciation." He simply fought the devil and said, "The Lord rebuke thee." So the South should resist the temptation, while "our enemies denounce us as traitors, pirates, rebels, and the like," to answer in "scathing reproachful words." Southern Christians should fight in the manner of Michael, without anger or hatred. "Let us imitate the manner and temper of the great angel . . . and then we shall not greatly err."[8]

In the long recovery from the Civil War, which claimed more American lives than any war before or since, Americans needed angels to show that hope and dignity had survived despite the terrible losses of life. This need was met in part by a profusion of public and private memorial art, much of which featured angels, who were no longer fighting males but females who were helping and healing and celebrating victory. Currier and Ives sold a print called *Angels of the Battlefield* that showed a female nurse on one side of an injured soldier and a female angel on the other. World War I added to the demand for memorials. As we saw in chapter 3, sculptors led by Augustus Saint-Gaudens (1848–1907) and

Daniel Chester French (1850–1931) used their commissions for memorials to place female angels in front of the White House, on the southeast corner of Central Park in New York, and in many other settings where religious imagery would not have been acceptable before.

A new form of angelic militancy, both populist and disturbingly close to fascism, emerged in American culture with the release of a motion picture called *Gabriel over the White House* in 1933. Produced by William Randolph Hearst and distributed by MGM, with a script reviewed by Franklin Delano Roosevelt himself, this film begins with the inauguration of a president of the United States, who appears, at first, to be a tame representative of business interests and of his political party (presumably Republican). An automobile accident almost kills the new president, but the archangel Gabriel (who is acknowledged by the president, but visually represented by nothing more dramatic than curtains moving in a window) keeps him alive and apparently takes control of his decisions. The revived president fires his cabinet, meets with the leader of an Army of the Unemployed marching on Washington, provides jobs for the unemployed in public works projects, then dismisses Congress and places the nation under martial law. He creates a federal police force that rounds up and executes gangsters without trial; the movie includes scenes of firing squads. He forces foreign countries to pay their debts to the United States from World War I and then presides at an international conference at which world leaders stand on the shore and observe as the navies of the world are sunk, after which he dies. Reflecting on these revolutions, the president's male secretary says that he had always thought of Gabriel as a "messenger of wrath," to which the president's (former) mistress replies, "Not always. To some, he was the angel of revelation, a messenger of God to men."

Gabriel over the White House marked a shift in the role of angels in American public religion. Where the angels of nineteenth-century paintings and monuments had been intended to serve as emblems of order—triumphant, but static, in victory or in death—angels could now be seen as agents of revolutionary change, comic disorder, and even redemptive violence. Angels of change appeared with increasing frequency in American culture through the twentieth and early twenty-first centuries. Though many were concerned with personal transformation and acted as therapists, others came to fight.

After 1934, Roman Catholics in the United States (and around the world) followed the instructions of Pope Pius XI to add a prayer to the archangel Michael after every Low Mass (the ordinary Mass said in churches several times a day and on Sundays) for the protection of Christians in Russia. The prayer never mentioned Russia or communism, but only Michael and the demons. It asked Michael to "defend us in the day of battle," to save us from "the wickedness and snares of the devil," and to "thrust down to hell Satan and all wicked spirits, who wander through the world for the ruin of souls."[9]

The wars of the twentieth century gave numerous opportunities for visions of angels, some of which came to America from across the Atlantic. At the Battle of Mons in World War I, a German advance was said to have been halted and reversed when thousands of white-robed figures appeared to the attackers. After the desperate air defense of Britain in World War II, Air Chief Marshal Lord Hugh Dowding was cited (by Billy Graham, among others) as a believer in eyewitness reports that angels had operated the aircraft of dead RAF pilots.[10]

In *A Guy Named Joe* (1944), MGM used the uncertain boundary between angels and dead people (a boundary blurred by the visionary Swedenborg, the Mormons, and the Spiritualists, among others) to tell a war story with patriotic (as well as implicitly New Age) religious lessons. The screenplay by Dalton Trumbo had the star, Spencer Tracy, playing a pilot named Pete Sandidge who is killed in an air battle and assigned by an afterlife general to train his replacement, while riding invisibly in the copilot's seat and giving instructions. At first reluctant to help, Pete becomes even more recalcitrant when the new pilot convinces Pete's former girlfriend to accept his proposal of marriage. His attitude changes after the general (called only "the general," and played by Lionel Barrymore) asks him if he ever heard music in the sky. The general explains: "It's the high, fine, beautiful sound of an earthbound creature who grew wings and flew up high and looked straight into the face of the future and caught just for an instant the unbelievable vision of a free man in a free world." Pete is asked to recognize that his own achievements as a pilot were inspired "by every man from the beginning of time who dreamt of wearing wings" and to join a fellowship of "all of us together, every man that ever flew." The general assures him that children would understand, because "they're going to fly like a generation of angels into the free air and the sunlight." Like Clarence in *It's a Wonderful Life*, Pete has to earn his "wings," or his role in the afterlife, by helping someone on Earth, but the wartime movie is much more concerned with the fate of humanity as a whole than with any individual. Pete has to let go of his earthly identity, say goodbye to his former girlfriend, and trust that "no man really dies unless he breaks faith with the future." At the end, he guides his former girlfriend (who has stolen a plane) in one last attack on an ammunition dump, then waves goodbye and fades away as the living couple embrace. The angels of *A Guy Named Joe* gave Americans at war a message that questioned concern for individual salvation even as it affirmed sacrifice for victory.

With the war against fascism won, a war against communism—which was often very hot, as in Korea and Vietnam, though it was called "cold"—began. The leading American prophet of that war, Billy Graham, saw it as a conflict involving angels. Graham recalled that on two occasions—at a meeting with Dean Rusk, President Lyndon B. Johnson's secretary of state, in 1967, and later with Henry Kissinger in the Gerald Ford administration—he told the nation's leaders that "the world was experiencing an unseen spiritual war in which the powers of darkness were attacking the forces of God."[11] In his 1975 book, *Angels: God's Secret Agents*, which sold about 2.5 million copies over the next twenty years, Graham set forth an expectation of how the war between Lucifer and God would go in a passage that reflected a consensus among many Southern Baptists and other evangelicals. As Graham wrote, "The Anti-Christ, who will be Satan's 'front,' will arrive on the scene for a brief time and seemingly be The Answer."[12] Dreams of world peace and unity, including harmony among the world's religions, could not be trusted because they fed into the satanic plan that would end with the rule of the Antichrist. The peace of that rule would prove false, for there can be "no final solution to the world's great problems until this spiritual warfare [between Lucifer and God] has been settled." The Antichrist's reign would end in "the last great war of history—Armageddon. Then Christ and His angelic armies will be the victor!"[13] The violent angels of Revelation seemed very much alive in Billy Graham's United States.

Graham presented his book on angels as a response to the outburst of interest in Satan in the 1960s and 1970s; he cited *The Exorcist* (1973) and the Rolling Stones' song "Sympathy for the Devil," among other cultural indicators.[14] The same sense that the Devil was gaining ground appeared in the best-selling nonfiction volume of the 1970s, *The Late, Great Planet Earth* (1970) by Hal Lindsey, who was a traveling spokesman for the Campus Crusade for Christ. According to Lindsey, drugs, meditation, astrology, and witchcraft all opened the minds of people to possession by the Devil, who would recruit those he possessed into a false world religion led at first by the pope and other religious leaders espousing ecumenism but eventually by the Antichrist himself.[15]

Plotting the End

The global context for all of this demonic activity included a definite plot for the end of the world. First, God had restored the Jews to Israel in 1948, fulfilling Ezekiel 36–37, so that the unfulfilled prophecies regarding Zion and the last days could take place. Soon Russia and an alliance of Arab and other states would invade the Near East, seeking to control its oil wealth and to conquer Israel, fulfilling the prophecies of an invasion of Israel by "Gog and Magog" in Ezekiel 38–39. God would miraculously save Israel from this invasion, but then a European confederacy—the spiritual revival of the Roman Empire, led by the Antichrist, fulfilling the prophecies of the Beast in Daniel 7 and Revelation 13—would emerge and negotiate a peace treaty with Israel. The Jewish Temple would be rebuilt, but a seven-year period of global suffering called the "Tribulation" would begin. The Antichrist would eventually declare himself the Messiah. After recovering from apparent death from a head wound, the Antichrist would pursue and put to death all who would not worship him or take his mark; he would rule the world during the Tribulation, but would be defeated at Armageddon. According to Lindsey, some would be converted to true Christianity during the seven-year period, but those who were born again before the Tribulation would be caught up to Heaven (or "raptured," as in 2 Thess. 4) before it began. In fact, he taught that the stage was set for the Rapture to occur any day.[16]

Lindsey did not create this perspective on spiritual warfare but inherited it from earlier evangelical theologians, including his teacher at Dallas Theological Seminary, John F. Walvoord, and Walvoord's teacher, J. Dwight Pentecost. Pentecost laid out the whole plot in his 1958 book, *Things to Come.*[17] He, in turn, had built on the work of Cyrus Scofield, a former Confederate soldier and Dallas pastor who edited the *Scofield Reference Bible* in 1909, and on the organization of history into dispensations by John Nelson Darby (1801–1882), an Irish Protestant theologian.[18] Elements like the role of Israel in marking the beginning of the end had appealed to Americans at least as far back as Cotton Mather, who asked the militia of Massachusetts Bay in 1691 to pray for the restoration of Jews to their land so that the last days might come.[19] All aspects of the apocalyptic plot became more widely disseminated with Hal Lindsey's book, however, because *The Late, Great Planet Earth* was incredibly popular: The 1977 edition claimed 10 million copies in print. The even larger sales of the *Left Behind* novels at the turn of the twenty-first century testified to a new readiness to accept this plot. The appeal of the story derived from several features of American culture, including fascination with the Jews and Israel; suspicion of Russia, the Arabs, and Europe; and fear of non-Christian religions and spiritual disciplines. Most importantly, the plot connected current events with the biblical sense of spiritual war.

Since the 1980s, American evangelicals working within that general plot for history have engaged with angels in spiritual warfare on two fronts, at home and abroad. Evangelical fiction and individual practice have dealt with demons and angels within the United States, especially in prayers for the deliverance of cities from spirits. Meanwhile, leaders of evangelical politics and practitioners of collective prayer have concentrated, in the manner of General Boykin, on territorial spirits occupying the Middle East.

No writer has ever given as many detailed descriptions of such a broad variety of angels and demons as Frank Peretti, a former Pentecostal pastor whose novel *This Present Darkness* (1986) sold 2.8 million copies in its first decade. Peretti's angels appeared as "giant men" who "descended to earth like glimmering, bluish-white comets, held aloft by rushing wings that swirled in a blur and burned like lightning." Once on Earth, the light from their clothes faded, "the shimmering wings gently subsided," and they seemed to be men of "towering stature . . . dressed in what looked like matching tan fatigues," with swords encased in scabbards of "dull copper" and "simple leather sandals" on their feet. All the good angels of Peretti's book are young male warriors, though they vary by ethnic group. At a gathering before battle, the "huge, burly, black-bearded" angel Guilo, who is called "the Strength of Many," surveys his companions, all wearing "the same tan tunics and breeches." There is "Nathan, the towering Arabian . . . who had taken demons by their ankles and used them as warclubs against their fellows." He sees "Armoth, the big African whose war cry and fierce countenance" often sent enemies fleeing before the fighting began, and with whom Guilo had once "battled the demon lords of villages in Brazil" while guarding "a family of missionaries on their many long treks through the jungles." Then he notes "Chimon, the meek European with the golden hair," renowned for "his ability to take blows simply as a shield for others and then to rally himself to defeat untold numbers alone." Other angels of less definite ethnicity include a blond named Triskal, the "tall, dark-haired" Krioni, and "a tall Oriental" named Signa. All these and more, in the angelic campaign of *This Present Darkness*, are marshaled under "Tal, the Captain of the Host," whom Guilo had seen "near the throne room of Heaven itself, in conference with none other than Michael." Despite belonging to ethnic groups, the angels of Frank Peretti are not former humans. None of the angels ever remembers a former life, and Guilo reflects that he and Tal had been "companions in the Lord's service before there had been any rebellion [among the angels] at all."

The rebel angels or demons of *This Present Darkness* appeared in much greater variety of gender, size, and character than the heavenly host. Some were generic breeds, named for the effects they had on people, including Complacency, Despair, Lust, and Deception. Spirits of Rebellion, Divination, and Sorcery possess a boy in an arcade of video games. Describing a spirit of Despair, Peretti conjures up "a high-strung little gargoyle, his hide a slimy, bottomless black, his body thin and spider-like," with "huge yellow cat-eyes" and breath that "came in short, sulfurous gasps, visible as glowing yellow vapor." Other demons work as spiritual companions, like the demon Madeleine, who meets a college student learning to meditate and nearly lures her to commit suicide. Chief demons tend to have ancient and biblically based names, such as "Ba-al Rafar, the Prince of Babylon," his lieutenant Lucius, and the commander of all the demons in this book, the Strongman (whose name derives from Matt. 12:29).

Rafar of Babylon is the most vivid evil presence in the book, claiming the title "Ba-al" that belonged to the Canaanite god who opposed Israel in biblical times. The good angels Tal and Guilo recall fighting an epic battle with Rafar when ancient Babylon fell, and the angelic plotline of this book involves their rematch over control of Ashton, a college town in the American Northwest. Rafar has "a lion-like face, fiery eyes, incredibly muscular body, and leathery wings that filled the room." Sometimes Rafar's wings "draped down behind him . . . like the robe of a monarch." He also has personal style: "His jet black hair hung like a mane to his shoulders, and on each wrist he wore a gold bracelet studded with sparkling stones; his fingers displayed several rings, and a ruby-red belt and scabbard adorned his waist."

On the human level, *This Present Darkness* told the story of a New Age religious group called the Universal Consciousness Society attempting to take over the American town of Ashton and the private college located there. This represented part of a larger plot involving "Babylon the Great," the "Great Harlot" of the unified world religion predicted (according to evangelical interpretations) in Revelation 17. At a New York meeting of the Universal Consciousness Society, angels Tal and Guilo watch "VIPs from many different nations and races" arriving in limousines that also carry "demons, large, black, warty, and fierce, their yellow eyes darting warily in every direction" as they sit with the passengers and perch on the roofs of the cars.

At every stage in the novel, human activity is entangled with angelic war. A college student named Sandy, hearing the gospel of universal consciousness from her boyfriend, thinks she is just appreciating her kinship with the trees and the birds, but all the while, "with very gentle, very subtle combing motions of his talons, Deception stood behind Sandy, stroking her red hair and speaking sweet words of comfort to her mind."[20] No character who is not born again in Christ is protected from such influence, and even the Christians can be oppressed (if not entirely possessed).

Meanwhile, although it might seem that the good angels should be guaranteed victory, since they are fighting on God's side, they actually need "prayer cover" from human saints to defeat their demonic foes. In the climactic battle of the book, Rafar of Babylon is about to defeat Tal when Rafar's sword snips off "a corner of Tal's wing." The air is "filled with the stench of sulfur" and "the evil darkness" becomes "thick like smoke." Tal uses the words of Michael from the letter of Jude, "The Lord rebuke you," but to no avail. Rafar asks, "Where is the Lord?" and strikes again; next, Tal's left hand is injured and he screams. But an elderly woman praying in an Ashton church receives a message from the Holy Spirit to pray, partly because of Tal's desperate pleas to God to tell the praying humans the name of his attacker. She tries to guess the name, comes up with "Raphael" and "Raving," and triggers the memories of a formerly possessed boy who had met Rafar and so recalls the name. When the woman, the boy, and the others in the church ask specifically that Rafar be bound, their prayer makes the sword of the demon miss, so that Tal can recover and win. From his "dripping, foaming jaws . . . through the tar and froth," the wounded Rafar gurgles, "But for your saints!" and falls.[21]

This causal relationship between human prayer and angelic victory expressed the theology of a movement called Third Wave Pentecostalism. In the first wave, beginning with revivals at Topeka, Kansas, in 1901 and Azusa Street, Los Angeles, in 1906, the gifts of speaking in tongues and healing predominated, and churches like the Assemblies of God, the Church of the Foursquare Gospel, and many others were born. The second wave began among the Jesus People of the 1960s and 1970s. It gave birth to charismatic movements within "mainstream" denominations like the Lutherans and Catholics, as well as such sometimes contradictory phenomena as megachurches, Christian rock, the prevalence of casual dress at worship, and an ideal of simple living that resonates in Peretti's novels. The Third Wave began in 1980s' California with an alliance of churches and leaders called the Vineyard movement, which found an intellectual center at the Fuller Theological Seminary among teachers like C. Peter Wagner and Charles H. Kraft. Peretti's *This Present Darkness* has been called the Bible of the Third Wave. Its distinguishing characteristic is prayer for the removal of spiritual obstacles (personified as evil spirits, fallen angels) to the conversion of individuals and the spread of the church. People of the Third Wave also routinely pray for guidance over all major decisions in their lives and for worldly success, including health and prosperity. They use prayer to direct angels even toward such mundane goals as the sale of a home while they seek to deliver themselves and the world from oppression by demons.

Not all evangelical Christians have bought into this worldview or these practices, but scores of millions in the United States (including major figures like Pat Robertson of the 700 Club) have been affected by them. Evangelical critics have focused on the lack of biblical basis for the idea that humans empower angels with their prayers or provide "prayer cover" for angels battling demons. Others have complained that Third Wave views of prayer and of angels diminish the control of God over events. Some have regretted that the Third Wave worldview cuts Christians off from many other people—including homosexuals, video game players, and practitioners of meditation—because people of the Third Wave tend to see such people as possessed by demons.

Despite all the critics, the image and practice of spiritual warfare promulgated by *This Present Darkness* has continued to appeal to millions. Spiritual warfare has given Christians a way to participate in a postmodern popular culture fascinated with spiritual power, as exemplified by *The Exorcist*, the *Star Wars* movies, and the film version of *The Lord of the Rings;* television shows like *Touched by an Angel, Buffy the Vampire Slayer,* and *Charmed;* and the Harry Potter novels. As Halloween became the second-largest holiday (measured in terms of per capita spending) in American life, and role-playing games like "Dungeons and Dragons" or "Diablo" and "Diablo II," or card games like "Magic: the Gathering" and video games like "Doom" spread a cross youth culture, serious Christians were barred by biblical prohibitions against sorcery and idolatry from taking part. Frank Peretti, who began his storytelling career as a counselor at a Christian camp, knew how to keep an entertaining supernatural tale within the bounds of Christianity.

Peretti's hypermasculine angels and their human allies also reinforced the norms of gender and culture that many New Age stories of angels and spiritual powers have called into question. Both in *This Present Darkness* and in its sequel, *Piercing the Darkness,* the angels of Frank Peretti fight to keep rural American towns free from demon-inspired international organizations that have gained a foothold through female educators who teach meditation. After the battle with demons and those they possessed is won, a safe and coherent world is reestablished, and the good angels fly off to another battle, while Peretti's human heroes gather in their redeemed families and churches.

Such domestic outcomes for spiritual warfare have extended beyond the fictions of Frank Peretti to every part of American culture. In the finale of the *Left Behind* series, *Glorious Appearing,* character Rayford

Steele feels, even after the final battle of Armageddon is over, that the members of his family will be "close, affectionate friends throughout the Millennium."[22] It is instructive to recall, in contrast to this modern American dream, that the English Puritan John Bunyan's classic tale *The Pilgrim's Progress* showed its hero vanquishing the demon Apollyon in hand-to-hand combat and then continuing his solitary flight to the Celestial City from the City of Destruction, where he had left his wife and children when they refused the gospel. American Third Wave Pentecostals believe that they can transform the world, not merely defeat the demons that infest it to gain salvation for themselves. Other American believers in angels, including liberal and New Age believers, have joined in this common American optimism. As shown later in this chapter, the Navajo ceremony in the film *The Prophecy* (1995) defeats an evil angel named Gabriel and sends him and Lucifer off to Hell, and the heroic female angels of *Touched by an Angel* cleanse a town where the satanic Patriot League once flourished. Chapter 7 discusses the heroic sisters of *Charmed*, who used witchcraft to vanquish demons every week. Meanwhile, the president of *Gabriel over the White House* solved the Depression, and the spirits of *A Guy Named Joe* won World War II. The concept that God's kingdom is "not of this world" (John 18:36) seems never to have gained much acceptance among Americans. As in the epic of ancient Israel and the conquest of the American continent, the pattern of aggressive defense allows a righteous nation to find itself with a peaceful home surrounded by an empire.

Angelic Geopolitics

Strategic spiritual warfare thinkers from the 1980s through the turn of the twenty-first century have focused on demonic occupation of the "10/40 Window," a huge rectangle extending in degrees of latitude from 10 to 40°N and from West Africa through Egypt and the Middle East to India, China, and Japan. Within that rectangle live 90 percent of those whose access to the Christian gospel is restricted by their governments and/or religious authorities. At the center stand the ruins of Babylon, located about 50 miles southeast of Baghdad and partially rebuilt by Saddam Hussein. Babylon was also known as Babel, the gate of Heaven, site of the tower from which humanity was scattered in Genesis 11.

For ancient Israel, Babylon was the focus of evil in the world, and early Christians used "Babylon" as a code word for the focus of evil in pagan Rome. Near Babylon, at least on the maps of spiritual warfare, lies an even more potent location: the site of the Garden of Eden, from which some say that the serpent never left. George Otis, Jr., an evangelist who began as Billy Graham's minister for evangelism to restricted nations, wrote that history provides "striking evidence that the serpent of Eden has established a global command and control center atop the oily residue of the Garden's once flourishing vegetation and animal life."[23]

According to Otis and other prominent evangelicals, including C. Peter Wagner of Fuller Seminary and David Barrett of the Southern Baptist Foreign Mission Board, fallen angels occupy much of the territory between West Africa and Japan and impede evangelism there. Otis has written of "mounting evidence that the demonic prince of Persia has recently been loosed from his cosmic struggle with the archangel Michael and is once again prowling the . . . Middle East." The prince of Persia who fought Gabriel, according to this theory, also possessed Ayatollah Khomeini and continues to inspire Iranian martyrs and the terrorists of Hezbollah; the Shi'ite emphasis on martyrdom translates this angel's ancient demand for human sacrifice into Islamic terms.[24] Daniel's demonic Prince of Greece may remain influential in Baalbek, a city of Lebanon's Bekaa Valley, because of the temples to Greek gods located there. The residue of "pagan cult worship" that occurred in Baalbek for centuries "attracts demonic spirits like flies to raw meat," Otis wrote.[25]

Outside the 10/40 window, demons have occupied some territory in many locales. Otis listed San Francisco, New Orleans, and Hollywood as "frontier strongholds" of demons in the United States. He gave a similar status to Athens and Delphi in Greece, Ville Bonheur in Haiti, and the "Mayan-Toltec areas" of Central America, among about two dozen others. He listed New York, London, Berlin, and Stockholm among fourteen "cities under siege." But the center remained Eden, and the forces of Christendom were closing in. Otis predicted in 1991 that "Christian soldiers from around the world will reenact the celebrated Allied link-up at the Elbe at the end of World War II; only this time their boots will be moistened by the great tributaries of Eden—the Tigris and Euphrates."[26]

Christians who engage in spiritual mapping and strategic spiritual warfare have recaptured much of the optimism that characterized the

Christian missionary movement of the nineteenth and early twentieth centuries. Like the Student Volunteer Movement workers of the years before World War I, they expect to convert the world to Christianity, and their hope should not be dismissed as ridiculous. George Otis and his cohort attend Anglican conferences in Africa, where the Anglicans are evangelical and interested in fighting evil spirits. In anthologies on spiritual warfare, professors from Fuller Seminary and other American centers share their analyses of stories of angels guarding missionaries and prayer driving demons from neighborhoods with scholars from Asia, Africa, Europe, and Latin America. As journalist Philip Jenkins and sociologist Rodney Stark have claimed, Christianity (particularly in its Pentecostal form) and not Islam is now both the largest and the fastest-growing religion in the world.[27] Untrammeled by denominational lines, the theorists and practitioners of spiritual warfare have proved willing to cooperate with Roman Catholics, Methodists, Baptists, Pentecostals, and independents; anyone who drives out demons is on the side of the angels. In fact, Otis and others began early in the twenty-first century to advocate that Christians of all churches in a city or region work as partners to take control of the whole culture, from business to entertainment to education. This new approach to mission work has been called "Transformationalism" because it aims to transform the world.

Now that troops from the United States have actually "moistened their boots" in the Euphrates, killing Iraqis in the tens of thousands and losing American lives in the thousands to reach the vicinity of Eden, a question arises regarding how harmful spiritual warfare may be. Those who see history as conflict between Satan and Christ, with legions of demons and angels serving as soldiers while some humans die for their cause or as a side effect of the struggle, have almost certainly supported the 2003 invasion of Iraq and the ongoing occupation in larger numbers than nonbelievers. Iran, the nation that George Otis identified as possessed by the demonic Prince of Persia, now seeks to develop nuclear weapons and intercontinental missiles. Should responsible scholars urge believers to change their minds before what Samuel Huntington called the "clash of civilizations" goes nuclear?

Scholarship has provided some basis for retaining the concept of spiritual warfare while interpreting it in a liberal direction. As far back as Origen, who was arguably the most creative Christian theologian of the third century, some have speculated that Satan might be saved through the conflict that he began. In our day, American writers as diverse as Catholic priest and novelist Andrew Greeley and angel therapist Doreen Virtue have claimed that Satan is not fallen at all but only misunderstood. Such writers tend to assert that Satan's function is to test humanity.

The most thorough liberal reading of spiritual warfare has come from Walter Wink, longtime professor of biblical interpretation at Auburn Seminary in New York, a Presbyterian school where the father of John Foster Dulles once taught. For Wink, the idea that nations have angels helps us to understand that nations are more than material entities; they are also spiritual beings. He pointed out that the U.S.-supported government of South Vietnam and the government of the Shah of Iran failed to survive even though they had armies more powerful than those of their opponents. "In both cases the spirit of the nation—the felt sense of its cohesiveness, stability, and power—had simply evaporated," he wrote.[28] Besides recognizing the angels of nations, Wink also asserted the wisdom of acknowledging the reality of angels of churches like those addressed in Revelation 2–3; of demons who exercise powers that the Greeks and Romans attributed to gods; and of spirits in the elements of physics and in living things. Wink was inspired to see these spirits as autonomous beings by the archetypal psychology of Carl Jung. His works also cited Dorothy Maclean of the Findhorn Community in England, who wrote *To Hear the Angels Sing* to teach people how to garden in cooperation with the spirits who govern plants (a perspective that has come to the United States in a community called Perelandra, located in Virginia).

Although Wink accepted the possibility of demonic possession, he wrote in *Unmasking the Powers* (1986) that the media had focused too much on individuals. "Why should Satan reveal himself . . . in individual cases," Wink asked, when he could "preside over an entire global culture that spreads out over the whole surface of the planet like a cancer: a civilization that systematically erodes traditional religions, that treats people like robots for producing and serving things . . . ?"[29] Only by acknowledging a personal power of evil in control, Wink wrote, could people grasp that the seemingly opposed Washington and Moscow of the Cold War were actually on the same side. With regard to nations becoming controlled by Satan, Wink dealt with the common assertion that the Germans of the Nazi era were possessed (a contention made by Jung in the 1930s) by saying that the possession is true if we do not conceive the angel of Nazism as a discarnate supernatural being but as the inner, spiritual life of the German people, "the Angel of Germany having turned its back on its vocation."[30] He approvingly quoted a German pastor who said that it was true that Germans were possessed, but that this was no excuse, because they let themselves be possessed.

Wink sought the spiritual meaning of atomic weapons in the New Testament attitude toward worship of "elements," against which Paul warned in Colossians 2:8. He cited Robert Oppenheimer's famous quote of the Bhagavad-Gita in response to the results of the first atomic test ("I am become Death, the shatterer of worlds") as evidence that humanity "brought to the elements of the world a request: give us the power of massive, unimaginable death," and that this request had been answered: "We are become death."[31]

On this point, liberal professor Walter Wink was joined by evangelical George Otis. In *The Last of the Giants* (1991), Otis also recalled Oppenheimer quoting "I am become Death, the shatterer of worlds." His interpretation differed from Wink's in its premises, but not much in its conclusion. Otis claimed that in the atomic blast, Oppenheimer saw no mere metaphor, but the power of Satan "enraged by the sure knowledge of his own impending doom." According to Otis, the words of the terrible Krishna in the Gita "were once [Satan's] inspiration," but that "the deeds are now his handiwork." He wrote that the same satanic rage manifest in the atom bomb produced "the bitter rhetoric of the Friday imams . . . the beating of an Algerian mission worker, the hanging of an Iranian [Christian] pastor, the torture of Egyptian teenage converts."[32] From their opposite ends of the political spectrum, Otis and Wink both saw the people of our time in danger of worshipping fallen angels rather than allowing good angels to reveal the transcendence that belonged to God.

Within this general agreement, however, American writers of the Left and the Right have tended to use the angels of war in very different ways. Evangelicals from Samuel Hopkins of the New England colonies through California Pentecostal Tim LaHaye, coauthor of the *Left Behind* series, have made angels into allies of God's people in their struggle for territory with demons, beings who occupy definite nations and places on the Earth. Not only have the two sides in this angelic warfare been fixed since Lucifer's fall, according to these authors, but the territories ruled by angels have also been fixed in their moral character, and they will remain so at least until the end of the world, when the war between good and evil will finally be won. More liberal writers on angelic war, such as the William Randolph Hearst of *Gabriel over the White House,* Dalton Trumbo of *A Guy Named Joe,* Martha Williamson of *Touched by an Angel,* or Walter Wink, are rarer, but they have made angels into agents of change with much less definite geographic and spiritual goals.

Angels in Apocalyptic Comedy

This difference between freedom and fate corresponds to the differences between apocalyptic and prophetic forms of discourse about war. Although apocalyptic stories tend to involve war, not all wars or discussions of war reach apocalyptic dimensions. The English word "apocalypse" comes from the Greek *kaluptein,* to cover, with a negative prefix, *apo,* and so invokes the action of removing a cover. The word "revelation" has an exactly analogous etymology from the Latin *velum,* veil. In apocalyptic writing, the war has already been lost. The world has become entirely dark, dominated by evil, but divine intervention, like a flash of lightning, enables a visionary to have a fleeting glimpse of good, though it may be clothed in dark and difficult symbols. In the case of ongoing or impending war, in contrast, prophetic rather than apocalyptic criteria apply. The word "prophecy" derives from *phetes,* speaker, and *pro,* before or for. The prophet is one who speaks for another or before an event. Having been taken to the court of God, or given the verdict of that court, the prophet announces that word to people.

So prophecy, on the one hand, gives a clear statement imposing ethical responsibility on the nation in very particular terms. Always the verdict is based on the past, but the sentence is conditional on future behavior: If the king and the nobles, the priests, and the people continue to act in a certain way (oppressing the poor, worshipping idols, or perverting justice, for example), God will visit them with this or that punishment (the Assyrians will burn the cities, Babylon will destroy the Temple). In an apocalyptic outlook, on the other hand, evil has already triumphed; the Temple has already been destroyed, the king and the nobles carried off into exile. The nation has no ethical choices to make. Questions about justice have yielded to issues of survival. The apocalyptic statement does offer an urgent choice of attitude, however. In the midst of darkness, God will strike. Those who hear the apocalyptic message can choose to side with the oppressors who hold places of authority, or they can remain true to the word of God as they understand it. They cannot affect the course of the battle, but they can refuse to take the mark of the Beast and await their deliverance, and their choice will determine their fate when the final judgment comes.

In apocalyptic writing, angels often take on strange and possibly symbolic forms, like the wheels and animals of Ezekiel, who wrote in the midst of the Babylonian exile. Such forms are suitable to myth, and apocalyptic literature uses all of the elements of myth, such as battles that include the stars and the sea, great monsters, and mountains. The Christian book of Revelation (sometimes called Apocalypse), which came out of the first persecutions of Christians by Rome, abounds in angels performing cosmic acts that believers have spent centuries interpreting. The angels of Revelation blow seven trumpets, pour out seven bowls, harvest humans from the Earth and gather them like grapes into the winepress of God; they dry up the river Euphrates so that the kings of the East can pass over with 200 million cavalry on the way to Armageddon. No book of the Bible contains more angelic activity and more angels acting on a cosmic scale than the twenty-two chapters of Revelation.

Angels also appear in prophecy, as in the famous vision from Isaiah 6, where the prophet sees the cherubim under God's throne and the seraphim around it. Before Revelation turns to apocalyptic symbols in its fourth chapter, it has two chapters of prophecies that give clear instructions to the angels of seven churches in the Roman province of Asia Minor (modern Turkey). Prophecy can also bring angels into visions of the end of the world, as in Matthew 25:31, where Jesus speaks of angels while describing the last judgment with great clarity—and stating a prophetic hope that those who hear his message will change.

When wars become so intense that they threaten the order of civilization, angels seem to proliferate, at least in Western history. The emergence of angels in ancient Persia, when prophet Zoroaster described the gods of the planets as warriors of the creator God in combat with Ahriman, an evil spirit, and his demonic hosts, probably related to a period of "conflict between the Iranians and the Indo-Aryans for the land of Iran"[33] more than 3,000 years ago. What historian of religion Norman Cohn has called "combat faith," featuring visions of war between angels, became important to Jews when they fought Syrians and Greeks in the days of the Maccabees, and to Jews and Christians in the era of persecutions by pagan Rome. The cult of St. Michael the Archangel, God's warrior, became very prominent in the times of the Crusades, and angels multiplied in art and philosophy during the religious wars of the Reformation and Renaissance. Over the past six decades, since the establishment of Pakistan and Israel as nations for Muslims and Jews, respectively, and the outbreak of the Cold War, which pitted the United States as a "nation under God" against "godless" communism, the world has entered another phase of wars explicitly motivated by religion, whatever forces of economics and politics are at work beneath the surface. The "War on Terror" since 2001 is only the latest of this series of religious wars, and it resembles the Cold War in the threat it poses to reduce civilization to chaos.

As people have tried to make sense of our chaotic history, apocalyptic and prophetic thinking about the end of the world has appeared in books, movies, poetry, and song, and angels have taken roles in many of these cultural expressions. Even in times of peace, humans seem to need what literary theorist Frank Kermode long ago called a "sense of an ending."[34] Without an ending, a story can have no definite shape or meaning, and history without an ending becomes reduced to meaningless detail, a random weather of events, in the manner of a soap opera. Some Buddhist, Hindu, and Jewish and Christian mystics apparently can live in such a state without succumbing to despair because they feel connected with an eternal dimension that contains all time, but the vast majority of the followers of any religion require a plot that redeems their history. Plots demand characters in conflict with each other, and the one true God can remain in conflict with no one for long. Angels, however, can fight through plots with real suspense.

Some of these plots can be comedies, even though they concern the end of the world. As professor of communication Stephen O'Leary pointed out in *Arguing the Apocalypse*, the literary form of the book of Revelation actually follows the plot line of comedy, a double line in which the evil side falls while the good rises, not the single, broken plot of tragedy with its rise, climax, and fall.[35] In American culture, angels have starred in comedy about the end since *The Horn Blows at Midnight* (1945), a radio story that turned into a movie vehicle for Jack Benny and provided many jokes for the comedian in his television career. In that movie, Benny plays Athaniel, an angel trumpeter buried deep in the massive orchestra of Heaven. Athaniel's life changes when the Deputy Chief for Small Planet Management calls him into his office, in a gigantic corporate headquarters, and assigns him to the job of destroying the Earth because its inhabitants have become "completely out of hand": They have been allowing themselves to indulge in "persecution and hatred everywhere." Athaniel is given this chance to distinguish himself because the usual "demolition expert" is unavailable; the reward will be a promotion in the orchestra—if successful, Athaniel may even get a solo or two. This comedy tries to teach that persecution and hatred could destroy the world, and also incidentally that Heaven is a bureaucracy.

Conflict soon begins, however, because the horn has to be blown exactly at midnight on New Year's Eve in New York City, and angels prove unequal to the temptations of the city. Athaniel is distracted by a girl and a penthouse party run by two fallen angels who have assumed human form. He tries unsuccessfully to play jazz, eats an amazing array of incompatible foods at an Automat, has no money to pay for the food, and loses his trumpet. As a female angel (Alexis Smith) descends to try to save Athaniel, the film sinks into a slapstick chase. It ends with Athaniel regaining the trumpet as he falls into a gigantic cup advertising Paradise Coffee on a billboard above Times Square. The radio show on which the film was based had a more sentimental ending, but the movie played it entirely for laughs.

More serious explorations of angels and apocalypse in the twentieth century came from such major writers as Wallace Stevens (1879–1955), whose poetry and prose referred to the sense of reality as a "necessary angel" who vanished as we caught a glimpse of him; and Sam Shepard (b. 1943), whose radio play *The War in Heaven*, broadcast in 1985, was a long monologue by a fallen angel afflicted by a loss of soul that Stevens would have recognized.[36] In 1957, Isaac Asimov (1920–1992) published a short story, "The Last Trump," in which the old Persian devil Ahriman (personified as American R.E. Mann), watches gleefully as the world ends and people realize how ghastly and boring life in the resurrection would be. The world is then saved temporarily by "a very junior seraph" named Etheriel, who makes his case to the "Chief" that the contract specifying the date of the end (January 1, 1957) cannot be valid until everyone on Earth counts years by the same system. As the story ends, R.E. Mann is beginning a campaign to have December 2, 1944, the day of the first nuclear explosion at Los Alamos, recognized as the start of the Atomic Era from which a valid 1,957 years could be counted.

In Tony Kushner's *Angels in America,* the seven angelic Principalities of the seven continents want history to stop so that God will become bored with humanity and return to the angels in Heaven. Their chosen prophet, the gay man and dying AIDS patient Prior Walter, takes the advice of a Mormon mother and wrestles the angel, demanding the blessing of more life, and history goes on. Even better, the young Mormon wife, whose husband has left her in search of his identity as a gay man, sees a vision of angels in which all those who die of AIDS rise into the skies and join hands, making "a great net of souls, and the souls were three-atom oxygen molecules," so that the hole in the ozone layer (that apocalyptic terror of the 1980s) is healed.[37] As Kushner has his prophet conclude, "The world only spins forward. We will be citizens. The time has come." His "we" is inclusive: He is referring not only to those onstage at the moment he is speaking—gay men, women, Jews, and African Americans—but also, presumably, to all humanity. Though the angels have resisted humanity, they have also strengthened humans and helped to stave off the end of the world.

While the *Left Behind* series and *Touched by an Angel* offered evangelical and liberal versions of angelic warfare to massive audiences, the 1995 horror film called *The Prophecy* (which cast Christopher Walken as the angel Gabriel gone bad) became a cult classic as it exemplified a New Age willingness to modify the biblical model and to integrate other religions. The Lucifer of *The Prophecy* helps humans to defeat Gabriel, who is said to have begun a second war in Heaven against Michael and his hosts. Gabriel seeks to win that war by coming to Earth to recruit for his side the soul of an American colonel who has become a cannibal in Vietnam, thereby reaching strength in evil surpassing that of the fallen angels. Through misadventure, this soul is breathed into a young Navajo girl, who becomes sick and begins to recite terrible memories of war. Her people use one of their strongest healing rituals, the Enemyway combination of sand painting and chanting, on a sacred site in their reservation. The ceremony works; the wicked soul is driven from the girl and killed. Lucifer then kills the human form of Gabriel, restoring peace and reopening Heaven, which had been opened by the sacrifice of Jesus but closed again because of the second angelic war.

Reflecting on all this, a fictional priest-turned-policeman in *The Prophecy* warns another human that angels spend their "whole existence praising God" but have "one wing dipped in blood." The policeman asks, "Every time God wants to punish someone or kill someone He sends an angel—did you ever wonder what such creatures would be like?" The film exaggerates slightly, allowing Gabriel to claim the deaths of the Egyptian first-born sons that the Bible ascribes to God Himself, but the point still has some validity. The basic plot of *The Prophecy* evokes a central aspect of Christian tradition: the idea of war in Heaven between angels. Most Christian thinkers over the past 2,000 years have traced the existence and power of evil in the world to the rebellion of Lucifer and the other angels who joined him. They have found comfort in the belief that Michael, an angel who is called "the great prince who has charge" of Judah in Daniel 12:1, and who will throw Lucifer (Satan) out of Heaven when the prophecies of Revelation 12 come to pass, can always defeat the rebels.

In America, the first statue of an angel carved by any Christian was probably done by a Catholic in the Spanish Empire and probably represented Michael the Archangel, dressed as a Renaissance prince and raising his sword, as he appears in chapter 3. That battle must have been symbolic, since Michael held scales of justice in the other hand; he was simply executing the judgment already passed.[38] A tradition of such statues flourished in Spanish, colonial New Mexico and continued through the nineteenth century.

A less courtly, Anglo-American version of Michael appears in *The Indwelling* (2000), the seventh volume of the *Left Behind* series of novels by Pentecostal minister Tim LaHaye and writer Jerry Jenkins. Among the characters in these books is an Israeli named Tsion Ben-Judah, who converts to Christianity and becomes the spiritual leader of a group of Americans fighting the Antichrist. As Tsion speaks with Michael in a vision, he feels "as if he dangled between the nose and cheekbone of some heavenly Mount Rushmore image." The face of the angel, "ringed with hair massive as prairie grass," is "kindly and yet not soft, loving and yet confident and firm."[39] The vision proceeds with Michael and Tsion approaching the divine throne, where they see Lucifer ask God to let him rule humanity. Lucifer responds to God's refusal by changing into a dragon filled with rage. As in Revelation 12, the dragon crouches near a woman about to give birth and seeks to devour her child. Finally, Tsion sees Michael "pull the golden sword from its sheath and swing it in a high arc over his head" as he pursues the dragon, who is driven with his followers from Heaven and proceeds to wreak havoc on Earth.[40]

This battle resumes in the twelfth volume of the *Left Behind* series, *Glorious Appearing* (2004), when Michael fights Satan before all humanity on judgment day. There Satan shifts shapes from dragon to serpent to lion, and the opponents tumble so close to the onlooking crowd that people have to back away. The "sinewy" arms of Michael bind the lion in a "long, heavy chain," but Satan turns back into an angel of light and slips out. Michael then flings a 20-foot length of chain after him, "catching him at the midsection," tackles the rebel angel, picks him up, and flies with him into the "smoldering, smoke-belching chasm" as the crowd cheers. Though the human hero of the novels, an American airline pilot named Rayford Steele, begins to worry when Michael does not immediately return, the angel reappears "with a key in his hand,"[41] fulfilling the story of Revelation 20.

Whatever one thinks of the truth or entertainment value of angelic wrestling, the coauthors of the *Left Behind* books undeniably succeeded in using Michael and Satan to translate biblical stories into images and settings comprehensible to contemporary Americans. A Michael with the stature of Mount Rushmore and hair like prairie grass, who tackles his cosmic opponent as a football player might tackle someone, has left behind medieval and European images such as those that prevailed in colonial New Mexico to become a Michael for modern Americans. One result of such recasting was to make scriptures from thousands of years ago available as guides for the geopolitics of the twenty-first century. The Michael of *Glorious Appearing* fought for Jesus, Israel, and an American corps of believers not only against Satan, but also against the great hypothetical enemies of most evangelicals and of other right-wing thinkers in the United States. This archangel helped to defeat a unified world religion and a world government, led by a human who had been possessed by Satan.

From closer to the center of the political spectrum, the television drama *Touched by an Angel* also showed angels at war. The twelfth episode of the show's first season (1994–1995) featured conflict over the opening of a hospice for people dying of AIDS in a small western town. When angelic "caseworker" Monica (Roma Downey) is sent to guard the Jewish woman doctor who wants to start the hospice, her supervisory angel, Tess (Della Reese), comes along to visit a man she had helped through part of a difficult childhood. The two angels arrive just in time to save the doctor from dying in a car bombing and find that Tess's former charge has become part of a group called the Patriot League. At a meeting of this group, the leader asks for "a big Aryan hand to our friends who stopped that Jew doctor and her homosexual friends." He preaches a gospel common among white supremacists: that because the Hebrew "Adam" can be related to the word for "red," only those who can blush, or "show blood in the face," are truly human. Other races resulted from the mixing of humans with demons or animals. As she hears this teaching, the black angel Tess recognizes the leader as Satan in human form. After a great deal of persuasion, the good angels finally lead people to take action. At a climactic moment, the man whom Tess once protected from his father's abuse prays to God to send Satan out of town, and his prayer is answered.

The characters in *Touched by an Angel* and those in the *Left Behind* books both fought evil, but the evil took a different form in the TV series than it did in the books. Week after week, the angels of the TV show waged spiritual warfare indirectly, through human beings, and they fought for liberal causes. The aspects of life they associated with Satan were racism, fascism, anti-Semitism, and homophobia, while in the *Left Behind* series, the Christians fought against the satanic world government, a satanic world religion, and Satan himself. Tess and Monica on *Touched* reflected the values of Martha Williamson, the born-again Methodist who produced *Touched by an Angel* and who wrote many of its episodes. For Pentecostal pastor and author Tim LaHaye and his characters in the *Left Behind* books, it was too late for angels or humans to work toward a better world; the end was inevitable, and a better world would only come with the return of Christ. The role of angels was not to help humans improve the world one good deed at a time, but to aid in overturning the forces of evil once and for all and so usher in the millennium.

Both the *Left Behind* series and *Touched by an Angel* sparked subsidiary culture wars among evangelicals and liberals. On one hand, some evangelicals complained that the angels of the CBS series sold "a seductive mix of truth and New Age sentiment," leaving repentance for sins (such as homosexuality) and faith in Christ out of their gospel. On the other hand, *New York Times* columnist Nicholas Kristof wrote an op-ed piece in 2004 characterizing the judgment scenes of *Glorious Appearing* as hate speech that would rightly alarm Americans if it came from a Muslim source.[42] Yet the audiences for the show and the novels were so enormous, and at the same time so selective for people interested in religious fiction, that millions of Americans probably affirmed *both* Martha Williamson's Tess and Tim LaHaye's Michael as they defeated very different Satans in very different ways. Angels have demonstrated remarkable power as symbols of unity. This power builds upon but goes beyond the power of the Bible, which about 30 percent of the U.S. population takes literally and 50 percent accepts as the inspired word of God, while 78 percent believe in angels.[43]

In almost all visions of the end, the apocalyptic war results in renewal as well as destruction. The human mind may have a constitutional bias against contemplating death without rebirth. One of the most popular visions of angels and apocalypse in recent American culture, the comedy *Dogma* (1999) by Kevin Smith, embodied many themes of this book in what Smith called "a love letter to faith." *Dogma* has been called a repackaging of Catholicism for Generation X and denounced as blasphemous by the Catholic League.

Angels and demons drive the plot of *Dogma*, merging Catholic theology with world religions and popular culture as they go. The story begins with two angels, Loki (Matt Damon) and Bartleby (Ben Affleck), who have been banished to Wisconsin because Loki, the former angel of death who destroyed Sodom and Gomorrah, among other places, was persuaded by Bartleby to quit in protest and lay down his flaming sword. Although their sentence is permanent, they are given hope by a demon, Azrael, who is temporarily out of Hell on the mission of possessing a human. Azrael sends the two angels a newspaper clipping about a plenary indulgence being offered to anyone who walks through the

In Kevin Smith's Dogma *(1999), Ben Affleck played the former Angel of Death, banished from heaven and attempting to regain it through a Roman Catholic plenary indulgence. The plan results in a violent black comedy, in which humans save God and the whole universe. (Miramax Films/Photofest)*

portal of St. Michael's Church in New Jersey on the day when Bishop Glick is to initiate a campaign of renewal called "Catholicism Wow!" Their plan threatens the existence of the cosmos, however, because it would involve God in the self-contradiction of forgiving those who had been irrevocably sentenced. In order to receive the plenary indulgence, the angels will have to become human, taking on mortality by cutting off their wings. They are foiled after many twists and turns, including the need to set God (played by singer Alanis Morissette) free from the body of a comatose human through the intervention of angel Metatron, the Voice of God. Metatron enlists various earthly and heavenly helpers, including a distantly descended niece of Jesus (Linda Fiorentino), two prophets (a comedy team called Jay and Silent Bob, played by Jason Mewes and Kevin Smith, the *auteur* of the movie), a black apostle named Rufus (Chris Rock) who was left out of the gospels, and a muse (Selma Hayek) who left Heaven to write on her own and found she could not, but there is no question that the angels are the agents whose motives make the story. Azrael and Bartleby even resurrect an ancient theme of speculative angelology, that the fallen angels are motivated by hatred of humanity for usurping their place with God. After evil appears to triumph, God intervenes in apocalyptic fashion, and *Dogma* reveals itself as a true comedy, affirming the world.

The names of the angels suggest a vision of unity between religions in *Dogma*. For example, Metatron is a name to conjure with in Talmudic lore. The rabbis apply that name to an angel more powerful than any other, the "little Jehovah" whose throne stands in the seventh heaven, closest to God, and who appears as a pillar of fire. In *Dogma*, Metatron comes to Jesus' niece Bethany as a pillar of fire and is greeted by a blast from her home fire extinguisher. He functions as the Voice of God, which is one of his roles in tradition. Azrael, who initiates the plot against God in *Dogma*, is the name of the angel of death in several Islamic traditions, especially in Persia. Loki, who is called the angel of death in *Dogma*, bears a name drawn from the trickster/devil whose hatred brings about the end of the world in Norse mythology. Loki's friend Bartleby derives from a Herman Melville story, "Bartleby the Scrivener," in which a mysterious lawyer's assistant refuses to do one thing after another until he dies, refusing to eat.

Though the angels of *Dogma* bear an unorthodox combination of names, avoiding the unquestionably biblical Michael and Gabriel and the fairly orthodox Raphael and Uriel, they do bear witness to some established theological traditions and to some that have become enshrined in the angel religion of American culture. On the traditional side, none of these angels are former humans; all of them remember and respond to the war in Heaven between Lucifer and the good angels; and none of them have even the capacity to have sex. When Bethany fears that Metatron may be a rapist, he pulls down his pants to show a smooth metal surface and calls himself "as anatomically deficient as a Ken doll." The muse, Serendipity, does a similar move later. In another affirmation of orthodoxy, God condemns angels to eternal damnation in *Dogma*. When Bartleby rails against the divine order, Loki at first protests that he has heard this before from "the Morningstar," Lucifer, and rejects the idea of rebellion. Ultimately, Loki goes along with Bartleby and is killed, along with Bartleby and the demon Azrael who started it all. Viewers are left to draw the orthodox conclusion that these angels go to Hell, where Azrael lived before his attempted escape.

On the side of heresy (or development of doctrine), the angels of *Dogma* stand very close to humanity. Unlike angels in traditional theology, they can renounce their status and become human by the physical act of cutting off their wings. For fallen angel Azrael, this has become impossible, but Bartleby and Loki can still "transubstantiate," as they inaccurately call it, misapplying the term for transforming bread and wine into the body and blood of Jesus. As in the films where angels become human by plunging from roofs to the street (*Wings of Desire, City of Angels*, an episode of *Touched by an Angel*), or in many books and movies and doctrines from Swedenborg to *The Gates Ajar* that contemplate people becoming angels, the gap in power between angels and humans in *Dogma* is not very great. Here *Dogma* shares a characteristic with television shows like *Buffy the Vampire Slayer* and *Charmed* in which humans can battle demons. In one episode of *Xena: Warrior Princess*, Xena (Lucy Lawless) says that she has the power to kill Michael the Archangel.[44]

Dogma suggests a similarly small distance separating all creatures from God. The female God of *Dogma* hugs angel Bartleby before she kills him with her voice, exploding his head with a shout. Azrael nearly succeeds in imprisoning God in the body of a man, which she had assumed in order to indulge her delight in playing an arcade game called Skee-Ball. God's imprisonment takes place through the simple expedient of having the man God has inhabited beaten into a coma by some demonic underlings. After this angelic rebellion is routed, God causes a pregnancy in the womb of Christ's hitherto barren, distantly descended niece, and Metatron tells her to take good care of the "package," because God will have a world of work for her to do. Finally, both faith and dogma are criticized in *Dogma:* Instead of faith, niece Bethany tells the black apostle that she now has "a good idea." As apostle Rufus had told her earlier, ideas about God are better than faith because ideas can be changed.

Dogma clearly used angels to set forth what I have called a transtheistic faith; it is accepting of many spiritual principles while retaining some commitment to an underlying unity. In 1999, however, the world was about to receive a new message from believers in the one true God. The most fitting angelic symbol of the times seemed to shift from Tony

Kushner's Angel of Bethesda in Central Park to General Boykin's photographs of demons. The next chapter will explore how theories regarding angels and images of angels have evolved further under the impact of 9/11 and the War on Terror.

Just as people see angels at moments of emergency, nations see angels in times of war. Whether such visions happen in emergencies and wars because God sends angels where they are needed, or because human nature has evolved with a capacity for people to see personal agents like angels when they are under stress, cannot be ascertained by reason or academic research. But one cannot help but wonder why so many Americans saw and talked with angels, and filled their culture with stories, images, and products that represented angels, at the end of the twentieth century, just as the United States was entering an era of religious war. The history of religions shows that this phenomenon is not unusual: Visions of angels have often proliferated in times of war.

Although the United States may be the most powerful nation on Earth, tens of millions of Americans live with the worldview that Satan is still the lord of this world and that his minions surround us. Even the image of the New Jerusalem from the book of Revelation asserts this theme—the city that descends from Heaven is filled with the saints but surrounded by darkness, "dogs and sorcerers and fornicators and murderers and idolaters" (Rev. 22:14–15). That same image—a city without gates, flooded with commerce—inspired President Ronald Reagan and his chief speechwriter, Peggy Noonan, as they invoked the "city on a hill" (from Matt. 5 and John Winthrop's speech on the *Arbella*) in Reagan's farewell speech of 1989. "How stands the city?" Reagan asked. He answered that it stood "tall on its granite ridge . . . no matter what storm" and that it was "still a magnet . . . for all the pilgrims from all the lost places who are hurtling *through the darkness*, toward home."[45] The United States of Ronald Reagan in 1989 still seemed surrounded by storms and by darkness, on the front line in the war with demons. Ever since the Spaniards and the English came to what they called the New World, Europeans in the Americas have described themselves in this way, and they still do today. Even while conquering empires and celebrating past victories, Americans call on angels for defense.

As the United States sent armies to the homeland of angels, the former Persian Empire, in 1991 and again in 2001 and 2003, angels immediately regained one of their most ancient functions, providing the narrative explanation for evil within a monotheist worldview. Meanwhile, responding to globalization, angels became more multicultural. New theories about matter and spirit led people to picture angels as more physical, or more involved with the physical world, than

The horrific and apparently antihuman angels of Ozark Prophecy *(on facing page) seem to make this painting an exception to the rule that Americans see angels as useful helpers, but even these angels are fulfilling some human desires. The artist, an Arkansan who is now completing a master's degree at the Yale University School of Art, went at the urging of friends to hear a preacher in the Ozarks during the millennial fervor that preceded the year 2000. In a camp meeting ground formed by trailers and filled with guns, the preacher inveighed against those who had taken the "mark of the Beast" from Revelation 13 by getting credit cards. He said that in the final battle such traitors would be slain by angels bearing "swords of fire" that would resemble the "muzzle flash of a machine gun." The image haunted Lane, who created this painting several years later. The interrupted barbecue and suburban streets of* Ozark Prophecy *brought angels and the Apocalypse into an intensely American setting. As Lane worked on his aggressive male angels, moviemaker Kevin Smith was casting the young and muscular actors Ben Affleck and Matt Damon as angels with machine guns, slaying people outside a New Jersey church in* Dogma *(1999). The angels of* Ozark Prophecy *and* Dogma *are actually much less violent than those of chapter 14 in the New Testament book of Revelation, which describes angels harvesting humans with sickles and throwing them into the "wine press of the wrath of God," where the humans are crushed until blood flows "as high as a horse's bridle" for two hundred miles. Andrew Lane (b. 1971),* Ozark Prophecy *(2000), 84 x 48 in., oil on canvas. (Reproduced with permission of the artist; photograph by William Gardella)*

ever before. Because the same events in politics, economics, and science affected all Americans, evangelicals and New Age thinkers both took part in these trends. Popular culture also both reflected and contributed to the development of angels. The superheroes of comic books and the characters and plots of science fiction, for example, expressed a longing for new angels and new stories. While the story of war with demons and "aggressive defense" accompanied the conquest of the continent and the first wars of overseas expansion, the new empire in which the United States found itself after 2001 required a new story, which is only now emerging. In the new world, animals and ancient goddesses can function alongside angels, and even Satan may be redeemed.

Multicultural Angels

Contemporary American culture and the ancient Persian heritage of angels came together in the movie *Crash*, which won the Academy Award for Best Picture of 2004. *Crash* introduces an angel when a Latino father, presumably Catholic or Pentecostal, comforts his very young daughter with a story about an invisible, magical cloak that a fairy gave him as a child (after knocking things in his room over with her wings). Though the girl had been hiding under her bed at night, terrified by gunfire from the neighborhood of Los Angeles where they live, the story of the fairy and the cloak reassures her. An unintended consequence takes place when the Latino father is threatened with a gun by an Iranian (Persian) immigrant who blames him because his store, where the Latino had tried unsuccessfully to repair a lock, has been plundered and spray-painted with ethnic slurs. When the little girl sees the store owner holding a gun on her father, she runs from their house and leaps into her father's arms to shield him with the fairy's cloak. The gun goes off, apparently injuring the girl, but it had been loaded with blanks by the Iranian's own daughter, an adult. As everyone recovers from the trauma, the Iranian tells his daughter that he was saved from becoming a killer by his *fravashi*, using the ancient Persian word for a guardian angel.

In ancient Persia, fravashis were the heavenly, spiritual aspects of people, described as "winged warriors, female like the Valkyries, living and very potent." The original battle between the good creator God (Ahura mazda, or Ohrmazd) and his evil enemy (Angra mainyu, or Ahriman) apparently had been won by evil, with the first human, the first ox, and all good spirits vanquished, when the fravashis turned the tide. The spirits of warriors killed by Ahriman kept the evil one from returning to his stronghold in the darkness where he could regain strength for new attacks. Trapped in the world of light made by Ohrmazd, Ahriman watched in horror as new life arose from the good aspects of the dead creation.

Fravashis gained their capacity to defeat cosmic evil from the unique place they held in Persian cosmology, which had several levels of beings that corresponded to later levels of angels. First in the creation after God were the seven immortals, personifying Wisdom, Truth, Justice, Devotion, Integrity, Immortality, and Obedience. These were the source of the seven archangels of Judeo-Christian tradition. Next came the Yazatas, one governing each day and others personifying stars and planets, natural forces, and abstract goods; some of these, like Mithra and Vayu, were gods of the Hindu pantheon. Both of the higher levels of spirits were present when Ohrmazd made a perfect material world, in which trees had no bark or thorns, the ox was perfectly white, and the original man, Gayomart, shone as bright as the sun. Behind the sky Ohrmazd imprisoned Ahriman, the personification of Evil Thought, but battle began when Ahriman broke free and made evil counterparts of every good thing: wolves to oppose dogs, Falsehood against Truth, Disease against Health. "Every archangel had an opposing arch-demon," according to John Hinnells, historian of Persian religion, and in the conflict the original man and ox and all good plants died. The fravashis changed the balance because Ohrmazd had made humans with a dual nature, material and spiritual. When human bodies died, their spirits went on fighting, and yet these spirits belonged in this lower world. Ohrmazd himself praised them for saving the material creation.[1]

Angels of recent American television have had more in common with these worldly fravashis than with the heavenly figures on war memorials and tombs from the early twentieth century. The hero of *Angel*, a television series that ended in 2004 after spinning off from the more successful *Buffy the Vampire Slayer*, was a reformed vampire who battled both vampires and demons, and he was also the semi-immortal spirit of a dead human. In *Charmed*, a series that ran from 1998 to 2006, beautiful witches were protected (and occasionally married) by "whitelighters," former people who had gained the angelic power to move instantly from one place and time to another. Even the more orthodox *Touched by an Angel,* where the angel Monica and her superior Tess were explicitly not former humans, had episodes in which Monica was given a human liability to feel physical cold and a temptation to marry, and Tess was certainly subject to anger. The ABC/Family series *Fallen,* which launched with a two-hour special in 2006 and was slated to run weekly in 2007, featured a teenaged boy in foster care who did not realize at the beginning of the show that he was among the *nephilim* (or "fallen ones") who resulted from the angel-human marriages of Genesis 6. By the end of the pilot episode, the boy/angel Aaron was learning to use the huge black wings and flaming sword that he could cause to appear at will. He needed the sword to fight off Thrones (a division of the traditional angelic hierarchy) who sought to kill him. He had found a mission of redeeming fallen angels, who apparently lived in many disguises in our world, and had a helper in a dog named Gabriel with whom he could speak. If current trends in angels continue, in future shows the canine Gabriel may reveal that he, too, is an angel.

Psychotherapist Doreen Virtue, who began channeling angels in the early 1990s, dramatically broadened the lists of spirits she contacted after the century turned. In 2003, she published a book called *Archangels and Ascended Masters* that brought St. Michael and his colleagues together with Gandhi and Martin Luther King Jr. Virtue had already published two different decks of Oracle Cards featuring angels and archangels, each resembling Tarot cards in their use for divination and in therapy, in the 1990s. After the millennium, she added Goddess Guidance Oracle Cards (2003) and Saints and Angels Oracle Cards (2005). The goddesses included Kwan Yin of China, Lakshmi of India, Isis of Egypt, White Tara of Tibet, Brigit of Ireland, and Aphrodite of Greece. Among the humans who combined with angels in the latter deck were Mother Teresa, Bernadette of Lourdes, Joan of Arc, Hildegard of Bingen, Padre Pio, and saints Anthony, Francis, and Cecilia. These conflations of spiritual categories reached a climax in Virtue's book *Goddesses and Angels* (2005), which recounted her visits to holy places in Great Britain, Ireland, Europe, and Australia. Here dolphins and turtles swam up to Virtue and imparted messages, one of which urged her to visit the site at Medjugorje, in Croatia, where people have been seeing the

Virgin Mary since 1981. She touched foreheads with the Dalai Lama, who urged her to do more meditation. As the new century progressed, the spirits that Virtue encountered and channeled belonged to more international and more nonhuman communities. They were also more likely to manifest in physical ways and to impart messages concerned with ecology, diet, exercise, breathing, and other kinds of physical practice.

In *From Angels to Aliens: Teenagers, the Media, and the Supernatural* (2003), sociologist Lynn Schofield Clark related current interest in supernatural beings to "the dark side of evangelicalism." Clark, whom the evangelical magazine *Christianity Today* identifies as a "longtime youth minister,"[2] argued that evangelical Christianity had opened Americans to the belief that a world of spiritual power was accessible. Drawing a contrast between believers in aliens and angels, she pointed out that those who affirmed the reality of aliens deliberately sought to take a position on the margins of American culture, which they often saw as complicit in a conspiracy to suppress the truth, while those who affirmed angels also affirmed their agreement with a broad religious and cultural community, even when the angel believers did not belong to a church or religious tradition.[3]

Though evangelical Christian writers on angels commonly try to turn readers to the Bible, warning against religious syncretism and what they criticize as New Age thinking, many of their books confirm Clark's observation that evangelicals participate in and sometimes drive the more general trends of American culture. Evangelicals write about angels with multinational identities and deep involvement in the material world. For example, while former Pentecostal leader and fiction writer Frank Peretti presents the New Age as a spiritual movement with roots in Hell, he also introduces angels like "Nathan, the towering Arabian," "Armoth, the big African," and "Chimon, the meek European with the golden hair, who bore on his arms the marks of a fading demon's last blows."[4] These angels are so physical that they can be wounded in battle, and they show scars from the healing of former wounds. The same can be said for Peretti's demons, who (as we saw in chapter 6) range from insectoid personifications of Despair, Envy, and other negative traits to dark princes like Rafar of Babylon, who wears rubies and carries his leathery wings as a cape.

Physical Angels and Demons

Twenty years after Peretti, Bill Wiese presented another vivid and even more physical vision of demons in his book *23 Minutes in Hell* (2006). Brought to Hell by God so that he could spread a word of warning to others (though he did not know it at the time), Wiese claimed he had been tormented by demons named Evil and Terror who resembled reptiles in human shape. "Their arms and legs were unequal in length, out of proportion—without symmetry. The first one had bumps and scales all over its grotesque body . . . a huge protruding jaw, gigantic teeth, and large sunken-in eyes." This creature, Evil, was "stout and powerful, with thick legs and abnormally large feet." It paced around the cell where Wiese was imprisoned. Meanwhile, the other demon, Terror, watched calmly. Terror was "taller and thinner, with very long arms and razor-sharp fins that covered its body. Protruding from its hands were claws . . . nearly a foot long." These demons spoke to one another in a language Wiese could not even identify, let alone understand, but he knew that they used "terrible, blasphemous language that spewed from their mouths expressing extreme hatred for God." Eventually, Evil threw Wiese against the cell wall, where he landed so hard that he felt that every bone in his body had been broken; next, Terror grabbed him "from behind in a bear hug" and pressed him into his chest so that the demon's "sharp fins pierced" Wiese's back. Terror then plunged his claws into Wiese's chest and "ripped them outward," leaving his flesh hanging "like ribbons." Yet he did not die and could not: "Death penetrated me, but eluded me."[5]

The physicality of Wiese's description from 2006 went far beyond that of Peretti's best-selling novels of 1986 and 1989. Such violence might be necessary to impress generations raised on video games, increasingly explicit horror movies, and the realities of terrorism and war. The details of Wiese's journey to Hell also had cultural references, starting with the names of the demons, "Evil" and "Terror"—both words that became very prominent in American political discourse after September 11, 2001. President George W. Bush sent Americans to war against "evildoers" and described an "Axis of Evil" that ran through Iraq, Iran, and North Korea. The invasions and occupations of Afghanistan and Iraq were justified as part of a "War on Terror." In Wiese's vision, the ungainly, semi-human forms of the demons, and their incomprehensible but somehow clearly blasphemous and hateful language, suggested American reactions to the pictures of men who appeared on television as our enemies, clad in Muslim garb, clambering among the rocks of Middle Eastern mountains and speaking Arabic. The calm yet hateful demeanor of the tall, thin demon, Terror, brought to mind media impressions of Osama bin Laden himself. The way that the demons handled Wiese, and his remark that "Death penetrated me," referenced another common, physical image of evil, suggesting prison rape and the well-known conditions in America's own prisons as they were both before and during the War on Terror. Wiese repeatedly described Hell as a prison with cells and bars. Satan, along with 13-foot giants who were conceived by fallen angels and human women in Genesis 6, ruled the place, but there were no guards to restrain the malice of prisoners against each other. He located the prison of Hell in a specific physical location, the center of the Earth, "approximately thirty-seven hundred miles deep."[6]

Although Wiese's book, which stood at 979 out of the millions of titles on the Amazon list in April 2007, has sold well enough so that its author, who has worked as a real estate agent, is now in demand as an evangelist, Bill Wiese does not have great authority among evangelicals. His *23 Minutes in Hell* built on the success of an even more prominent book by a Southern Baptist minister, Don Piper, called *90 Minutes in Heaven* (2004), which ranked 116th on Amazon and held fifth place among the *New York Times* paperback best-sellers as of April 15, 2007. While Piper did not claim to have seen physical angels or demons, he did feel an angel who "clutched" his hand with a "strong, powerful touch" as he lay near death from a car accident.[7] Piper also described meeting very physical dead people (whom some might call angels, as we have seen) in Heaven, including a high school friend who put his arm around Piper's shoulders and a great-grandmother who suffered in life from osteoporosis but who stood up straight in the afterlife. Piper's Heaven was physically vivid—the gates were literally pearly, with an "iridescent" surface, the streets were made of gold bricks, and the songs, sung both by angels and by heavenly humans, were overpowering.[8]

Max Lucado, the pastor of the Oak Hills Church of Christ in San Antonio, who has been named "America's Pastor" by *Christianity*

Today magazine, has also provided some physical descriptions of angels among his more than fifty books. For example, the opening pages of *When Christ Comes*, a meditation on the end of this world that Lucado published in 1999, pictured a stunned individual hearing a trumpet blast, then looking up to see "an endless fleet of angels" spread across the whole sky. "Thousands of silvery wings rise and fall in unison," as humanity watches, "and over the sound of the trumpets, you can hear the cherubim and seraphim chanting, 'Holy, Holy, Holy!'"[9] Three years later, in 2002, Lucado published a novella telling the Christmas story from the standpoint of the angels. *An Angel's Story* began with the single word, "Gabriel," then described Gabriel's reactions to hearing God say his name. "Just the sound of my King's voice stirred my heart. I left my post at the entryway and stepped into the throne room. . . . I entered the circle of unending Light, folded my wings before me to cover my face, and knelt before Him."[10]

Though Lucado's denomination, the Church of Christ, has an austere tradition that rejects all instrumental music or decorations (including pictures of angels) in its churches, Lucado's writings have often invoked angels in very physical ways. On his website, the daily message for October 25, 2006, repeated the story of a missionary in Vietnam who was driven to his hotel by two angels in a taxi. Lucado drew the lesson that "God sends his best troops to oversee your life." He asked readers to "imagine the president assigning the Secret Service to protect you, telling his agents to motorcade your car through traffic," and to think about how they would sleep if they "knew D.C.'s finest guarded your door?" Even better, "How *will* you sleep knowing heaven's finest are doing just that?"[11]

One of the most spectacular examples of physical angels in recent times has come from Roland Buck, the pastor of the Central Assembly of God in Boise, Idaho, who began to report visitations by angels starting on June 18, 1978. Buck's account, *Angels on Assignment*, has sold more than a million copies since 1979 and is now available in its entirety on the Internet. According to Buck, the angel Chrioni, who accompanied Gabriel on a visit to Idaho, stood 7 feet tall and weighed some 400 pounds. Buck saw a blue glow from the room where the angels gathered because their clothing, skin, and especially eyes all shone. During a visit from Michael, Buck noted, "the copper color of his skin was . . . brilliant with the radiation that flows out of him from having been in the presence of God." As if to show that their images were more than insubstantial appearances, the angels who visited Buck did physical things. Chrioni scratched the ears and stomach of Buck's dog Queenie. Leaving Buck's house (not by flying or dematerializing, but by walking through the back patio doors) after a visit during which six inches of snow fell outside, the angels "took three steps, which pressed the snow down all the way to the ground, and carried them close to fifteen feet, nearly five feet per step," and then they vanished, leaving "huge footprints in the snow."[12] These very physical angels also had physical effects on Pastor Buck. On one visit, Gabriel gave him "a round wafer approximately five inches in diameter and 5/8 inch thick, that looked like bread." When Buck ate the wafer (along with water the angel provided from a silver ladle), he found that he not only felt "rivers of praise . . . bubbling up out of my innermost being," but also lost five pounds a day for four days, about a pound a day for some time after that, and felt a great increase in strength and stamina.[13]

Angelic aid in weight loss linked this Pentecostal pastor with New Age therapists like Doreen Virtue, whose *Healing with the Angels* (1999) taught that angels give advice on diet to help humans "increase the 'vibrational frequency' of our bodies." In pursuit of this goal, angels urge people to avoid toxins and hormones in foods, pesticides, and the nitrates in cured meats. Virtue reported that people who speak with angels often become vegetarians or vegans. Eventually, Virtue predicted, humans will attain "a lifestyle of 'breatharianism,' where we'll receive all of our nourishment from the *prana* that is in the air." People will attain such "high-frequency bodies" that they will "teletransport, dematerialize, and withstand events that would traumatize a denser, lower-frequency body." Although such angelic humans would not really need food, they could create it: "Higher-vibrating minds will be able to manifest any required foods or other supplies."[14] The same transformation of humanity into energy beings, beginning with vegetarianism, took place without angelic guidance in James Redfield's best-seller, *The Celestine Prophecy* (1993).

Although evangelical theorists have described the same mixed realm of spirits and bodies, their advice often opposes that of Redfield, Virtue, and other New Age thinkers. During the 1980s, Rebecca Brown, a physician, produced several books, sold in Barnes and Noble as well as in Christian bookstores, that emphasized a triadic relationship between spirits, bodies, and souls. Brown explained spiritual healing and out-of-body travel by means of two main concepts: that "human spirits have the same capabilities as demon and angel spirits," and that all of these spirits "can manipulate and change the physical body." Unlike Virtue and Redfield, however, Brown saw vegetarianism as a demonic trap. Because "spiritual battling results in an acute loss of protein from our physical bodies," Brown wrote, it is very important to "increase our intake of high-quality protein during times of intensive spiritual battle." She noted that ever since the days of Noah, "Satan and his demons have been trying to stop people from eating meat." The demons, she said, wish to regain the physical access they had prior to the flood, when fallen angels had sex with human women; God then gave Noah permission to eat meat in order that people might be strong enough to resist the demons. Meanwhile, Brown said, people who practice religions that she considers "forms of demon worship," including Hindus and other followers of Eastern religions, as well as New Age teachers, naturally advocate vegetarianism.[15]

Another evangelical who offered physical experiences and teachings about angels at the turn of the millennium was John Loren Sandford, a Congregational pastor and spiritual therapist from Idaho. Descended from the Osage nation of Native Americans, Sandford drew upon the heritage of his people in his book *Healing the Nations* (2000) to set Christians free from a dualism of matter and spirit. He pointed out that "Satan is a spiritual being" and that, beyond demons and angels and humans, "animals have their own kind of spirit." He used Paul's description of a whole creation longing for redemption in Romans 8:19–21, as well as the "speech" of creation in Psalm 19, to support his contention that "all of creation has spirit flowing in and through it." Only when Christians recognize this truth and pray for the deliverance of nature from satanic domination could redemption be complete.

The final battles, Sandford said, would involve the participation of angels. In several visions, he was taken to the "councils of God," where he saw angels giving crowns and batons to people of various nations, including "a large, well-muscled black man on our right . . . [and] a man on our left who looked to be Middle Eastern, with a sharply trimmed beard and long, flowing robe and turban." God spoke to him during one of these councils, saying that "a rift has occurred in history . . . between heaven and earth." Sandford reflected that in biblical times, "angels often appeared in power and glory among humans and performed wonders." Now, "Satan's master plan" had succeeded in so weakening "belief in anything supernatural" that many people no longer expected angels, while others "trivialized, commercialized, and even idolized" them, so that angels "no longer feel free to come among us in the fullness of who they are." Humanity, he wrote, must repent, because "in the coming warfare for the nations, there will be need for angels and mankind to fight alongside one another—they on their plane, we on ours."[16]

To further explain the program of spiritual warfare that he wanted other Christians to take up, Sandford described his travels to Germany, Japan, England, and Australia and among the Osage in the United States, where he had tried to break generational curses that bound these nations. For example, because generations of Japanese emperors have taken office by having ritual intercourse with the sun goddess Amaterasu, who is actually "a demonic succuba spirit," there has been "a virulent descendancy of sexual infidelity and perversion among Japanese men." Strongholds of spiritual evil of this type do not yield overnight, or to any one person, Sandford taught, but Christians should band together and seek to overcome them. Their prayers would someday be answered, in part through the intervention of angels. One prayer that Sandford recommended asked God, "Risk sending Your angels to war for us. I will not let You down by quitting too soon or by not believing that Your redemption is going to happen."[17] Such a sense that humans and angels fought on the same side and needed each other had also appeared in the fiction of Frank Peretti and in the preaching of many in the Vineyard movement, a school of Pentecostal theology and church fellowship that continues to spread.

Though Sandford condemned New Age thinking, he also paid it a tribute of sorts by defining the New Age movement as "an attempt to make mankind into all he is intended to be without death to self in Christ Jesus."[18] The New Age and Sandford's brand of evangelical Christianity shared a vision of the high spiritual destiny of humanity. As the millennium turned, evangelicals and New Age thinkers both predicted the coming of a new community between humans and angels. They often agreed in their visions of the future while disagreeing on the means whereby people would become angelic.

A former Billy Graham associate named Terry Law, for example, rejected both the New Age and the methods of spiritual warfare taught by John Loren Sandford, yet set forth a worldview that accepted elements from both. In *The Truth about Angels* (1994), Law speculated that "the devil is enjoying all this attention" devoted to spirits who dominate nations because it was leading Christians to waste their time praying for the defeat of demons already defeated by Christ. Law also warned that in the New Age, Satan was using the "neo-Pentecostal (or charismatic)" emphasis on "the supernatural gifts of the Holy Spirit" for his own purposes. Pentecostal gifts were being "translated by the world into interest in the occult," Law complained. A spiritual movement that sought return to "the basics of the faith" was being "translated in the secular world as a 'back to the earth' movement, back to one's roots in nature." Yet, there was no doubt that a new approach of angels to humanity was taking place. "God is showing us that we need to know about angels," Law wrote, because they would soon become as commonly known as in "the early church." At such a time as this, Christians needed to be on guard, because Satan would use the moment to "thrust his 'ringers' forward, catching the world's attention."[19]

While criticizing those who prayed to pull down territorial demons, Law affirmed the existence and activities of such demons. He ascribed the "long chain of tyrannical rulers" in Mesopotamia, the status of Haiti as a "social and economic eyesore," the high murder rates of "Andean nations," particularly Colombia, and the difficulty of spreading Christianity in Japan to demonic activity. As for good angels, Law had met Roland Buck, the visionary Idaho pastor of *Angels on Assignment,* and he endorsed Buck's character and his visions, testifying that angels told Buck things about Law's spiritual life that Law had told no one. At times, Law implied the same close connection between spirits and the material world that appeared in the visions of Buck and the works of Doreen Virtue and Rebecca Brown. He taught that sacrificial worship in biblical times provided "a legal right for the angels to ascend and descend to and from God's throne bringing help to the saints." Following this model, Christians today should think of their praise and worship and of their suffering as material sacrifices that would "activate angels on our behalf." With regard to finances, Christians should know that "sacrificial giving activates angels as much as sacrificial praise." Those who give sacrificially can also "tell the ministering angels to go and bring forth" what they themselves need.[20]

In the same year that Law published his book, I was trying to repair and sell my family's old home, and a Pentecostal contractor told me that angels had helped him to find a buyer for his own father's house. The house had languished on the market, he said, until he prayed in the Spirit and "dispatched angels to the north, west, east, and south" to bring buyers. The next day, he had offers above the list price. Though a cynic might see this as the Pentecostal equivalent of the Catholic superstition I followed, burying a statue of St. Joseph upside-down near the "For Sale" sign, there were qualitative differences. The contractor felt he could command spirits and that he was entirely justified in doing so, while I somewhat guiltily hoped that discomfort in the spiritual realm, perhaps stemming from the desire of St. Joseph to be released, would bring a buyer. The Pentecostal believed both in angels and in the angelic authority of his own spirit. His faith was Christian, but his confidence and the intimate interaction between spirit and matter in his practice also belonged to the New Age.

A merging of Christian and New Age teaching on angels appeared in Betty J. Eadie's *Embraced by the Light* (1992), an account of a near-death experience (NDE) that reached number one on the *Publishers' Weekly* nonfiction best-seller list on February 7, 1993, and was sold to Bantam paperbacks for $1.5 million. After a partial hysterectomy, Eadie apparently hemorrhaged twice and became clinically dead long enough to have a discussion with angels and then with Jesus himself. She described a vision of three men wearing "beautiful, light brown robes" tied with "gold-braided belt[s] . . . with the ends hanging down." Both the men and Eadie had bodies that glowed. As she spoke with these men, who appeared to be about eighty years old, she found that they had known her long before she was born on Earth. While they had functioned as "guardian angels during [her] life on earth," in her larger life they were "ministering angels."[21] Reassured by these spirits, she went through a dark tunnel to Jesus, who was the "Light" of the title. She was surprised to find that Jesus "was a separate being from God, with his own divine purpose." Many readers have suspected that Mormon doctrine about Jesus and God informed Eadie's theology.

With regard to angels, Eadie exemplified many trends of the millennial turn. Her angels and humans melted into each other: Some angels were future humans, some had already lived on Earth, and others had chosen to remain in Heaven to serve as guardians or warriors against Satan's army. Those who had been human had been spirits first, and the line between spirit and matter was blurred. "All people as spirits in the pre-mortal world took part in the creation of the earth," Eadie wrote. "Everything was created of *spirit matter* before it was created physically. . . . I was told by the Savior that the spirit creation could be compared to one of our photographic prints; the spirit creation would be like a sharp, brilliant print, and the earth would be like its dark negative."[22]

Eadie saw warring angels, who resembled those of evangelical novelist Frank Peretti and Assembly of God pastor Roland Buck, though her powers of description were weaker than theirs. These spiritual warriors were "giant men, very muscularly built," and "actually dressed like warriors, in head dress and armor." Looking at the Earth, she saw people calling angels in the form of lights shooting up "like broad laser beams," others that "resembled the illumination of small pen lights," and some that were "mere sparks." Each light was a prayer, and she "saw angels rushing to answer the prayers." The angels "literally flew from person to person, from prayer to prayer, and they were filled with love and joy by their work." Like other angel writers, such as Sophy Burnham, Eadie advanced a theory of effectual prayer in which doubt and fear and suffering had to be supplanted by confidence and faith. Eventually—again echoing Sophy Burnham, but also expressing a Mormon doctrine—Eadie promised that "we may become like the angels themselves."[23]

Several times in her journey, Eadie was told that her death had been premature. Now she faced a council of twelve men who told her that she must return to Earth. At first, she was resentful of the all-male composition of the council, but she received an insight into the differences between men and women that led her to accept the roles of the council members and her own. She suddenly "understood the peril women faced from Satan," who "would attack women through their restlessness." Adam had been satisfied in Eden, but Eve wanted to become a mother and so disrupted the garden, consciously beginning both progress and death. Eadie had felt the same restlessness and resentment, but she now understood. Asked by the council to review her life before returning to the body, she learned "that many of my experiences had been orchestrated by guardian angels." After she reluctantly accepted the mission to return, she found that "thousands of angels surrounded" her. She "heard their cheering," then listened as they "began to sing . . . spontaneously, parts not so much memorized as instantly known, instantly felt." When the song ended she saw the Earth again, "with its billions of people on it," but now she also saw that "angels knew the people by name and watched over them closely." She "saw that we could literally call down thousands of angels in our aid if we ask in faith," and that "we are all equal in their eyes." Eadie concluded, "We are all precious and carefully watched over. Their love never fails us."[24]

Changes, Remakes, and New Songs

The elaborate account of angels in *Embraced by the Light* showed how much American culture had changed over the two decades since the publication of psychiatrist Raymond A. Moody's *Life after Life* (1975), the book that first generated widespread interest in near-death experiences in America. For Moody, reports of a "being of light" who communicated specific questions and answers seemed a common theme among the 150 cases he had reviewed of people who had come back from nearly dying. Moody wrote that many Christians called the being Christ, that "a Jewish man and woman identified the light as an 'angel,'" but that no one had said the being of light "had wings, played a harp, or even had a human shape or appearance."[25] Between Moody's vague description and Betty Eadie's octogenarian guardian angels and armored warriors came the writings of scores of other Americans who described angels.

At the movies, the differences between two versions of *Angels in the Outfield*, the original from 1951 and the Disney version from 1994, illustrated how much had changed since mid-century, even though the same writer, Dorothy Kingsley, worked on screenplays for both films.[26] The second movie featured a baseball team, the California Angels, that wears halos topping the A's on their caps and that did not exist in 1951; the first version involved the Pittsburgh Pirates. There is some question whether it would have been acceptable for a professional sports team to be called "the Angels," even in Los Angeles, in 1951.

In the 1951 movie, the action begins because of sin, or at least because of a disruption of moral norms: The Pirates manager swears too much. Invisible spirits speak to him, offering that if he gives up swearing they will help the Pirates win. Complications ensue when an orphan boy from a school run by nuns sees the angels on the field and talks about them in the hearing of newspaper reporters, including a wicked sportscaster who is an enemy of the Pirates manager. As the Pirates win more and more games in semimiraculous fashion, speculation arises that the manager might be insane because he is talking with angels. The scandal requires resolution, and so there is a hearing before the commissioner of baseball. The issue is resolved by formal religion when a minister, a rabbi, and a priest testify before the commissioner that each of their religions affirms the reality of angels, after which the three go together to a Pirates game. As the manager reflects on his angelic helpers, he realizes that they were former human beings, deceased baseball greats.

The Disney version of *Angels in the Outfield* from 1994 neither identifies angels with dead people nor precludes that possibility. Here the spirits come in response to the prayer of a boy in foster care who desperately wants to restore his family. His father has left, saying that they will only be reunited when the California Angels win the pennant—a remote possibility, given the Angels' record that season. As in both evangelical and New Age theory of the 1990s and beyond, however, human prayer can direct angels. Several of them come to help the Angels team, miracles occur on the ballfield, and the boy gets his wish.

Where the angels of the 1951 movie are invisible onscreen and act only subtly to change game outcomes, the angels of the later film intervene in more dramatic ways. In one scene, they lift a player to superhuman heights as he leaps to catch a potential home run, and in another an angel swings with a batter to hit a ball so hard that it tears through a fielder's glove. To viewers of the 1994 movie, the angels, led by actor Christopher Lloyd, appear in swirling special effects, their bodies in robes. As in the earlier movie, the manager is charged with insanity, but this time he is saved not by clergy but by the boy's foster mother, who points out that no one laughs when football players pray after scoring touchdowns. She wonders aloud why asking for help from angels should be wrong if asking God is acceptable. Formal religion was not needed to validate angels by 1994, and the question of faith in angels had become

The spirits of the 1994 version of Angels in the Outfield *became much more*
physical and vivid than those of the first movie, which was released in 1951.
(Buena Vista/Photofest)

equal to the question of faith in God. While the first movie ends on an
elegiac note, with the manager musing about great games that "angels"
like Babe Ruth must play in Heaven, in 1994 the angels have the last
word, careening manically across the screen and away with the promise
that "we're always watching." The writers and producers of the 1994
film clearly felt more comfortable with prominent, independent, and
physically active angels than did their predecessors of 1951.

A less dramatic but still significant shift in the direction of more physical angels took place with the release of the 1997 animated version of
The Littlest Angel, which features a plot twist that did not appear in the
classic children's book that Charles Tazewell wrote in 1939. As mentioned in chapter 3, in the original book a box of treasures from the
Littlest Angel's boyhood is declared the most pleasing gift of all to the
Christ child and is changed into the Star of Bethlehem, showing that
items from the material world can have high value. In the animated version, however, this climax is insufficient. After the transformation of

the box, the Littlest Angel leads three other angels, who had once criticized his behavior, to a place called the Elysian Fields, where he teaches them to make mud squish between their toes, to climb trees, and to fish—all earthly pleasures he had regretted losing, and that he never recovered in the original book.

By 2003, when a religion journalist named Anthony De Stefano published *A Travel Guide to Heaven,* images of the afterlife, including very personal angels, had become as concrete as they were in the heyday of Spiritualism when Mark Twain satirized them in *Extract from Captain Stormfield's Visit to Heaven* (1909). Although De Stefano remained orthodox about angels not being former humans and not having physical bodies, his depiction of Heaven was amazingly physical (including human bodies "made up of atoms and molecules and cells," living on a renewed planet Earth), and his account of how angels related to humans was remarkably intimate. Your own guardian angel is "now watching you read," De Stefano wrote. "He's got his own special . . . personality . . . with unique talents and powers that he's used before to help you at various moments." One of the joys of Heaven will be talking with our angels about the times when they helped us, he said, but De Stefano urged his readers to begin the conversation now. Since the Bible says that angels "rejoice," people should realize that angels have feelings and acknowledge them, ask them for help, thank them, and "even give our angel a name."

De Stefano's advice on naming a guardian angel was reminiscent of that of many angel therapists as well as of ordinary devotees, like Arthur Young, professor of English and communication at Cabrini College in Pennsylvania. Young described his attachment to an angel named Khalib in *Love Somewhat Incarnate: Angels in Everyday Life,* a short film about angels made by Cabrini religion professor Leonard Primiano and documentary filmmaker Will Luers in 1999. The "Somewhat Incarnate" of the title, taken from a phrase that angel visionary and therapist Penny Wright uses in the film, well expressed the feelings of those who knew that angels were supposed to be immaterial beings but who still wanted to relate to them as distinct personalities with human feelings.

As I have already noted in the chapters on angels in love and angels in the material world, popular songs about angels generally have used angels as a metaphor for transcendent or particularly intense human love, at least until 1998, when the soundtrack for the movie *City of Angels* was released. On that album, Sarah McLachlan's "Angel," the Goo Goo Dolls' "Iris," and U2's "If God Will Send His Angels" all seemed to be written with real angels, rather than girlfriends or boyfriends, in mind. Only one song before this, Jimi Hendrix's "Angel" (posthumously released in 1971) actually dealt with an angel-human romance, though Madonna's witchy and ambiguous "Angel" (1989) came close. As the millennium turned, two more songs linked humans and angels: "Calling All Angels" by Train, which sought help in solving environmental and social woes (as we saw in chapter 1) and "Angels," a 1999 song and music video from English artist Robbie Williams that was turned into a hit by Jessica Simpson in 2004. "Angels" celebrated guardian angels not as romantic lovers, however, but as beings who can help the singer to transcend the world.

The lyrics of "Angels" begin with the singer wondering, "Does an angel contemplate my fate?" That fate includes what will happen to the singer in old age and after death. The singer has heard that human "salvation" is what "lets their wings unfold." The song evokes a person lying in bed isolated, thinking, and deciding that "I'm loving angels instead." Triumphal music accompanies assertions that the angel offers not only "protection" but also "love and affection" whether the singer is "right or wrong." The "instead" of the line about loving angels refers by implication to other lovers and other sources of assurance that the singer has rejected. By "loving angels instead," the singer gains a source of support that will never fail. Even as the singer goes "down the waterfall" of life, the song asserts, angels will keep him or her from being broken, remaining faithful to the end.

At the beginning of Robbie Williams's MTV music video of "Angels," the singer is walking on a roof at night. As he sings about loving angels, he watches drunks and prostitutes and other humans having sex in a terrible urban neighborhood. By the time the song repeats its assertions about angels loving us "right or wrong," and staying through all the "waterfalls" of life, all the people the singer has seen are turning from their previous behavior and flapping their arms like wings, apparently inspired by the song to love angels instead.

Jessica Simpson made no video, but she did the song in many concerts that could be viewed on YouTube (pending copyright infringement actions) in 2007. For her, the lyrics seemed to function as an anthem of her own status as a born-again Christian. The message merged with what the rest of American culture (both evangelical and New Age) was saying: Claim an angel for your own; love angels and so improve your life.

Fairies and Superheroes

If angels seemed too disembodied or theologically serious, American culture began to provide other supernatural beings to serve the same functions. As we have seen, therapists like Doreen Virtue offered communication with ancient goddesses, saints, and even dolphins. Fairies (or "faeries") began after 2000 to proliferate in bookstores and on collectible shelves. Though winged like angels, the origins of fairies among pagan Celts and other European peoples made them more flexible, and especially more flirtatious or mischievous, than biblical spirits. The statues could be scantily dressed rather than gowned. For example, a young American artist a few years out of the University of Toledo, Jessica Galbreth, had a line of Zodiac Fairies in stores in 2006, which were being sold alongside a book featuring Queen Mab and her crew by veteran artist Amy Brown. One of the first new characters and female muppets on *Sesame Street* in thirty-seven years had her debut on August 14, 2006: Abby Cadabby, a pink and fuzzy "fairy godchild" with wings and a magic wand. Greeted with protests from the Campaign for a Commercial Free Childhood and from *New York Daily News* columnist Lenore Skenazy,[27] Abby seemed destined to teach a generation of girls both to stay in touch with their mothers on their cell phones (as Abby often did in her first appearance) and to aspire after magical powers.

Superheroes have been the most dramatic angel equivalents produced by American culture in the past eighty years. Beginning with Superman and extending through Batman, Captain Marvel, Captain America, the Flash, and most recently Hellboy, who is actually a demon fighting for good, superheroes initiated a universe of modern myth that now extends into science fiction and video games. These characters have roots among American Jews, bearers of the same tradition that brought the Persian idea of angelic warfare into the Western world. Almost all of the superheroes were invented by Jewish writers and drawn by Jewish artists.[28] Endowed with special powers because they were refugees from destroyed planets or chosen by mysterious beings, the heroes repeated themes from Jewish history; behind their stories stood Samson and the Golem (a hero brought to life from clay by a medieval rabbi to defend the Jewish people). Even though the American heroes did not begin as angels, they developed more and more angelic powers as the decades passed. The freedom of America allowed for larger dreams, and the advances of technology demanded them.

For example, when Jerry Siegel and Joe Shuster began to write and to draw Superman in 1938, the powers of the Man of Steel were great but also limited. He could not fly, but he could jump a third of a mile at a time. He was not invulnerable, but he could catch artillery shells in his hands and throw the shells back at Nazi U-boats. As the introductory announcer from the television show (which ran from 1953 to 1957, and infinitely after in syndication) used to intone, "Faster than a speeding bullet; more powerful than a locomotive; able to leap tall buildings in a single bound!" After World War II, when DC Comics editor Mort Weisinger took over the direction of Superman comic books, the hero became much more powerful.[29] The television show represented some of these new powers: Superman could now fly, not just jump, and he developed X-ray vision to see through walls. In the comics, with their larger scope for imagination, the Superman of the 1950s and 1960s could now fly through the centers of stars, move planets in or out of their courses, and travel in time by flying faster than the speed of light. The Superman movies that starred Christopher Reeve in the 1970s and 1980s showed him causing time to flow backward, not just for himself but for the whole world. He had the traditional powers of an angel (flying, moving planets, traveling through time) and perhaps even those of a god.

Unlike a god but like an angel, Superman always remained subordinate. His subordination was to higher principles, such as the "Truth, Justice, and the American Way" affirmed by the television introduction, but it was also personal. Superman fell from the sky in a space capsule designed by his father, Jor-El (whose name was another Jewish touch), who launched his son toward Earth in order to preserve him from the destruction of their home planet, Krypton. The baby, named Kal-El, landed in the fields of the Kent family in Kansas—the home territory of angels in America, as we saw in chapter 1—and learned obedience and respect from his human foster parents. As Superman's powers grew in

Superman could only leap tall buildings in the 1930s, but he gained the powers of a guardian angel long before this portrayal by Brandon Routh in Superman Returns *(2006). (Warner Brothers/Photofest)*

later versions, he subordinated himself to other authorities, including editor Perry White of the *Daily Planet* newspaper and his deceased father, who had sent recordings from Krypton to guide his son's progress.

In all of his permutations, Superman functioned as a guardian angel, sometimes for a woman named Lois Lane, the colleague of his alter ego Clark Kent; sometimes for the United States; and sometimes for the entire world. One key aspect of his appeal, and a constant element in his plots, particularly on the television show, was the way that he suddenly appeared to save the day, amazing the tormentors of the good. Such plots recalled stories of angel rescue from popular books and also the biblical stories of Jews in Babylon, where angels had saved Shadrach, Meshach, and Abednego in the fiery furnace and Daniel in the lion's den. Superman's assumption of a secret identity recalled the disguise of the angel Raphael in the biblical book of Tobit. Engaging a range of villains that shifted with the times, Superman fought corrupt politicians, stock manipulators, and fascists in the 1930s and 1940s, communists and generic crooks in the 1950s, supervillains and mad scientist Lex Luthor in the 1960s and 1970s, and the threat of nuclear annihilation in the 1980s. In an issue of DC Comics written by George Perez and Russell Braun that was published in October 1991, just months after an American-led coalition routed Saddam Hussein in the first Gulf War, Superman took part in a complex war that sent a coalition of gods and superheroes against enemies including the goddess Tiamat and her husband Kingu, who were the villains of the Mesopotamian creation story, the *Enuma elish*.

Although Superman has remained the archetype of American superheroes, he has been joined by numerous competitors and collaborators. First came the merely human (but costumed and technologically empowered) Batman, invented by another Jewish American, Bob Kane (born Robert Kahn). Batman's limited powers might have kept him from connecting with the realm of gods and angels, but by the early 1990s his adversaries included Azrael, a product of medical experimentation who was named for the Muslim angel of death, and Ra's Al Ghul ("Demon's Head"), an Arabian scientist. From the beginning, Batman's black cape was intended to evoke the wings of bats and demons.

The closest competitor that Superman ever had was Captain Marvel, arguably a Gentile superhero, who was created by Bill Parker and C.C. Beck, the son of a Lutheran minister. Even this hero had a biblical basis, since the wizard who enabled an American boy named Billy Batson to turn himself into Captain Marvel by saying the word "Shazam" was an Egyptian who had once advised King Solomon. The magic word (also the wizard's name) was an acronym that combined the Bible with gods, humans, and demigods from Greece and Rome: S for Solomon's wisdom, H for the strength of Hercules, A for the stamina of Atlas, Z for the power of Zeus, A for the courage of Achilles, and M for the speed of Mercury. For a few years in the 1940s, Captain Marvel outsold Superman, but the story of a hero from another planet had more staying power than that of a boy who could make himself a hero by magic. Ultimately, despite the enormous differences between the characters, the settlement of Superman's lawsuit for copyright infringement led to Captain Marvel's disappearance in 1953.

Among other first-generation superheroes were the Human Torch, who could turn his body into flame and fly; the Flash, who at first could run at the speed of light and later at ten times that speed; the Green Lantern, who flew with the aid of alien technology; and Hawkman, who flew with enormous wings. The resemblance of these heroes to angels lay not only in their powers, but also in their attitudes. Superheroes were good servants of humanity, humorless and sexless, subject to superior authority and liable to struggle but always victorious in the end. Their opponents resembled demons in that they also had great powers but acted on their own, seeking tyranny or wealth or simply to destroy. A new breed of flawed hero arose in the 1960s, when Stan Lee (born Stanley Lieberman), who had drawn for Marvel Comics as a teenager in the 1930s, took over the company and created superheroes with flaws and doubts.

Lee at first used radiation as the gimmick to give his characters their powers: The Fantastic Four began as astronauts exposed to radiation in space, and Spiderman was a teenager bitten by a radioactive spider. After their transformations, these humans did not always want to use their abilities for good, and even when they began to fight evil they were beset with doubts, jealousies, and simple human needs like money. Despite these more human conditions, however, the tendency for heroes to evolve into angels proved irresistible. Lee created characters like the mighty Thor, a human who became a Norse god by picking up the magic hammer Mjolnir; Doctor Strange, a magician who fought evil on many levels of the spirit; and Galacticus, a cosmic villain who lived by eating planets. Combat and cooperation with such entities pulled Lee's most human heroes into higher realms. Plots involving the concepts of Ragnarok (the Norse apocalypse), the Ring cycle, and the biblical Armageddon became normal in comic books around the year 2000 and after.

With the 1990s came the first directly angelic superheroes. Mike Mignola's Hellboy began as a demonic infant who had been summoned from Hell (the realm of the seven gods of chaos) by the Nazis during the last days of World War II and captured by the Allies. The child decided to stay in the human realm after he tasted pancakes. As an adult, he regularly filed the long curling horns that grew from his head into two nearly flat discs to avoid alarming humans, although his enormous body and flaming red skin still stood out, as did a huge right hand made of stone. He worked for the Bureau of Paranormal Research and Defense guarding the world against attacks from evil spirits who, like him, had taken very physical form on Earth. In a movie version in 2004, Hellboy vanquished Sammael, a demon sometimes equated with Satan in Jewish tradition.

Another angelic hero, Dream, appeared in a series of graphic novels published as *The Sandman* between 1987 and 1996. Dream was also called Morpheus, lord of sleep, and he belonged to a family of seven spirits known as the Endless: Dream, Destiny, Death, Destruction, Desire, Despair, and Delirium. This family engaged in conflicts with each other and in cosmic wars in which many angels struggled to rule Earth and Hell. Alongside the Endless, *The Sandman* featured such familiar fallen angels as Lucifer, Beelzebub, and Azazel, as well as more esoteric angels named Duma (angel of Egypt and of death in the *Zohar* and Yiddish folklore), Remiel (one of the seven archangels on some lists), and Mazikeen (a female descendent of Lilith, the demonic first wife of Adam). Unlike most superhero stories, *The Sandman* series did not center on human concerns; humans played only peripheral roles in rivalries among immortal spirits.

The author of *The Sandman*, Neil Gaiman, formed part of a movement that both fulfilled and expanded the stereotype of the superhero creator. Gaiman is a Jew who makes explicit use of Jewish tradition; he was born in England, but he has married an American and settled in Minnesota. His sophisticated graphic novels are published by the same company, DC (the former Detective Comics of the 1930s), that published the original Superman. In the 1960s and 1970s, DC Comics seemed to have resigned itself to stodginess, giving up the cutting edge to Stan Lee and Marvel. Gaiman formed part of a "Brit wave" of comics creators who worked for DC beginning in the late 1980s, starting with Alan Moore's graphic novel *Watchmen*. Another member of this group, Jamie Delano, wrote the series that emerged from comics into the movie *Constantine* (2004), in which Lucifer helps the human visionary John Constantine to save the world by stripping the angel Gabriel (played by Tilda Swinton) of her angelic powers. Among artists of the Brit wave, the trend toward merging humans, heroes, and angels continued, but the idealism that had motivated heroes from Superman to Hellboy diminished radically. Even the stories of more conventional superheroes became edgier and more cynical, particularly when those stories projected heroes into the future.

For several years in the 1990s, Marvel Comics published a series under the umbrella title of *2099*, featuring future versions of Spider-man, Thor, and other heroes in an America dominated by corporations. Where the Superman of 1950s' television fought "for the American Way," these heroes fought for freedom *against* the U.S. government. The first superheroes arose against a background of the Great Depression, crime, and fascism, with a frightening implicit message that order could only be restored through violence, but the heroes, gods, and angels of century's end lived in an imaginary world so fundamentally flawed that violence seemed preferable to order. Figures like Neil Gaiman's Dream, the red-suited Daredevil, the magical Doctor Strange, and the many spirits and gods of Thor comics showed that comic superheroes could approach both angelic and demonic status at the same time.

Human Angels of Science Fiction

Just as comic books combined art and text to tell stories on a mythic scale, so science-fiction television shows and movies reached the level of myth in the 1960s. The first successes of the space program helped to provoke this development, as did advances in special effects technology and a new cultural freedom to speculate about matters of the spirit. In earlier science fiction, Jules Verne's lunar explorers and their successors in America, such as Buck Rogers and Flash Gordon, rode rockets into stories that stressed human heroism and human triumphs over evil aliens, but now science-fiction heroes broke free of their bodies and gained the ability to materialize instantly at almost any point in space and time. They traveled backward and forward in time, moved and destroyed planets and stars, and interacted with the energy beings they were destined to become. They regularly engaged in conflict over the fate of the universe. In other words, the science-fiction heroes of the 1960s and after approached the powers and status of angels.

First to cross the threshold of angelic power were the crew of the starship *Enterprise* on the original *Star Trek* series. The show ran from 1966 to 1969 and went off the air less than two months before U.S. astronauts first reached the moon. In *Star Trek*, humans practiced angelic morality, vowing to explore and to communicate but not to interfere with alien cultures on pain of death. The show was driven by confidence in technological advance. In an age when the moon was within reach and Mars and the other planets seemed attainable in a few more years, the idea of a united Earth at the center of a Federation of Planets that could send ships to distant parts of the galaxy by the 2200s seemed plausible. Our solar system, the setting for earlier science-fiction stories, became only the local neighborhood.

At the same time, the fiction of *Star Trek* actually drove technological concepts. Harvard dropout Bill Gates (and many other undergraduates) watched Captain Kirk and others on the *Enterprise* talking with computers on their desks and wanted the same for themselves. On late models of the *Enterprise*, computer controls responded not to toggle switches or even to keyboards but to colored screens activated by touch. Members of the crew pulled "communicators" from their pockets, flipped them open with a chirping sound, and spoke over vast distances without wires, prefiguring the cell phone and realizing the dreams of Swedenborg and others about instant communication among the angels. Most importantly, the *Enterprise* crew could move with the speed and stealth of angels, not only by traveling in their ship faster than the speed of light but by "beaming," or teleporting, to the surface of planets as the ship was in orbit. In this process, the molecules and atoms of the travelers were translated into information and sent instantaneously to a place where the "transporter beam" reassembled surrounding matter into the travelers. The effect, accompanied by appropriate musical notes, was that of bodies materializing out of the air, just as in appearances of angels. The combination of these magical visions of technology and the politics of the show proved compelling for Americans long after the initial run of the television series. Not only has the original *Star Trek* continued to this day in syndication, but it gave rise to ten movies and to four new television series that remained on the air in new episodes continuously from 1987 to 2005, with two different series about the *Star Trek* universe running at the same time between 1994 and 1999.

In an article for the *Boston Globe* in 1986, I argued that the original *Star Trek* presented a very Protestant and very American view of the world.[30]

This worldview also resembled that of angel therapists like Doreen Virtue, even though the *Star Trek* vision began without connections to religion. Born from the mind of Gene Roddenberry, a Southern Baptist from El Paso, Texas, who took up secular humanism, the morality of *Star Trek* hinged on the Prime Directive, a rule against interfering with native cultures that bore an uncanny resemblance to the Categorical Imperative of German philosopher Immanuel Kant (1724–1804). Kant decreed that no act could be moral unless it was based on a maxim (or principle) that could be willed as a universal law. Kant also made respect for autonomy, both in oneself and others, a basic moral principle. Angels follow this principle, according to many of the angel therapists who wrote in the 1990s. People are not always helped because angels have to wait until humans ask them to intervene. Both the Prime Directive and the Categorical Imperative prevent interference with others except in cases of dire emergency. As Doreen Virtue wrote, angels could act without permission only in "a life-threatening situation that occurs before it's 'our time' to go."[31] Yet, in practice, whether on the *Enterprise*, in angel stories, or in American foreign policy, occasions for violating these purist rules arose during the *Star Trek* age with amazing frequency. Like angels or U.S. military advisers in Vietnam, members of the *Enterprise* crew were supposed to function as professional emissaries from a distant central power, but they entered into involvements that more closely resembled those of the fallen angels in Genesis 6. Commonly, Captain Kirk saved an alien culture by beating up a male villain and kissing a crucial female. A little later he would dematerialize, vanishing from the surface of the planet to appear again in *Star Trek*'s equivalent of Heaven (the bridge of the *Enterprise*, with its all-seeing viewscreen).

In many of the shows produced after Gene Roddenberry's death in 1991—*The Next Generation* (1987–1994); *Deep Space Nine* (1993–1999); *Voyager* (1995–2001); and *Enterprise* (2001–2005)—religious content became much more explicit as members of the crews went beyond exercising angelic technical powers to play explicitly religious roles. Captain Picard of *The Next Generation* had to live out parts resembling those of Gilgamesh and the sun god Shamash, both from Mesopotamian myth, in order to survive encounters with two different civilizations, one that communicated only through myth and another that died and left behind an interactive museum. Commander Worf, who appeared in two of the *Star Trek* series as a member of the warlike Klingon people, grew from ignorance of Klingon religion to devoted participation in its rituals and its hopes, which included cloning a messiah. Captain Sisko of *Deep Space Nine* functioned as an "emissary" for the people of the planet Bajor because he was chosen by their "prophets," a set of god-like beings who lived outside of time and knew the future. The original series encountered religions only to debunk them (as in an episode in which Kirk fought an alien who had been known on Earth as Apollo), but the later incarnations of *Star Trek* were guided by Rick Berman (an American Jew) into acceptance of many forms of practice and belief. One common denominator among the *Star Trek* religions was the role of technology, in the broadest sense of the root *techne*, meaning art or skill. All of the religions that survived into the future on *Star Trek*, from the Vulcan meditation of Mr. Spock and others to the use of Bajoran orbs of prophecy, involved techniques with real effects on the physical world. On its travels through the twenty-third and twenty-fourth centuries, Starfleet neither included nor encountered any Jews, Christians, or Muslims who simply prayed, kept their holidays, and read their scriptures out of faith in an invisible God.

Star Trek became most angelic when dealing with the ultimate destiny of humanity. On several occasions in the last two series, *Voyager* and *Enterprise,* the crews of the starships encountered colleagues from the twenty-ninth century, when management of the timeline had become the purpose of Starfleet. The final episodes of *The Next Generation* involved a long-retired Captain Picard solving a temporal anomaly that threatened to destroy humanity, with a climax in which versions of the *Enterprise* from three different times came together. Beyond all such crises, people were apparently destined to become beings of pure energy (as in angel books by Doreen Virtue and Sophy Burnham and in *The Celestine Prophecy*). This transformation was foreshadowed in many episodes going back to the original series, and especially in stories from *The Next Generation* involving a being called simply "the Traveler" and his interactions with teenager Wesley Crusher. When *Star Trek* showed energy beings, they were generally shapes of light that flew in the manner of abstract angels.

The human race also evolved into energy beings in the conclusion of *Babylon 5*, a science-fiction series that aired from 1993 to 1998. Before that transformation occurred, *Babylon 5* showed humans and other material forms of sentient life battling demonic beings called "Shadows," aided by mysterious "Vorlons," who hid their powerful brightness in "encounter suits" but sometimes appeared as angels of light. In *Stargate SG-1*, a series that began in 1997 and continues in 2007, ordinary soldiers from the contemporary United States go to planets across the galaxy by means of "gates" through time and space left by an ancient race. Caught up in cosmic war as they use their angelic power to travel instantly, these American soldiers have fought a race that was once worshipped as the Egyptian gods and a form of demonic energy beings called "the Wraith." They have found allies in the "Asgardians," a species that has appeared as Norse gods. One of the American soldiers has "ascended" into the dimension where those who made the stargates now dwell.

In all of these dreams of superheroes and science fiction, Americans have expressed their faith in progress and perfectibility. Though we plod through life on knees that need replacement, filling our arteries with cholesterol and challenging our lungs and livers with tobacco and alcohol, someday we will travel faster than light. People like us will dissolve into beams of energy and reassemble, or perhaps even live as pure energy, traveling the cosmos with no need of a vehicle. As with the superheroes who grew darker toward century's end, however, science-fiction versions of transformation revealed a negative potential.

According to *The Matrix* (1999) and its successors, human destiny involves our transformation from flesh and blood to information, bundles of data within a vast simulation run by artificially intelligent computers that use human bodies as batteries. Within the simulation, people who know the secret can operate as avatars, flying and enjoying the near-invulnerability of angels. They fight "agents" of the computers, avatars who are demonic in their complete emptiness of everything except hatred for humanity. The creators of *The Matrix*, the Wachowski brothers of Chicago, expanded the angelic and demonic existence of avatars from computer games into the world of large-scale spectacle.

Although the long series of *Star Wars* movies (the first three of which appeared in 1977, 1980, and 1983, and the last three in 1999, 2002, and 2005) did not show humanity evolving into energy beings, angelic and demonic themes also figured in the vision of George Lucas, who wrote and produced that epic. The two sides of the conflict, the Jedi and the

Sith, consisted of material beings (not all human) who manipulated matter with an invisible and at least partly spiritual energy called "the Force." The Jedi focus on the light side of the Force by using meditation techniques, and Sith focus on the dark side, which is accessible through anger and hatred. In a sense, all six movies culminated in the creation of a satanic figure, Darth Vader, who began as a powerful Jedi and went over to the dark side. The ultimate message of the series, that the Force has to be rebalanced by Darth Vader and his son Luke Skywalker, implied a science-fiction version of the redemption of Satan. The third-century Christian theologian Origen was charged by his opponents with having proposed Satan's redemption as the end of the Christian story, but that proposition was condemned by the Second Council of Constantinople in 553 and has rarely been defended since.[32]

Redeeming Lucifer

Sympathy for the Devil—not in the sarcastic sense of the Rolling Stones' 1969 hit song, where Satan remained a figure of unmitigated evil, but as a serious proposition that no spirit, including Satan or Lucifer, should be understood as lost forever—has become a common theme of American culture over the past few decades. In 1988, the Catholic priest, novelist, and sociologist Andrew Greeley had a female angel named Gabriella exclaim to the human she guarded that "Lucifer was not a demon, he was a good spirit, he never defied the Most High, he was brilliant and kind. . . . And deeply devout."[33] She urged humans to trust the book of Job, where Satan is one of the "sons of God," rather than "Iranian mythology" and John Milton, the seventeenth-century British author of *Paradise Lost*. Gabriella's passion on this subject in Greeley's novel, *Angel Fire*, arose from her marriage to Lucifer, who had died in the sort of accident that could kill the highly evolved, energy beings that humans call angels.

According to *Ask Your Angels* (1992), which provided more elaborate instructions for meditation than any other book in the angel-therapy genre, angels told authors Alma Daniel, Timothy Wyllie, and Andrew Ramer that Lucifer had simply accepted God's call for volunteers to "go down to Earth and help strengthen humanity's spiritual resolve by offering constant temptation." Lucifer had "loving intentions"—in fact, he began as the "guardian of the planet Venus," the planet of love. His mission was simply "to teach us about the necessary dark side of life," and people should understand "Christ and Lucifer" as spirits "on the same side, integral parts of the same whole."[34] Meanwhile, at the movies, both *The Prophecy* (1995) and *Constantine* (2004) showed Lucifer helping to save humanity from evil versions of the angel Gabriel (played by Christopher Walken and Tilda Swinton, respectively), who has become destructive out of frustration with the inconclusive war in Heaven.

On the Web, a young artist named Allison A. Carmichael draws comics (available at www.mangapunksai.com) that split Lucifer and Satan, presenting Lucifer as a foppish rebel with attitude and Satan as an earnest young angel assigned to keep Lucifer and his friend Azrael in Hell. The tone is frequently light. In a Christmas special from 2004, Lucifer and Azrael escape to Earth to steal eggnog and candy from a convenience store, but they find when they succeed that the fires of Hell spoil the eggnog and melt the candy. Often the series plays with gender, as when Michael becomes enraged with Lucifer's suggestion that he and Gabriel are lovers, or when artist Carmichael draws herself into a strip in which she makes Satan female, much to his embarrassment and Lucifer's delight. And yet the thirty-page comic that started the series, *The Story from Hell*, offers a serious reinterpretation. Lucifer revolted because of God's violence against people, who were made weak so that they would offer slavish devotion and also sin, so provoking wrath. According to Lucifer, God made humanity only in order to receive adulation and exercise power. Although Satan believes he is doing God's will by tormenting damned humans and keeping Lucifer imprisoned, he has not seen God for thousands of years and has begun to doubt. A similar but more sophisticated sympathetic account of Lucifer and the origins of Hell appeared in the novel *Memnoch the Devil* (1996), one of many bestsellers by Anne Rice. Because that story centered on sex, I considered it more fully in chapter 5.

Alongside sympathy and humor, belief in Satan and in his relevance to politics has prevailed in America since World War II. When playwright Arthur Miller wrote *The Crucible* in 1952, he clearly intended his play about the witch trials at Salem as a metaphor for the McCarthy hearings about Communist infiltration. Miller's play teaches that such witch hunts are themselves morally wrong, but many Americans during the Cold War actually believed that Satan was at work in communism as he had been in Hitler. During the 1980s, following a time in which *The Exorcist* had packed American movie theaters, and in which children with "recovered memories" had charged their caregivers with satanic ritual abuse, almost 70 percent of Americans were ready to believe in Satan and witches. The collapse of that scare over witchcraft caused belief in Satan to recede to 55 percent by 1994, but it returned to 70 percent by 2004, probably as one effect of the War on Terror.[35] Immediately after the attacks of September 11, 2001, pictures appeared on the Web showing a demon, sometimes identified as Satan, in the clouds rolling out of the World Trade Center. Searching Google Images under "world trade center devil" still reveals such pictures nearly six years later.

Throughout the 1990s, television host Pat Robertson of *The 700 Club*, the founder of the Christian Coalition, popularized a worldview centered on conflict between the United States and Satan. In 1991, Robertson wrote, "The Persian Gulf War has now brought into sharp focus the great cleavage that has existed in the human race since the early beginnings of civilization in the Tigris-Euphrates Valley," where Robertson located the Garden of Eden. That cleavage separated "those who build monuments to humanity under the inspiration of Satan" from the people of God, who follow "the Abrahamic, monotheistic tradition." Robertson expected Satan to use a charismatic leader, the Antichrist, to bring the world together under the United Nations and the World Bank. With the unbelieving world united, he said, "Satan will launch a war against the Christian people." Four fallen angels, now bound "at the mouth of the river Euphrates" (Rev. 9:14), would be loosed to slay a third of the human race, fulfilling the hopes for a smaller population that Robertson attributed to New Age ecologists. Although the return of Christ would finally defeat the satanic powers, Robertson hoped for a partial victory before Armageddon. He worked and spoke and began political organizations in order to insure that America would remain free of the world coalition. "With America still free and at large, Satan's schemes will at best be only partially successful," Robertson wrote. "An independent America could point out Satan's lies." Those who find these visions ridiculous should take note of their effects on politics. Robertson's hope that a coalition against "one-world globalism" would produce "a pro-freedom majority in the United States Senate in 1992, and a reversal of leadership in the House of Representatives by 1996" appear to have succeeded.[36]

After 2001, as we saw in chapter 6, not only evangelists but soldiers like Lieutenant General William Boykin saw themselves as fighting for the United States against Satan. Preachers now detected Satan's influence not only in humanism but also in Islam. Southern Baptist pastor Jerry Vines of Jacksonville, Florida, a former president of the Southern Baptist Convention, notoriously preached at that denomination's 2002 annual meeting that the Prophet Muhammad's claim to revelation and his marriage to the nine-year-old Ayesha showed that he was "a demon-possessed pedophile."[37] John Hagee, the pastor of the 18,000-member Cornerstone Church in San Antonio, Texas, quoted the Qur'an in 2006 to support his contention that "the god of Islam works with Satan and demons to lead people astray in order to populate the hell he created (Surah 6:39, 126; 32:13; 43:36–37)." Hagee predicted a battle of Armageddon in which "the satanic trinity consisting of Satan, his chief son the Antichrist, and the demonized spiritual leader called the false prophet" would lead many nations, including the United States, to war on the soil of Israel.[38]

At times the whole political and cultural discourse of the United States seemed to fall into a pattern of satanic rhetoric. In late September 2006, Jerry Falwell, the late pastor of Liberty Baptist Church and founder of Liberty University, told the crowd at a Values Voter Summit in Washington, D.C., that he hoped Senator Hillary Clinton would be the Democratic nominee for president in 2008 because nothing would energize his constituency more. "If Lucifer ran" for president, he wouldn't have the same impact as Senator Clinton, according to Falwell.[39] On that same September Sunday, the *New York Times* ran an op-ed piece by Frank Rich claiming that in Iraq, although the United States claimed to oppose an evil ideology in the name of civilization, we were in fact cooperating with Shi'ite militias and so "handing the very devil the keys" to Baghdad.[40] Such statements reflected a culture of dualistic thinking that also appeared in reality shows and energized the shouting news commentators of radio and cable television. During a casual discussion of presidential prospects with *Newsweek* editor Howard Feinman on October 11, 2006, then nationally syndicated radio host Don Imus exclaimed that Hillary Clinton was "Satan," later concurring with one of his staff that "she has the horns, she has the cape."

According to French theorist René Girard, the power of Satan emerged when the rivalries that naturally arose in human societies were carried to a point at which an execution of one person by the group (understood as ritual murder or human sacrifice) was necessary to restore order. After the ritual, which gradually developed less violent forms such as animal sacrifice, exorcism, and tragic or horrific drama, people went home satisfied, feeling that evil had been purged from the community. Then the tension of rivalries again rose to the point at which release was necessary, when Satan again appeared in some form and needed to be expelled.[41]

A similar mechanism of rivalries and rituals of expulsion seemed to be at work in the discourse about angels and Satan in America during the early 2000s. For evangelicals like Terry Law, John Loren Sandford, and some writers in *Christianity Today* magazine, New Age writers on angels were stealing biblical themes and using them to spread demonic ideas. New Age writers, in turn, accused evangelicals of succumbing to an "illusion of fear and loathing" and projecting their own "negativity onto a fictitious devil, or fallen angels, or onto other people."[42]

Some of the scholars who studied New Age and evangelical influence in America reinforced the sense of rivalry. According to Diana Eck, founder of the Harvard Pluralism Project, the New Age designated a broad and important "way of thinking and living that tries to break free of the dualistic opposition of science and spirit, outer and inner, body and mind." In an assertion that would fulfill the darkest evangelical fears, Eck stated that by the year 2000, New Age thinking and action had "gradually saturated the whole of American culture with essentially Hindu, more broadly Asian, ideas without speaking of them as such."[43] On the other side of the question, sociologists Roger Finke and Rodney Stark concluded in their 1992 book (and in their revised edition of 2005) that the New Age was "more of an amusement than a religion." Far from justifying the attention paid to it by scholars and the fears of evangelicals, they said the New Age had no more impact than "an audience cult"; it was a set of "pseudoscientific activities and techniques" that affected people about as much as "reading astrology columns."[44] As Stark developed his theory further in his later books, including *One True God* (2003) and *For the Glory of God* (2004), he argued that only monotheism could generate religious movements that changed the world.

With regard to angels, perspectives like that of Lynn Schofield Clark in *From Angels to Aliens* may point a way past this dualism. Clark called interest in the supernatural the "dark side of evangelicalism"; but perhaps interest in angels also represents the light (or the evangelical and/or Christian) side of the New Age. The intense marketing of angels brings to mind another recent book, David Chidester's *Authentic Fakes: Religion and American Popular Culture* (2005). Chidester has no index entry for "angels" but posited that popular culture does real "religious work," not simply attracting audiences but also providing both the "opiate" of which Marx complained and the prophetic, transcendent word of the prophets.[45] Angels—especially when broadly understood to include the angels of movies and songs, the superheroes of comics, and the heroes of science-fiction stories—are certainly the most eminent idols and icons of the past seven decades. The angels of the marketplace function as idols and icons both in the negative sense of those words for evangelical Protestants and in the positive senses that they have for Hindus and Orthodox Christians.

Coalescence and Empire

Just as the technologies of the nineteenth century, such as the telegraph, photography, and the telephone, affected that era's perception of spirits, so the motion picture, the comic book, the television, the computer, and space exploration have affected ours.[46] Our yearnings for spiritual power have grown to remain ahead of our physical techniques. Because evangelicals, New Age thinkers, conventional believers, and secularized Americans share the same technologies, they feel the attractions of similar dreams. An evangelical may reject the magical travel of "whitelighters" on *Charmed* but enjoy the faster-than-light flying of Superman or the transporter beam of *Star Trek*. A secular or New Age American may reject the angel visions of General Boykin and Roland Buck or the warnings of Pat Robertson but enjoy the visions of war with angels and demons in *The Prophecy* or *Constantine*.[47]

As sociologist Emile Durkheim suggested a century ago, people who share a political and social structure tend to share the same religion. This phenomenon seems to shape the contemporary American cult of angels. Religions are both systems of nonrational commitments that hold life together and networks of relationships, as I have argued in chapter 1 and elsewhere,[48] and so religions change in order to hold life together under specific conditions, including politics. In the days of the Persian and Greek empires, angels proliferated in ancient Israelite religion. The many powers of Heaven corresponded to the many powers that buffeted Israel. Those who live in empires tend to be prolific in imagining angels and hierarchies of spirits: The people of Persia, China, medieval Islam, and nineteenth-century Britain all have done so. Angels are messengers, and as my college-age son has reminded me, empires need good postal services.

The empire in which Americans live today is not simply an American empire, but something more like the international order that Pat Robertson feared in 1991. The U.S. government may hold most of the world's executive power by virtue of its worldwide military presence, but it remains subject to checks on the highest level by the G8 nations and the UN Security Council, as Michael Hardt and Antonio Negri argued in *Empire* (2000). According to Hardt and Negri, economic organizations like the World Bank, the Organization of the Petroleum Exporting Countries, and international corporations operate as a kind of Roman Senate in the world's de facto government, directing the executive and seeking stability for trade and wealth, while international networks like the Roman Catholic Church, the Red Cross, Amnesty International, Greenpeace, and some news organizations and celebrities try to represent the common people and the common interests of the world.[49]

In such an international and decentralized empire, angels have become dramatically multicultural. American movie audiences have seen the Persian *fravashi* in *Crash*, the Muslim angel of death Azrael in *Dogma* (renamed Asphodel in *A Prairie Home Companion*), and the Assyrian demon Pazuzu in *The Exorcist*. Doreen Virtue's Angel Oracle Cards topped the best-seller list in Australia, and her 2005 book took her there to encounter the spirits of dolphins. For the past decade, American young people have watched Japanese *anime* featuring evil angels who attack the Earth (*Neon Genesis Evangelion*), a modern schoolgirl fighting demons in medieval Japan (*Inuyasha*), and spirits who personify Christian deadly sins like Lust, Wrath, and Gluttony (*Full Metal Alchemist*).

Some of the angels of recent times have brought explicitly globalist messages. According to Gordon Davidson, an investment guru who founded socially responsible mutual funds and worked for years at the United Nations, daily meditation in the UN chapel led him to sense the presence of a spirit. Davidson testified that he felt "an Avatar of Synthesis" whose purpose was to "focus energy on the United Nations General Assembly, to assist the efforts of humanity in . . . strengthening a slowly growing will to unity."[50] Ted Turner, the inventor of Cable News Network, developed a cartoon show about a superhero, named Captain Planet, who serves as a flying crusader against ecological crime. According to the official website of the show, he is "a composite of the five Planeteers"—that is, children from each of five continents (Africa, Europe, Asia, and North and South America) who have been given magic rings and special powers by Gaia, the spirit of the Earth. In each adventure, they fight "eco-villains." The television series ceased production in 1993, but as global warming threatens to drown or bake the world, this superhero may regain his relevance.

American Angel Theories

As in so many other fields of thought, the American philosopher and pioneer psychologist William James, who died in 1910, anticipated this global way of thinking about supernatural beings. In *A Pluralistic Universe* (1909), James noted that "men have always made fables about angels, dwelling in the light, needing no earthly food or drink, messengers between ourselves and God." Now science had revealed the planets as such beings, James said; Earth was a planet of great beauty in which all the elements affected each other and us. "Yes! the earth is our great common guardian angel, who watches over all our interests combined," he concluded.[51] Angels suited James's argument that concrete experience demanded an account of the universe that included not just one but a plurality of spirits beyond humanity. Almost a century after James, the Gaia hypothesis—the notion that Earth acts as a single organism—attained enough popularity for *People* magazine to name Gaia one of the twenty-five most interesting people of 1989, and a theologian named Lawrence Osborn called Gaia an angel without noting that James had this idea first.[52]

Another important American philosopher, Mortimer Adler (1902–2001), made angels the center of his approach to anthropology and political thought. Adler was a partially self-taught child prodigy of a philosopher who was awarded a Columbia doctorate after teaching there without a high school diploma or bachelor's degree in the 1920s. He went in 1930 to the University of Chicago, where his neo-Thomist approach found a sympathetic reception. This approach was a form of philosophy most often practiced among Catholics, following Thomas Aquinas, and drew from the work of classical philosophers, especially Aristotle. Adler first wrote on angels in 1945, when he was working with Robert Hutchins, then president of the University of Chicago, on an index to the collection of great books they were publishing. Out of 102 "great ideas" indexed in their fifty-four volumes of Great Books of the Western World, Adler listed "Angel" as the first by alphabetical order. He recalled that Senator William Benton, who then served as president of the Encyclopedia Britannica company, which was publishing the collection, was "flabbergasted" and even "in a temper" about the choice. Hutchins and others on the editorial board also proved "querulous" about including "Angel" as a great idea, but Adler persisted.[53] He wrote a 5,000-word essay on the idea and found references to angels that ran to nine closely printed, double-column pages in the index of the great books, from Homer to Freud, which comprised the set. In the essay, Adler argued that angels were useful as concepts to illuminate "discussions of God and man, of matter, mind, and soul, of knowledge and love, and even of time, space, and motion," whether one believed in the existence of angels or not.[54]

After the Great Books of the Western World and their two-volume index, or "Syntopicon," beginning with Angel, were finally published in 1952—an event that spawned great books discussion groups in libraries across the country—Adler lectured on angels occasionally, including a talk to designers working on angel figurines for Steuben Glass. When a lecture at the Aspen Institute in 1978 drew a large audience—Adler called it "an audience larger than any I have ever enjoyed in the last thirty years"—he decided to write a book on the subject. *The Angels and Us* first appeared in 1982 and came out again during the angel craze of 1993. As the title implied, the book focused on what angels could tell us about reality and humanity. The concept of mind without body fascinated Adler, as did the related ideas of motion without continuous travel through space and knowledge without sensation. He clearly explained the philosophy of Thomas Aquinas and others on these matters, relating angels to quantum physics and modern psychology.

The practical climax of Adler's book was a critique of "angelistic fallacies in modern thought." These fallacies, he said, consisted in expecting people to practice a disembodied ethics, following Kant and Descartes and Plato, rather than what Adler saw as the more realistic anthropology of Aristotle and Aquinas, who described humanity as "predominantly a corporeal substance" only touching the incorporeal by virtue of a small part of the intellect. In contrast with angels, a human being was "dependent on a body for its operation."[55] Led by his philosophical research, Adler changed his identification as a self-described "pagan" (or a very secular Jew) to be baptized as an Episcopalian in 1984; he continued his spiritual journey by converting to Roman Catholicism at the age of ninety-seven, in December 1999.[56] Because Adler was resolutely Thomistic in his concept of angels, supporting Aquinas even against other medieval thinkers by insisting that angels were entirely incorporeal, he worked against the trend of Americans to endow angels with bodies. And yet, he was very American in emphasizing the practicality of angels for human purposes and their importance as a topic for serious consideration.

William James and Mortimer Adler were joined at the end of the twentieth century by many Americans who advanced bolder theories about angels. Priest and novelist Andrew Greeley included angels who were energy beings among the characters of his novels starting in 1988, as described in chapter 5. Though Greeley's angel Gabriella spent most of her time explaining the physics and biology of her species and using them to make love with Greeley's hero and kill his enemies, she was also believer enough to be pleased when the hero began to pray. Gabriella had never seen God, but she did love patterns, including those of the Catholic faith.[57]

Angel theories made more extensive use of science during the 1990s. As I mentioned at the end of chapter 2, Donald Cowan, a physicist and professor at the University of Dallas, speculated that angels might be forms of awareness inhabiting "that original void, that nothingness out of which the world was made." Since this void has not disappeared, but continues to permeate the universe, angels "might get around easily in it, able to transpose instantly to any target locus, according to their mission." Such angels would not be evolutionary products of our system like Greeley's energy beings, who were limited to the speed of light and so in a way less angelic than the explorers of *Star Trek.* Instead, Cowan wrote, they would be sets of positive or negative quanta that preceded the emergence of our energy and matter, "and hence angels are not subject to gravity nor limited by the speed of light as we are." Cowan drew globalist, multicultural arguments from his theory, concluding that "angels in other lands, times, and cultures . . . are not simply *like* our own but indeed *are* our own." He challenged readers of a 1994 anthology on angels to study the angels of other cultures, so that they might "unify all these signals from the spiritual inner space that permeates all existence."[58] Writing in the same anthology, poet and University of Texas professor Frederick Turner posited angels as creatures of the future. Because they were our descendants, angels were properly pictured as children "winged with incalculable power and complexity of purpose," visiting us in their past to nurture an evolutionary process that has only begun to attain self-consciousness. Evolutionary angelology was a central assertion of *Angels: Ministers of Grace* (1988) by Geddes MacGregor, an emeritus professor of philosophy at the University of Southern California. MacGregor hoped that considering angels as our evolutionary superiors might help people find their way between thinking of themselves as God's ultimate achievement or as an utterly independent "exercise in survival."[59]

In *The Physics of Angels* (1996), a former Dominican monk and later Episcopal priest named Matthew Fox, who pioneered a movement called Creation Spirituality, teamed with biologist Rupert Sheldrake in a dialogue on how passages on angels from Dionysius the Areopagite, Thomas Aquinas, and Hildegard of Bingen could combine with modern science to contribute to a new cosmology. Fox built on the idea of Aquinas that an angel was not in a place but inhabited space by acting on it, so that the place was contained in the angel as the human body is contained in the soul. Both he and Sheldrake saw this way of conceiving the relation of angels to space as analogous to the scientific concept of the field, as in gravitational and electromagnetic fields.[60] If the entire cosmos is conceived as the field of action in which God constantly gives being to matter and energy, individual angels might be sent as the mediators of God's action to each place in the cosmos.

All of these mixtures of angelology with scientific theory have led me to recall a theory of my own from several years ago, when I was working on some (still unpublished) alternative versions of Bible stories. Considering the angels who swarm through accounts of creation and judgment from Job through the book of Revelation, I noted then that angels could be the expressions of divine power bringing each moment of time and space into existence. Each angel could therefore connect time with eternity, conscious of the whole and of one other moment, the particular moment to which that particular angel is sent. Angels would not need or have continuous memories, though they could become perfectly aware of any moment at will. Fallen angels could be those who freely chose to reject the pattern of creation, to break from their awareness of the whole and to concentrate on their own moment, so that they know only themselves and the missions of destruction that they chose. As John Milton had Lucifer observe in *Paradise Lost,* wherever "I fly is Hell; myself am Hell," and "The mind is its own place, and in itself / Can make a Heav'n of Hell, a Hell of Heav'n."[61] While such beings might move from one moment in space and time to another, attempting to draw people into their choice, they could neither regain the vision of the whole by their own power nor be forced to do so, at least if the integrity of their creation and their will as intellectual beings was to be respected. For these angels to be redeemed by God, their paths from eternity into time would have to be destroyed and recreated so that they could be sent again on the missions they refused. But would they then be the same angels?

Humans could play a key role in this story. As creatures limited to continuous movement through a certain span of space and time, but endowed with continuous memory and the potential to passively receive an awareness of the whole, humans could become the media whereby fallen angels are restored. Each fallen angel who entered the soul of a human would, at the moment when that human attained the beatific vision, have an opportunity to see the whole again. In the classic *Cur Deus Homo* (c. 1000), St. Anselm of Canterbury argued that humans were made to replace the fallen angels. Perhaps we were also made as lifeboats to make their return possible.

Paul Klee's Angelus Novus *(1920) inspired Walter Benjamin with pessimistic European reflections on history. Oil transfer and watercolor on paper. 31.8 x 24.2 cm. (The Israel Museum, Jerusalem. Gift of Fania and Gershom Scholem, Jerusalem; John Herring, Marlene and Paul Herring, Jo Carole and Ronald Lauder, New York. Copyright Artists Rights Society (ARS), New York/VG Bild-Kunst, Bonn)*

A Serenity angel ornament, designed by Ceal Bialobrzeski, expresses an American faith in the future. (Photograph by William Gardella)

Though Origen was accused of teaching that Satan would eventually be saved, he denied the charge, and he surely never proposed a theory as optimistic and human-centered as mine. However mercenary or sentimental American uses of angels may have appeared in the course of this book, Americans have generally retained this spirit of practical optimism. A final contrast between European and American culture may make this point more concretely.

Among the greatest angel artists of the twentieth century was a Swiss named Paul Klee (1879–1940), who made line sketches and paintings of angels that far surpassed Andy Warhol's in sophistication and wit. Klee's *Angelus Novus* appealed to Walter Benjamin, the Austrian thinker who committed suicide when he was thwarted in his attempt to flee the Nazis in 1940. Benjamin saw this message in *Angelus Novus:*

> A Klee painting named "Angelus Novus" shows an angel looking as though he is about to move away from something he is fixedly contemplating. His eyes are staring, his mouth is open, his wings are spread. This is how one pictures the angel of history. His face is turned toward the past. Where we perceive a chain of events, he sees one single catastrophe which keeps piling wreckage and hurls it in front of his feet. The angel would like to stay, awaken the dead, and make whole what has been smashed. But a storm is blowing in from Paradise; it has got caught in his wings with such a violence that the angel can no longer close them. The storm irresistibly propels him into the future to which his back is turned, while the pile of debris before him grows skyward. This storm is what we call progress.[62]

In contrast to this tragic and expressive European pessimism, Americans in 2007 can find in many gift shops and on many websites a Christmas ornament or pin from the Serenity angels collection, produced by Seasons of Cannon Falls based in Cannon Falls, Minnesota, called *Angel of the Future*. A thin female in pewter with a long gown and large wings, the angel was designed by Ceal Bialobrzeski, who is said to be "inspired by her childhood guardian angel."[63] *Angel of the Future* has a quotation from Eleanor Roosevelt inscribed on her skirt: "The future belongs to those who believe in the beauty of their dreams." For better and for worse, from Pat Robertson and General Boykin to Tony Kushner, Superman, and the Hallmark stores, that is the message of the American religion of angels.

Notes

CHAPTER 1. USEFUL SPIRITS OF AMERICAN CULTURE

1. Doreen Virtue, *Angel Therapy: Healing Messages for Every Area of Your Life* (Carlsbad, CA: Hay House, 1997), 217.

2. The comparison to Albertus Magnus comes from an account of recent philosophical thinking and neuroscience in Larissa MacFarquhar, "Two Heads," *The New Yorker*, February 12, 2007, 60.

3. Diana Eck, *A New Religious America: How a "Christian Country" Has Become the World's Most Religiously Diverse Nation* (San Francisco: HarperSanFrancisco, 2001), 77.

4. Elizabeth Reis, "The Trouble with Angels," *Common-place: The Interactive Journal of Early American Life* 1, no. 3 (April 2001), http://www.common-place.org/vol-01/no-03/reis/ [October 18, 2005].

5. Charlton T. Lewis and Charles Short, *A Latin Dictionary* (1879; Oxford: Clarendon Press, 1969), 1556.

6. William James, *The Varieties of Religious Experience* (1902), Lecture Two.

7. Clifford Geertz, *The Interpretation of Cultures* (New York: Basic Books, 1973), 87–125; Robert Orsi, *Between Heaven and Earth: The Religious Worlds People Make and the Scholars Who Study Them* (Princeton, NJ: Princeton University Press, 2005), 2–5.

8. Peter Gardella, *Domestic Religion: Work, Food, Sex and Other Commitments* (Cleveland, OH: Pilgrim Press, 1998), 1–5.

9. Robert N. Bellah, "Civil Religion in America," *Daedalus* (Winter 1967).

10. Colleen McDannell, *The Christian Home in Victorian America* (Bloomington: Indiana University Press, 1986); Gardella, *Domestic Religion*.

11. For conservative Protestants, see A. C. Gaebelein, *The Angels of God* (Grand Rapids, MI: Baker Book House, 1924), and Ron Rhodes, *Angels among Us* (Eugene, OR: Harvest House, 1994). For conservative Catholics, see James D. Collins, *The Thomistic Philosophy of the Angels* (Washington, DC: Catholic University of America Press, 1947). For Jews, see Morris R. Margolies, *A Gathering of Angels: Angels in Jewish Life and Literature* (New York: Ballantine, 1994). For Muslims, a popular book in the United States is Shayk 'Abdu'l-Hamid Kishk, *The World of the Angels* (London: Dar Al-Taqwa, 1994).

12. For Swedenborgians, see Emanuel Swedenborg, *Heaven and Hell*, translated by George F. Dole, introduction by Bernhard Lang (West Chester, PA:

Swedenborg Foundation, 2000). For the Church Universal and Triumphant, see Elizabeth Clare Prophet, *Fallen Angels and the Origins of Evil* (Corwin Springs, MT: Summit University Press, 2000).

13. For exorcists, see Michael Cuneo, *American Exorcism: Expelling Demons in the Land of Plenty* (New York: Doubleday, 2001). For Satanism, see the chapter "Satan in the Suburbs" in John Godwin, *Occult America* (New York: Doubleday, 1973), 229–251, and for a more recent account Bill Ellis, *Raising the Devil: Satan, New Religions, and the Media* (Lexington: University Press of Kentucky, 2000).

14. Oscar W. McConkie, *Angels* (Salt Lake City: Deseret, 1975).

15. Gustav Davidson, *A Dictionary of Angels* (New York: Free Press, 1967), 20.

16. Max Weber, "Science as a Vocation," 1919, in H. H. Gerth and C. Wright Mills, eds., *From Max Weber* (New York: Oxford University Press, 1958).

17. James Robert Parish, *Ghosts and Angels in Hollywood Films: Plots, Critiques, Casts and Credits for 264 Theatrical and Made-for-Television Releases* (Jefferson, NC: McFarland, 1994).

18. Lewis and Short, *Latin Dictionary*, 1066.

19. See http://www.census.gov/population/www/pop-profile/geomob.html [January 2, 2006].

CHAPTER 2. ANGELS IN THE MATERIAL WORLD

1. Steven May, "Abbott Thayer: The Nature of Art," National Museum of American Art, Washington, DC, http://www.antiquesandthearts.com/archive/thayer.htm [January 4, 2007].

2. Peter Gardella, *Innocent Ecstasy: How Christianity Gave America an Ethic of Sexual Pleasure* (New York: Oxford University Press, 1985).

3. See http://planetdiablo.com/diablo/act/story [January 4, 2007].

4. See http://www.mangapunksai.com [January 4, 2007].

5. All three volumes by Allen and Linda Anderson, published by New World Library. See http://www.angelanimals.net [January 5, 2007].

6. Badr Azimabadi, *The World of Angels* (New Delhi: Adam Publishers, 2002), 24.

7. See http://www.willowtree.info/interview.html [January 5, 2007].

8. Personal e-mail communication from Karen Lordi, March 14, 2007.

9. See http://www.cecsa.org/newsletters/20050524.pdf [January 5, 2007].

10. See http://www.preciousmoments.com/content.cfm/precious_moments_history_timeline [January 5, 2007].

11. See http://www.preciousmoments.com/content.cfm/park_chapel [January 4, 2007].

12. See http://www.aspecialgift.com/Pavillion_Gift/kneeded_angels_1 .asp [July 18, 2006].

13. Leigh Eric Schmidt, *Consumer Rites: The Buying and Selling of American Holidays* (Princeton, NJ: Princeton University Press, 1995), 97–102.

14. "Facts about Hallmark Cards, Inc.," http://pressroom.hallmark.com/ hmk_fact_sheet_html [March 14, 2006].

15. Morris B. Margolies, *A Gathering of Angels* (New York: Ballantine, 1994).

16. Nancy V. Workman, "From Victoria to Victoria's Secret: The Foundations of Modern Erotic Wear," *Journal of Popular Culture* 30 (Fall 1996), 61–73. See also Shaun Frentner, "Victoria's Secret," http://www.bookrags.com/ history/popculture/victorias-secret-sjpc–05.html [July 15, 2006].

17. See http://www.toospoiledfashion.com/victorias_secret_is_too_spoiled [July 14, 2006].

18. Ross Bainbridge, "A Look at Roman Seraphim Angels," http://www .figurine-dot.com/articles/A_Look_at_Roman_Seraphim_Angels.html [March 25, 2006].

19. See http://corporate.americangreetings.com/aboutus.html [January 5, 2007].

20. David Chidester, *Authentic Fakes: Religion and American Popular Culture* (Berkeley: University of California Press, 2005), 61–64; Roland Barthes, *Mythologies* (French 1957; English ed, New York: Hill and Wang, 1972).

21. Joan Wester Anderson, "Miracle at Wal-Mart," copyright 2004, http:// www.ibelieveinangels.com/Angel-Stories/Miracle-at-Wal-Mart–27.html [April 18, 2006].

22. Howard Finster, as told to Tom Patterson, *Howard Finster, Stranger from Another World: Man of Visions Now on This Earth* (New York: Abbeville Press, 1989), 33–35.

23. John Foster, "Smudging the Edges: Folk Art Goes Commercial," *Folk Art Messenger* 16, no. 1 (Spring 2003), http://www.folkart.org/mag/foster/foster .htm [July 25, 2006].

24. Finster, in Patterson, *Howard Finster, Stranger from Another World*, 122.

25. Ibid., 178–184.

26. Andy Lakey and Paul Robert Walker, *Andy Lakey: Art, Angels, and Miracles* (Atlanta: Turner Publishing, 1996), 20–22.

27. Finster, in Patterson, *Howard Finster, Stranger from Another World,* 133.

28. Lakey and Walker, *Andy Lakey,* 134–135, 150–152.

29. Ibid., 98.

30. Ibid., 139–142.

31. See, for example, Doreen Virtue and the Angelic Realm, *Angel Therapy: Healing Messages for Every Area of Your Life* (Carlsbad, CA: Hay House, 1997), 162. For a fictional version, see Andrew Greeley, *Angel Fire* (New York: Warner, 1988), 165, 172.

32. Mignon F. Ballard, *Shadow of an Angel* (New York: St. Martin's Minotaur, 2002).

33. Virtue and the Angelic Realm, *Angel Therapy,* 217.

34. Doreen Virtue, *Messages from Your Angels Oracle Cards: What Your Angels Want You to Know* (Carlsbad, CA: Hay House, 2002), 10.

35. Andy Warhol, *Angels, Angels, Angels* (Boston: Little, Brown, 1994).

36. Harold Bloom, *The American Religion: The Emergence of the Post-Christian Nation* (New York: Simon & Schuster, 1992), 81.

37. David Morgan, *Visual Piety: A History and Theory of Popular Religious Images* (Berkeley: University of California Press, 1998), 26–58.

38. Robert Sardello, "Angels and the Spiral of Creation," in Robert Sardello, ed., *The Angels* (Dallas: Dallas Institute of Humanities and Culture, 1994), 56.

39. Donald Cowan, "Angels and the Evidence of Things Not Seen," in Robert Sardello, ed., *The Angels* (Dallas: Dallas Institute of Humanities and Culture, 1994), 77.

40. Larry Dossey, "Angels: The Missing Link," in Robert Sardello, ed., *The Angels* (Dallas: Dallas Institute of Humanities and Culture, 1994), 90–91.

CHAPTER 3. ANGELS COME FROM PERSIA

1. John R. Hinnells, *Persian Mythology* (London: Hamlyn, 1973), 50–54.

2. Mark Kermode, *The Exorcist* (1997; rev. ed., London: British Film Institute, 2003), 25.

3. Gunnar Berefeldt, *A Study on the Winged Angel: The Origin of a Motif* (Stockholm: Almqvist and Wiksells, 1968), 55.

4. Increase Mather, *Angelographia* (Boston: B. Green and J. Allen, 1696), 11.

5. John Deetz, *In Small Things Forgotten: The Archaeology of Early American Life* (New York: Anchor Press, 1977), cited in Janet L. Heywood, *Behold the Angels of Mount Auburn* (Cambridge: Friends of Mount Auburn Cemetery, 2005), 6.

6. Larry Frank, *New Kingdom of the Saints: Religious Art of New Mexico, 1780–1907* (Santa Fe: Red Crane Books, 1992), ii, 23 et passim.

7. Missionaries of the American Indian Bible Mission, *Satanic Forces at Work among the Navajos* (Farmington, NM: American Indian Bible Mission, 1970).

8. Jorge Cañizares-Esguerra, *Puritan Conquistadors: Iberianizing the Atlantic, 1550–1700* (Stanford, CA: Stanford University Press, 2006), 9, 67, 80, 158–160.

9. Mather, *Angelographia*, 9–14, 27–34, 44.

10. Stuart Schneiderman, *An Angel Passes: How the Sexes Became Undivided* (New York: New York University Press, 1988), 85.

11. Mather, *Angelographia*, A10–A11, 103.

12. Robert H. West, *Milton and the Angels* (Athens: University of Georgia Press, 1955), 22.

13. Mather, *Angelographia*, 16–18, 113.

14. Cotton Mather, *The Wonders of the Invisible World* (Boston: John Dunton, 1693), 184.

15. Perry Miller, *Errand into the Wilderness* (Cambridge: Belknap Press of Harvard University Press, 1956); Paul Boyer and Stephen Nissenbaum, *Salem Possessed: The Social Origins of Witchcraft* (Cambridge: Harvard University Press, 1974), 22–30.

16. Jonathan Edwards, *The Works of Jonathan Edwards*, vol. 2 (1834; reprint, Carlisle, PA: Banner of Truth Trust, 1995), 604, 615. Also accessible through the Christian Classics Ethereal Library at Calvin College (http://www.ccel.org/e/edwards/works2/htm/i.htm).

17. Joseph Fish, *Angels Ministering to the People of GOD, for their Safety and Comfort in Times of Danger and Distress. A Sermon, Preached at Westerly, R.I., August 27, 1755* (Newport, RI: J. Franklin, 1755), 9–10, 22.

18. Emanuel Swedenborg, *Heaven and Its Wonders and Hell, from Things Heard and Seen* (Latin ed., London, 1758; 52nd printing, English ed., New York: Swendenborg Foundation, 1964), 178, para. 311.

19. "Testimony of the Prophet Joseph Smith," preface to *The Book of Mormon* (Salt Lake City: Church of Jesus Christ of Latter-Day Saints).

20. Oscar W. McConkie, *Angels* (Salt Lake City: Deseret, 1975), 22–23, 80, 93–111.

21. These themes have been explored in Leigh Schmidt, *Hearing Things: Religion, Illusion, and the American Enlightenment* (Cambridge: Harvard University Press, 2000), and Ann Braude, *Radical Spirits: Spiritualism and Women's Rights in Nineteenth-Century America* (Boston: Beacon Press, 1989).

22. Joseph F. Berg, *Abaddon, and Mahanaim; or, Demons and Guardian Angels* (Philadelphia: Higgins and Perkenpine, 1856), 5–6, 229–230.

23. Lewis R. Dunn, *The Angels of God* (New York: Phillips & Hunt, 1881), 288, 29–30.

24. Ralph Waldo Emerson, "Uriel" (1846), http://vcu.edu/engweb/transcendentalism/authors/emerson/poems/uriel.html [June 17, 2004].

25. Herman Melville, *Moby Dick; or, The Whale* (1851; Chicago: Encyclopedia Britannica, 1952), 419.

26. Walt Whitman, *Leaves of Grass* (1892; New York: Bantam Books, 1983), 353–354.

27. Quentin Anderson, *The Imperial Self* (New York: Alfred A. Knopf, 1971).

28. Henry Wadsworth Longfellow, *The Poetical Works of Longfellow* (Boston: Houghton Mifflin, 1975), 200–201.

29. Ibid., 432, 463.

30. H. D. [Hilda Doolittle], *Tribute to the Angels* (Oxford: Oxford University Press, 1944).

31. Elizabeth Stuart Phelps, *The Gates Ajar* (1868; Boston: Fields, Osgood, 1870), 89–92.

32. Ibid., 166–167.

33. Golden Light [W. W. Hicks], *Angels' Visits to My Farm in Florida* (New York: John W. Lovell, 1892), 207–209.

34. Mark Twain, *The Mysterious Stranger and Other Stories* (New York: Harper & Row, 1922), 231.

35. Ibid., 250–253.

36. Ibid., 256, 262, 264.

37. Ibid., 277.

38. Ibid., 231.

39. William Gibson, in Mark Twain, *The Mysterious Stranger*, edited with an introduction by William M. Gibson (Berkeley: University of California Press, 1969), 1–2.

40. Ibid., 114.

41. Ibid., 404–405.

42. Dunn, *The Angels of God*, 62, 114, 121.

43. Nathalia Wright, *Horatio Greenough: The First American Sculptor* (Philadelphia: University of Pennsylvania Press, 1963), 98.

44. Ibid., 208.

45. David Edwin, "Apotheosis of Washington," Smithsonian National Museum of American Art, c. 1800.

46. David Morgan and Sally M. Promey, *Exhibiting the Visual Culture of American Religions* (Valparaiso, IN: Brauer Museum of Art, Valparaiso University, 2000), 75.

47. Morgan and Promey, *Exhibiting the Visual Culture of American Religions,* 20–23.

48. Metropolitan Museum of Art, *Memorial Exhibition of the Work of Abbot Henderson Thayer* (New York: Metropolitan Museum of Art, 1922), plates 31, 32, 45, 54, 59, 65, 69, 74, 78.

49. Michael Richman, *Daniel Chester French: An American Sculptor* (New York: National Trust for Historic Preservation, 1976), 187–194.

50. Richman, *Daniel Chester French,* 71–79.

51. Adeline Adams, *Daniel Chester French, Sculptor* (Boston: Houghton Mifflin, 1932), 78.

52. Troy Taylor, *Beyond the Grave: The History of America's Most Haunted Graveyards* (Decatur, IL: Whitechapel Press, 2005); see excerpt at http://www.prairieghosts.com/oakland.html [June 27, 2005].

53. Adams, *Daniel Chester French,* 70.

54. K. L. Nichols, "The Women's Building at the 1893 Exposition," http://members.cox.net/academia/cassatt5.html [June 27, 2005].

55. Ann Douglas, *The Feminization of American Culture* (New York: Alfred A. Knopf, 1977). See also Carl G. Jung, *Answer to Job* (German ed., 1952; English trans., Princeton, NJ: Princeton University Press, 1958).

56. Tom Longden, "Famous Iowans: Tazewell, Charles," *Des Moines Register,* June 7, 2005, http://desmoinesregister.com [August 1, 2006].

57. Charles Tazewell, *The Littlest Angel,* illustrated by Paul Michich (1946; Nashville, TN: Ideals Children's Books, 2002).

58. John Culhane, *Walt Disney's Fantasia* (New York: Harry N. Abrams, 1989), 182.

59. Kevin Burk, "Walt's Boyhood Home—Marceline, Missouri," http://www.startedbyamouse.com/features/Marceline01.shtml [January 5, 2007].

60. Jeanine Basinger, *The It's a Wonderful Life Book* (New York: Alfred A. Knopf, 1986), 95–102.

61. Ibid., 103–107.

62. For these definitions of religion, see Robert A. Orsi, *Between Heaven and Earth: The Religious Worlds People Make and the Scholars Who Study Them*

(Princeton, NJ: Princeton University Press, 2005), 2–5, and Peter Gardella, *Domestic Religion: Work, Food, Sex, and Other Commitments* (Cleveland: Pilgrim Press, 1998), 1–5.

63. Basinger, *The It's a Wonderful Life Book*, 66.

64. All of these television shows are available for viewing at *The Museum of Television & Radio*, 25 West 52nd Street, New York, NY 10019.

CHAPTER 4. ANGELS, THERAPISTS, AND EXORCISTS

1. Sophy Burnham, *A Book of Angels* (New York: Ballantine, 1990), 6, 203, 233.

2. Ibid., 4–6, 228.

3. Ibid., 239.

4. Ibid., 67–71.

5. Ibid., 114.

6. Ibid., 21–22.

7. Ibid., 17, 136–138, 140, 158.

8. Ibid., 245.

9. Ibid., 238.

10. Ibid., 249.

11. Diana Eck, *A New Religious America* (New York: Doubleday, 2001), 111.

12. Burnham, *A Book of Angels*, 223–226.

13. See http://www.joanwanderson.com [July 19, 2005].

14. Joan Wester Anderson, *Where Angels Walk: True Stories of Heavenly Visitors* (Sea Cliff, NY: Barton and Brett, 1992), 207.

15. Ron Rhodes, *Angels among Us* (Eugene, OR: Harvest House, 1994), 27–28; Kenneth L. Woodward, "Angels," *Newsweek* 122, no. 26 (December 27, 1993), 52.

16. Janice T. Connell, *Angel Power* (New York: Ballantine, 1995), xiii.

17. Ibid., xvi.

18. Ibid., 23.

19. Ibid., 26.

20. Ibid., 69.

21. Ibid., 205.

22. Ibid., 32–42.

23. Ibid., 244–270.

24. Ibid., 296; see also pp. 283, 289.

25. Ibid., 156, 201.

26. For gross receipts for *The Exorcist,* see http://www.the-numbers.com/movies/series/Exorcist.php [July 24, 2005]; see also http://www.filmsite.org/exor.html [July 24, 2005]; http://horror.about.com/od/faq/f/boxoffice.htm [July 24, 2005].

27. Michael Cuneo, *American Exorcism: Expelling Demons in the Land of Plenty* (New York: Doubleday, 2001), 273, 69.

28. Gallup Poll News Service, "Eternal Destinations: Americans Believe in Heaven, Hell," May 25, 2004, http://www.religionfacts.com/chrisitanity/beliefs/angels_demons.htm [July 9, 2005]; George Gallup, Jr., *Religion in America: 1996 Report* (Princeton, NJ: Princeton Religion Research Center, 1996), 20.

29. Win Worley, *The Curse of Jezebel* (1983; reprint, Mesquite, TX: WRW Publications, 1990), 23.

30. Ibid., 160.

31. Mark Kermode, *The Exorcist* (1997; rev. ed., London: British Film Institute, 2003), 12.

32. M. Scott Peck, *Glimpses of the Devil: A Psychiatrist's Personal Accounts of Possession, Exorcism, and Redemption* (New York: Simon & Schuster, 2005), 2.

33. Confraternity of Christian Doctrine of the Archdiocese of St. Paul, *The Commandments: A Manual for Catholic Pupils Attending the Senior High Schools* (1942; 24th printing, St. Paul, MN: Confraternity of Christian Doctrine, 1958), 33.

34. Win Worley, *Curses and Soul Ties, Binding and Loosing Spirits* (1983; reprint, Mesquite, TX: WRW Publications, 1993), 4.

35. For the entire *Malleus Maleficarum,* see Heinrich Kramer and Jacob Sprenger, *The Malleus Maleficarum,* translated and with an introduction by Montague Summers (1486; London: Pushkin Press, 1948). Selections containing the points cited here can be found in Elizabeth T. Clark and Herbert W. Richardson, eds., *Women and Religion* (New York: Harper & Row, 1977).

36. This account of the show and of Gina's exorcism is based partly on Cuneo, *American Exorcism,* 61–68, and partly on viewing a tape of the show itself.

37. Malachi Martin, *Hostage to the Devil* (New York: Reader's Digest Press, 1976). For Martin's appearance on *Oprah,* see Cuneo, *American Exorcism,* 55–57.

38. Martin, *Hostage to the Devil,* 409ff.

39. Susan Brill, "Martha's Angels," *Christianity Today* 39, no. 13 (November 13, 1995), 65.

40. Robert S. Waliszewski, "Jolted by an Angel," *Focus on the Family Magazine*, 2001, http://www.family.org/fofmag/pp/a0023968.cfm [July 20, 2005].

41. Mark Morning, "He Was My Everything," *Christianity Today*, February 22, 2005, http://www.christianitytoday.com/movies/interviews/michael landonjr.html [April 19, 2007].

42. Karl Marx, *Deutsch-Französische Jahrbücher*, February 1844. Often translated as *Economic and Philosophical Manuscripts of 1844*.

43. Doreen Virtue and the Angelic Realm, *Angel Therapy: Healing Messages for Every Area of Your Life* (Carlsbad, CA: Hay House, 1997), 172.

44. Doreen Virtue, *Healing with the Angels* (Carlsbad, CA: Hay House, 1999), 149.

45. Ibid., 155.

46. Ibid.

47. Ibid., 7.

48. Virtue and the Angelic Realm, *Angel Therapy*, 178.

49. Ibid., 27.

50. Alma Daniel, Timothy Wyllie, and Andrew Ramer, *Ask Your Angels* (New York: Ballantine, 1992), 25, 108–111, 161–165.

51. Ibid., 164–165, 228–229.

52. Ibid., 339–343.

53. Ibid., 98.

54. Ibid., 27–28.

55. Ibid., 128–129.

56. Eileen Elias Freeman, *Touched by Angels* (New York: Warner, 1993), 147.

57. Ibid., 6–7.

58. Ibid., 12.

59. Sharon Beekman, *Enticed by the Light: The Terrifying Story of One Woman's Encounter with the New Age* (Grand Rapids, MI: Zondervan, 1997), 144, 190.

CHAPTER 5. ANGELS, LOVE, AND SEX

1. Erika Doss, private communication, November 13, 2006.

2. Kevin P. Sullivan, *Wrestling with Angels: A Study of the Relationship between Angels and Humans in Ancient Jewish Literature and the New Testament* (Leiden: Brill, 2004), 11, 200. For evidence of the routine nature of this interpretation over the past sixty years, see notes on Genesis 6:1–4 in Bruce M. Metzger and Roland E. Murphy, eds., *The New Oxford Annotated Bible* (New York: Oxford University Press, 1991), and W.D. Stacey, "Children [Sons] of God," in Frederick C.

Grant and H. H. Rowley, eds., *Dictionary of the Bible* (New York: Charles Scribner's Sons, 1963), 134. Even Bernard J. Bamberger, who argued against the existence of *fallen* angels in his *Fallen Angels* (Philadelphia: Jewish Publication Society of America, 1952), conceded that Genesis 6:1 depicted angels having sex with women; Bamberger simply insisted that these angels were not demons.

3. Sullivan, *Wrestling with Angels*, 202–203.

4. John R. Hinnells, *Persian Mythology* (London: Hamlyn, 1973), 50–52.

5. Ibid., 32–33, 58.

6. Augustine, *The City of God*, Book XV, Chapter 23. See Thomas Aquinas, *Summa Theologica*, Part I, Q LI, Article 1, on angels having no bodies; on angels having no sex, see I.51.3, especially the reply to objection 6.

7. J. H. Heertz, ed., *The Pentateuch and Haftorahs* (1937; London: Soncino Press, 1988), 19.

8. John Calvin, *Commentary on Genesis*, chapter 6, http://www.ccel.org/c/calvin/comment3/comm_vol01/htm/xii.htm [August 21, 2005]; Jonathan Edwards, *A History of the Work of Redemption*, Part I: From the Fall to the Flood, http://www.ccel.org/ccel/edwards/works1.html [August 21, 2005].

9. Gunnar Berefeldt, *A Study on the Winged Angel: The Origin of a Motif* (Stockholm: Almqvist and Wiksell, 1968).

10. Adeline Adams, *Daniel Chester French, Sculptor* (Boston: Houghton Mifflin, 1932), 71–73.

11. James Robert Parish, *Ghosts and Angels in Hollywood Films: Plots, Critiques, Casts and Credits for 264 Theatrical and Made-for-Television Releases* (Jefferson, NC: McFarland, 1994), 203–206.

12. Ibid., 33.

13. Thomas Aquinas, *Summa Contra Gentiles*, Part IV.

14. For lyrics and other information, see http://www.oracleband.net/Lyrics/earth_angel.htm [August 10, 2005].

15. For lyrics, see http://www.oracleband.net/Lyrics/my_special_angel.htm [August 10, 2005].

16. Data at http://oldies.about.com/od/oldieshistory/a/february8.htm [August 10, 2005].

17. See www.oldielyrics.com/lyrics/mark_dinning/teen_angel.html [August 10, 2005].

18. For lyrics, see http://www.oldielyrics.com/lyrics/bobby_vee/devil_or_angel.html [August 10, 2005].

19. For lyrics, see http://showaddywaddy.net/pretty.htm [August 10,

2005]; for record of success, see http://www.thepeaches.com/music/60s/ [August 10, 2005].

20. For lyrics, see http://www.ntl.matrix.com.br/pfilho/html/lyrics/j/ johnny_angel.txt [August 10, 2005]; for sales standing for 1962, see http:// www.classicbands.com/top20.htm [August 10, 2005].

21. For lyrics, see http://rushmerilee.lyrics-online.net/AngelOfTheMorn ing.html [August 10, 2005].

22. Burt Bacharach and Hal David, "Close to You," sung by the Carpenters, 1972; copyright U.S. Songs, 1963, 1969; for lyrics, see http://www.lyricsfreak .com [January 10, 2006].

23. Peter Gardella, *Innocent Ecstasy: How Christianity Gave America an Ethic of Sexual Pleasure* (New York: Oxford University Press, 1985).

24. Heinrich Kramer and Jacob Sprenger, *Malleus Maleficarum* (1486). A good selection can be found in Elizabeth T. Clark and Herbert W. Richardson, eds., *Women and Religion* (New York: Harper & Row, 1977).

25. Andrew Greeley, *Angel Fire* (New York: Warner, 1988), 170, 256–257.

26. Ibid., 60.

27. Ibid., 87–89.

28. Ibid., 62.

29. Andrew M. Greeley, *Angel Light* (New York: Tom Doherty Associates, 1995), 113.

30. Greeley, *Angel Fire*, 144.

31. Greeley, *Angel Light*, 61.

32. Parish, *Ghosts and Angels*, 72–73.

33. Dawn Cole, review of *Michael* with letters from readers, http://www .christananswers.net/spotlight/movies/pre2000/i-mchl.html [August 16, 2005].

34. See http://www.lyricsfreak.com/g/goo-goo-dolls/61324.html [August 10, 2005].

35. Ranking data from http://www.songfacts.com/details.lasso?id=660 [August 10, 2005].

36. See http://www.lyricsfreak.com/s/sarah-mclachlan/121956.html [August 10, 2005].

37. See http://www.lyricsfreak.com/u/u2/141468.html [August 11, 2005].

38. Robin Taylor, "'Angels' CD a Soundtrack for Gen-X's Spiritual Quest," *National Catholic Reporter* 34, no. 33 (July 3, 1998), 20.

39. See http://www.touched.com/episodeguide/seasonseven/723.html [July 5, 2005].

40. Ann Rice, *Memnoch the Devil* (New York: Alfred A. Knopf, 1995), 221.

41. Ibid., 224–228.

42. Ibid., 234.

43. Ibid., 241.

44. Ibid., 242.

45. Ibid., 270.

46. Tony Kushner, *Angels in America, Part Two: Perestroika*, Act II, Scene ii (1992; New York: Theatre Communications Group, 1995), 175.

47. Ibid.

48. Ibid.

49. Ibid., Epilogue, 280.

50. Ibid., Act I, scene iv, 153.

51. English culture in the nineteenth century had produced some literature and art about sex between angels, but not about sex between angels and humans. See Gayle Shadduck, *England's Amorous Angels, 1813–1823* (New York: University Press of America, 1990), and the art of Edmund Bourne-Jones, among others.

52. Terry Law, *The Truth about Angels* (Lake Mary, FL: Charisma House, 2006), 220–223.

53. "Angel," New Life Community Church, Stafford, Virginia, http://new-life .net/angel01.htm [October 22, 2006].

CHAPTER 6. ANGELS OF WAR AND APOCALYPSE

1. Robert Marus, "Army General's Comments Renew Controversy over Islam," *Biblical Recorder: North Carolina Baptists' News Journal*, October 24, 2003, http://www.moralgroup.com/NewsItems/Islam/p14.htm [July 1, 2005].

2. John Yeats, "First Person: Chastening a Man of Valor," *Baptist Press News*, November 13, 2003, http://www.bpnews.net/bpcolumn.asp?ID=1189 [July 1, 2005].

3. CBS News, "The Holy Warrior," September 15, 2004, http://www.cbs news.com/stories/2004/09/15/main643650.shmtl [July 1, 2005].

4. Jorge Cañizares-Esguerra, *Puritan Conquistadors: Iberianizing the Atlantic, 1550–1700* (Stanford, CA: Stanford University Press, 2006).

5. Samuel Hopkins, *A Treatise on the Millennium* (1793; reprint, New York: Arno Press, 1972), 96–97, 119, 115, 102.

6. Ken Burns, "Gunpowder Entertainment," in *The West,* Episode 7, "The Geography of Hope," PBS Paramount, 1996.

7. Heber C. Kimball, quoted in Oscar W. McConkie, Jr., *Angels* (Salt Lake City: Deseret, 1975), 99–100.

8. Evangelical Tract Society, *Christian Duty to the Times* (Petersburg, VA: Evangelical Tract Society, 1861), 1–2.

9. Dom Gaspar Lefebvre, O.S.B., *The Saint Andrew Daily Missal* (St. Paul, MN: E.M. Lohmann, 1951), 988–989.

10. Billy Graham, *Angels: God's Secret Agents* (1975; rev. ed., Dallas: Word Publishing, 1994), 181.

11. Ibid., 85.

12. Ibid., 86.

13. Ibid., 72.

14. Ibid., 7–8.

15. Hal Lindsey, *The Late, Great Planet Earth* (1970; Grand Rapids, MI: Zondervan, 1977), 103–123.

16. Ibid., 132.

17. J. Dwight Pentecost, *Things to Come: A Study in Biblical Eschatology* (1958; 19th printing, Grand Rapids, MI: Zondervan, 1980).

18. Paul Boyer, *When Time Shall Be No More* (Cambridge: Harvard University Press, 1992), 87, 97.

19. Peter Gardella, "Gentile Zionism," *Midstream* (May 1991), 29–32.

20. Frank Peretti, *This Present Darkness* (Wheaton, IL: Crossway Books, 1986), 370–372.

21. Ibid., 119.

22. Tim LaHaye and Jerry B. Jenkins, *Glorious Appearing* (Wheaton, IL: Tyndale House, 2004), 397.

23. George Otis, Jr., *The Last of the Giants* (Tarrytown, NY: Fleming H. Revell, 1991), 99.

24. Ibid., 121, 137.

25. Ibid., 133.

26. Ibid., 161.

27. Philip Jenkins, *The Next Christendom: The Coming of Global Christianity* (New York: Oxford University Press, 2003), 5.

28. Walter Wink, *Unmasking the Powers* (Philadelphia: Fortress Press, 1986), 91–92.

29. Ibid., 28.

30. Ibid., 54.

31. Ibid., 129, 137.

32. Otis, *The Last of the Giants*, 143.

33. Norman Cohn, *Cosmos, Chaos, and the World to Come: The Ancient Roots of Apocalyptic Faith* (New Haven, CT: Yale University Press, 1993), 92.

34. Frank Kermode, *The Sense of an Ending: Studies in the Theory of Fiction* (New York: Oxford University Press, 1966).

35. Stephen D. O'Leary, *Arguing the Apocalypse: A Theory of Millennial Rhetoric* (New York: Oxford University Press, 1994), 201.

36. Sam Shepard, "The War in Heaven: Angel's Monologue," in *A Lie of the Mind* (New York: New American Library, 1986).

37. Tony Kushner, *Angels in America, Part Two: Perestroika*, Act V, scene x (New York: Theatre Communications Group, 1995), 275.

38. Larry Frank, *New Kingdom of the Saints: Religious Art in New Mexico, 1780–1907* (Santa Fe: Red Crane Books, 1992), 23.

39. Tim LaHaye and Jerry B. Jenkins, *The Indwelling* (Wheaton, IL: Tyndale House, 2000), 241–242.

40. Ibid., 248.

41. LaHaye and Jenkins, *Glorious Appearing*, 27–329.

42. Nicholas Kristof, "Jesus and Jihad," *New York Times*, July 17, 2004.

43. George H. Gallup, Jr., *Religion in America 1996* (Princeton, NJ: Princeton Religion Research Center, 1996), 19; see also http://www.religionfacts.com/christianity/beliefs/angels_demons.htm [July 9, 2005].

44. *Xena: Warrior Princess*, season 6, episode 12. See http://www.xenaville.com/epguide.html [January 9, 2007].

45. Ronald Reagan, "Farewell Address," January 11, 1989, http://www.ronaldreagan.com/sp_21.html [January 8, 2007]. Emphasis mine.

CHAPTER 7. NEW ANGELS AND SUPERHEROES

1. John R. Hinnells, *Persian Mythology* (London: Hamlyn, 1973), 57–59; Norman Cohn, *Cosmos, Chaos, and the World to Come: The Ancient Roots of Apocalyptic Faith* (New Haven, CT: Yale University Press, 1993), 90–91.

2. Interview with Lynn Schofield Clark, "Are Evangelicals Fueling Teen Fascination with the Powers of Darkness?" *Christianity Today*, July 1, 2003, http://ctlibrary.com/10627 [April 16, 2007].

3. Lynn Schofield Clark, *From Angels to Aliens: Teenagers, the Media, and the Supernatural* (New York: Oxford University Press, 2003), 45, 221.

4. Frank Peretti, *This Present Darkness* (Wheaton, IL: Crossway Books, 1986), 44.

5. Bill Wiese, *23 Minutes in Hell* (Lake Mary, FL: Charisma House, 2006), 2–6.

6. Ibid., 107, 116, 125, 134.

7. Don Piper (with Cecil Murphey), *90 Minutes in Heaven* (Grand Rapids, MI: Revell, 2004), 44, 135.

8. Ibid., 34.

9. Max Lucado, *When Christ Comes* (Nashville: Thomas Nelson, 1999), xv–xvi.

10. Max Lucado, *An Angel's Story* (Nashville: Thomas Nelson, 2002), 1–2.

11. Max Lucado, "Angels Watching Over You," http://www.maxlucado .com/email/2006/10/25.html [April 16, 2007].

12. Charles and Frances Hunter, as told by Roland Buck, *Angels on Assignment* (New Kensington, PA: Whitaker House, n.d.), 44–45, 169–171.

13. Ibid., 42.

14. Doreen Virtue, *Healing with the Angels* (Carlsbad, CA: Hay House, 1999), 13–14, 54.

15. Rebecca Brown, *Prepare for War* (New Kensington, PA: Whitaker House, 1987), 276, 290.

16. John Loren Sandford, *Healing the Nations* (Grand Rapids, MI: Chosen Books, 2000), 140, 145–146, 214–215, 221.

17. Ibid., 185–194, 248–249.

18. Ibid., 179.

19. Terry Law, *The Truth about Angels* (Lake Mary, FL: Charisma House, 1994), 162–163, 209–210.

20. Ibid., 173, 192–195, 204–207.

21. Betty J. Eadie, *Embraced by the Light* (Placerville, CA: Gold Leaf Press, 1992), 30–32.

22. Ibid., 47–48. Emphasis mine.

23. Ibid., 103–104, 107.

24. Ibid., 110, 115, 120–121.

25. Raymond A. Moody, Jr., *Life after Life: The Investigation of a Phenomenon—Survival after Bodily Death*, with an introduction by Elisabeth Kubler-Ross (1975; large print ed., New York: Walker and Company, 1987), 68–69.

26. Hal Erikson, "Dorothy Kingsley," *All Movie Guide*, http://movies2 .nytimes.com/gst/movies/filmography.html?p_id=97482 [April 19, 2007].

27. Lenore Skenazy, "Cute, Pink, Fuzzy—and Toxic to Little Girls," *New York Daily News*, August 13, 2006, 38.

28. Danny Fingeroth, *Disguised as Clark Kent: Jews, Comics, and the Creation of the Superhero* (New York: Continuum, 2006).

29. Bradford W. Wright, *Comic Book Nation: The Transformation of Youth Culture in America* (Baltimore: Johns Hopkins University Press, 2001), 60.

30. Peter Gardella, "*Star Trek:* American Fantasy on a Cosmic Scale," *Boston Globe*, November 29, 1986, 11.

31. Doreen Virtue, *Healing with the Angels*, 47.

32. David Chidester, *Christianity: A Global History* (San Francisco: Harper-SanFrancisco, 2000), 149–150.

33. Andrew Greeley, *Angel Fire* (New York: Warner, 1988), 70.

34. Alma Daniel, Timothy Wyllie, and Andrew Ramer, *Ask Your Angels* (New York: Ballantine, 1992), 28.

35. Gallup Poll News Service, May 25, 2004, http://www.religionfacts.com/christianity/beliefs/angels_demons.htm [July 9, 2005]; see also George H. Gallup, Jr., *Religion in America 1996* (Princeton, NJ: Princeton Religion Research Center, 1996), 20.

36. Pat Robertson, *The New World Order* (Dallas: Word Publishing, 1991), 252–261.

37. *Biblical Recorder*, June 14, 2002, http://www.biblicalrecorder.org/content/news/2002/6_14_2002/ne140602vines.shtml [October 9, 2006].

38. John Hagee, *Jerusalem Countdown* (Lake Mary, FL: FrontLine, 2006), 41–42, 119.

39. Peter Wallsten, "Falwell Says Faithful Fear Clinton More Than Devil," *Los Angeles Times*, September 24, 2006, http://www.latimes.com/news/nationworld/la-na-falwell24sep,0,4255550.story?coll=la-home-headlines [September 24, 2006].

40. Frank Rich, "Stuff Happens Again in Baghdad," *New York Times*, September 24, 2006, WK12.

41. René Girard, *I See Satan Fall like Lightning*, translated by James G. Williams (Maryknoll, NY: Orbis Books, 2001), 49–70.

42. Daniel et al., *Ask Your Angels*, 29.

43. Diana Eck, *A New Religious America: How a "Christian Country" Has Become the World's Most Religiously Diverse Nation* (San Francisco: HarperSanFrancisco, 2001), 111–112.

44. Roger Finke and Rodney Stark, *The Churching of America, 1776–2005: Winners and Losers in Our Religious Economy* (1992; 2d ed., New Brunswick, NJ: Rutgers University Press, 2005), 239.

45. David Chidester, *Authentic Fakes: Religion and American Popular Culture* (Berkeley: University of California Press, 2005), 230–231.

46. For the nineteenth-century story, see Leigh Eric Schmidt, *Hearing Things* (Cambridge: Harvard University Press, 2000), and *Telegrams from the Dead* (videorecording, PBS American Experience, 1994).

47. David Taylor, arts minister at Hope Chapel in Austin, Texas, posted such a commentary on the *Christianity Today* website in 2005. See http://www.christianitytoday.com/movies/commentaries/horrors.html [April 19, 2007].

48. Peter Gardella, *Domestic Religion: Work, Food, Sex and Other Commitments* (Cleveland, OH: Pilgrim Press, 1998), 1.

49. Michael Hardt and Antonio Negri, *Empire* (Cambridge: Harvard University Press, 2000), 309–314.

50. Corinne McLaughlin and Gordon Davidson, *Spiritual Politics: Changing the World from the Inside Out* (New York: Ballantine, 1994), 318.

51. William James, *A Pluralistic Universe* (1909; New York: Longmans, Green, 1932), 164.

52. Lawrence Osborn, "Archetypes, Angels, and Gaia," *Ecotheology: Journal of Religion, Nature and the Environment,* January 2001, 9.

53. Mortimer J. Adler, *The Angels and Us* (New York: Macmillan, 1982), xi–xii.

54. Mortimer J. Adler, "Angel," in Mortimer J. Adler, ed., *The Great Ideas: A Syntopicon of Great Books of the Western World,* vol. 1 (Chicago: Encyclopedia Britannica, 1952), 1.

55. Adler, *The Angels and Us,* 182–183.

56. "Dr. Adler's Biography," in *The Mortimer J. Adler Archive,* http://radical academy.com/adlerbio.htm [October 14, 2006].

57. Greeley, *Angel Fire,* 87–91.

58. Donald Cowan, "Angels and the Evidence of Things Not Seen," in Robert Sardello, ed., *The Angels* (Dallas: Dallas Institute of Humanities and Culture, 1994), 76–77.

59. Frederick Turner, "Angels from the Time to Come," in Robert Sardello, ed., *The Angels* (Dallas: Dallas Institute of Humanities and Culture, 1994), 109. See also Geddes MacGregor, *Angels: Ministers of Grace* (New York: Paragon House, 1988), 201–202.

60. Matthew Fox and Rupert Sheldrake, *The Physics of Angels* (San Francisco: HarperSanFrancisco, 1996), 99, 42.

61. John Milton, *Paradise Lost*, Book IV, line 75, and Book I, lines 254–255.

62. Walter Benjamin, "On the Concept of History," *Gesammelte Schriften* I, 691–704 (Frankfurt am Main: SuhrkampVerlag, 1974). For English translation, see Walter Benjamin, *Selected Writings*, vol. 4, *1938–1940*, ed. Howard Eiland and Michael W. Jennings (Cambridge: Harvard University Press, 2003), 392–393.

63. See http://www.midwestofcannonfalls.com/consumer_site/HTML/artists/CealB.html [October 15, 2006].

Bibliography

SECONDARY SOURCES

Anderson, Quentin. *The Imperial Self.* New York: Alfred A. Knopf, 1971.

Berefeldt, Gunnar. *A Study on the Winged Angel: The Origin of a Motif.* Stockholm: Almqvist and Wiksells, 1968.

Bloom, Harold. *The American Religion: The Emergence of the Post-Christian Nation.* New York: Simon & Schuster, 1992.

———. *Omens of Millennium: The Gnosis of Angels, Dreams, and Resurrection.* New York: Riverhead Books, 1996.

Boyer, Paul. *When Time Shall Be No More.* Cambridge: Harvard University Press, 1992.

Boyer, Paul, and Stephen Nissenbaum. *Salem Possessed: The Social Origins of Witchcraft.* Cambridge: Harvard University Press, 1974.

Braude, Ann. *Radical Spirits: Spiritualism and Women's Rights in Nineteenth-Century America.* Boston: Beacon Press, 1989.

Cañizares-Esguerra, Jorge. *Puritan Conquistadors: Iberianizing the Atlantic, 1550–1700.* Stanford, CA: Stanford University Press, 2006.

Chidester, David. *Authentic Fakes: Religion and American Popular Culture.* Berkeley: University of California Press, 2005.

Clark, Elizabeth T., and Herbert W. Richardson, eds. *Women and Religion.* New York: Harper & Row, 1977.

Clark, Lynn Schofield. *From Angels to Aliens: Teenagers, the Media, and the Supernatural.* New York: Oxford University Press, 2003.

Cohn, Norman. *Cosmos, Chaos, and the World to Come: The Ancient Roots of Apocalyptic Faith.* New Haven, CT: Yale University Press, 1993.

Cuneo, Michael. *American Exorcism: Expelling Demons in the Land of Plenty.* New York: Doubleday, 2001.

Davidson, Gustav. *A Dictionary of Angels.* New York: Free Press, 1967.

Douglas, Ann. *The Feminization of American Culture.* New York: Alfred A. Knopf, 1977.

Eck, Diana. *A New Religious America: How a "Christian Country" Has Become the World's Most Religiously Diverse Nation.* San Francisco: HarperSanFrancisco, 2001.

Fingeroth, Danny. *Disguised as Clark Kent: Jews, Comics, and the Creation of the Superhero.* New York: Continuum, 2006.

Finke, Roger, and Rodney Stark. *The Churching of America, 1776–2005: Winners and Losers in Our Religious Economy.* 1992; 2d ed., New Brunswick, NJ: Rutgers University Press, 2005.

Frank, Larry. *New Kingdom of the Saints: Religious Art in New Mexico, 1780–1907.* Santa Fe: Red Crane Books, 1992.

Gallup, George H., Jr. *Religion in America, 1996.* Princeton, NJ: Princeton Religion Research Center, 1996.

Gardella, Peter. *Domestic Religion: Work, Food, Sex and Other Commitments.* Cleveland, OH: Pilgrim Press, 1998.

———. *Innocent Ecstasy: How Christianity Gave America an Ethic of Sexual Pleasure.* New York: Oxford University Press, 1985.

Gibson, William. "Introduction," in Mark Twain, *The Mysterious Stranger.* Berkeley: University of California Press, 1969.

Girard, Rene. *I See Satan Fall like Lightning.* Translated by James G. Williams. Maryknoll, NY: Orbis Books, 2001.

Hardt, Michael, and Antonio Negri. *Empire.* Cambridge: Harvard University Press, 2000.

Heywood, Janet L. *Behold the Angels of Mount Auburn.* Cambridge: Friends of Mount Auburn Cemetery, 2005.

Hinnells, John R. *Persian Mythology.* London: Hamlyn, 1973.

Jenkins, Philip. *The Next Christendom: The Coming of Global Christianity.* New York: Oxford University Press, 2003.

Keck, David. *Angels and Angelology in the Middle Ages.* New York: Oxford University Press, 1998.

Kermode, Frank. *The Sense of an Ending: Studies in the Theory of Fiction.* New York: Oxford University Press, 1966.

Kermode, Mark. *The Exorcist.* 1997; rev. ed., London: British Film Institute, 2003.

McDannell, Colleen. *The Christian Home in Victorian America.* Bloomington, IN: Indiana University Press, 1986.

Metropolitan Museum of Art, *Memorial Exhibition of the Work of Abbot Henderson Thayer.* New York: Metropolitan Museum of Art, 1922.

Miller, Perry. *Errand into the Wilderness.* Cambridge: Belknap Press of Harvard University Press, 1956.

Morgan, David. *Visual Piety: A History and Theory of Popular Religious Images.* Berkeley: University of California Press, 1998.

Morgan, David, and Sally M. Promey. *Exhibiting the Visual Culture of American Religions.* Valparaiso, IN: Brauer Museum of Art, Valparaiso University, 2000.

O'Leary, Stephen D. *Arguing the Apocalypse: A Theory of Millennial Rhetoric.* New York: Oxford University Press, 1994.

Orsi, Robert A. *Between Heaven and Earth: The Religious Worlds People Make and the Scholars Who Study Them.* Princeton, NJ: Princeton University Press, 2005.

Parish, James Robert. *Ghosts and Angels in Hollywood Films: Plots, Critiques, Casts and Credits for 264 Theatrical and Made-for-Television Releases.* Jefferson, NC: McFarland, 1994.

Reis, Elizabeth. "The Trouble with Angels," *Common-place: The Interactive Journal of Early American Life* 1, no. 3 (April 2001), http://www.common-place.org/vol–01/no–03/reis/ [October 18, 2005].

Schmidt, Leigh Eric. *Consumer Rites: The Buying and Selling of American Holidays.* Princeton, NJ: Princeton University Press, 1995.

———. *Hearing Things: Religion, Illusion, and the American Enlightenment.* Cambridge: Harvard University Press, 2000.

Schneiderman, Stuart. *An Angel Passes: How the Sexes Became Undivided.* New York: New York University Press, 1988.

Shadduck, Gayle. *England's Amorous Angels, 1813–1823.* New York: University Press of America, 1990.

Sullivan, Kevin P. *Wrestling with Angels: A Study of the Relationship between Angels and Humans in Ancient Jewish Literature and the New Testament.* Leiden: Brill, 2004.

Taylor, Troy. *Beyond the Grave: The History of America's Most Haunted Graveyards.* Decatur, IL: Whitechapel Press, 2005.

West, Robert H. *Milton and the Angels.* Athens: University of Georgia Press, 1955.

Woodward, Kenneth L. "Angels," *Newsweek* 122, no. 26, December 27, 1993.

Wright, Bradford W. *Comic Book Nation: The Transformation of Youth Culture in America.* Baltimore: Johns Hopkins University Press, 2001.

Wright, Nathalia. *Horatio Greenough: The First American Sculptor.* Philadelphia: University of Pennsylvania Press, 1963.

PRIMARY SOURCES

Adams, Adeline. *Daniel Chester French, Sculptor.* Boston: Houghton Mifflin, 1932.

Adler, Mortimer J. *The Angels and Us.* New York: Macmillan, 1982.

Anderson, Joan Wester. *Where Angels Walk: True Stories of Heavenly Visitors.* Sea Cliff, NY: Barton and Brett, 1992.

Azimabadi, Badr. *The World of Angels.* New Delhi: Adam Publishers, 2002.

Ballard, Mignon F. *Shadow of an Angel.* New York: St. Martin's Minotaur, 2002.

Barthes, Roland. *Mythologies.* French ed., 1957; English trans., New York: Hill and Wang, 1972.

Basinger, Jeanine. *The It's a Wonderful Life Book.* New York: Alfred A. Knopf, 1986.

Beekman, Sharon. *Enticed by the Light: The Terrifying Story of One Woman's Encounter with the New Age.* Grand Rapids, MI: Zondervan, 1997.

Benjamin, Walter. *Selected Writings,* vol. 4, *1938–1940.* Edited by Howard Eiland and Michael W. Jennings. Cambridge: Harvard University Press, 2003.

Berg, Joseph F. *Abaddon, and Mahanaim; or, Demons and Guardian Angels.* Philadelphia: Higgins and Perkenpine, 1856.

Brill, Susan. "Martha's Angels," *Christianity Today* 39, no. 13, November 13, 1995.

Brown, Rebecca. *Prepare for War.* New Kensington, PA: Whitaker House, 1987.

Burnham, Sophy. *A Book of Angels.* New York: Ballantine, 1990.

Confraternity of Christian Doctrine of the Archdiocese of St. Paul. *The Commandments: A Manual for Catholic Pupils Attending the Senior High Schools.* 1942; 24th printing, St. Paul, MN: Confraternity of Christian Doctrine, 1958.

Connell, Janice T. *Angel Power.* New York: Ballantine, 1995.

Culhane, John. *Walt Disney's Fantasia.* New York: Harry N. Abrams, 1989.

Daniel, Alma, Timothy Wyllie, and Andrew Ramer. *Ask Your Angels.* New York: Ballantine, 1992.

Doolittle, Hilda [H. D.]. *Tribute to the Angels.* Oxford: Oxford University Press, 1944.

Dunn, Lewis R. *The Angels of God.* New York: Phillips & Hunt, 1881.

Eadie, Betty J. *Embraced by the Light.* Placerville, CA: Gold Leaf Press, 1992.

Edwards, Jonathan. *The Works of Jonathan Edwards,* vol. 2. 1834; reprint, Carlisle, PA: Banner of Truth Trust, 1995.

Evangelical Tract Society. *Christian Duty to the Times.* Petersburg, VA: Evangelical Tract Society, 1861.

Finster, Howard, as told to Tom Patterson. *Howard Finster, Stranger from Another World: Man of Visions Now on This Earth.* New York: Abbeville Press, 1989.

Fish, Joseph. *Angels Ministering to the People of GOD, for their Safety and Comfort in Times of Danger and Distress. A Sermon, Preached at Westerly, R.I., August 27, 1755.* Newport, RI: J. Franklin, 1755.

Fox, Matthew, and Rupert Sheldrake. *The Physics of Angels.* San Francisco: HarperSanFrancisco, 1996.

Freeman, Eileen Elias. *Touched by Angels.* New York: Warner, 1993.

Golden Light [W.W. Hicks]. *Angels' Visits to My Farm in Florida.* New York: John W. Lovell, 1892.

Graham, Billy. *Angels: God's Secret Agents.* 1975; rev. ed., Dallas: Word Publishing, 1994.

Greeley, Andrew. *Angel Fire.* New York: Warner, 1988.

———. *Angel Light.* New York: Tom Doherty Associates, 1995.

Hagee, John. *Jerusalem Countdown.* Lake Mary, FL: FrontLine, 2006.

Hopkins, Samuel. *A Treatise on the Millennium.* 1793; reprint, New York: Arno Press, 1972.

Hunter, Charles, and Frances Hunter, as told by Roland Buck. *Angels on Assignment.* New Kensington, PA: Whitaker House, n.d.

James, William. *A Pluralistic Universe.* 1909; New York: Longmans, Green, 1932.

Jung, Carl G. *Answer to Job.* German ed., 1952; English trans., Princeton, NJ: Princeton University Press, 1958.

Kramer, Heinrich, and Jacob Sprenger. *The Malleus Maleficarum.* Translated and with an introduction by Montague Summers. 1486; London: Pushkin Press, 1948.

Kushner, Tony. *Angels in America.* New York: Theatre Communications Group, 1995.

LaHaye, Tim, and Jerry B. Jenkins. *The Indwelling.* Wheaton, IL: Tyndale House, 2000.

———. *Glorious Appearing.* Wheaton, IL: Tyndale House, 2004.

Lakey, Andy, and Paul Robert Walker. *Andy Lakey: Art, Angels, and Miracles.* Atlanta: Turner Publishing, 1996.

Law, Terry. *The Truth about Angels.* Lake Mary, FL: Charisma House, 2006.

Lefebvre, Dom Gaspar, O.S.B. *The Saint Andrew Daily Missal.* St. Paul, MN: E.M. Lohmann, 1951.

Lindsey, Hal. *The Late, Great Planet Earth.* 1970; Grand Rapids, MI: Zondervan, 1977.

Longfellow, Henry Wadsworth. *The Poetical Works of Longfellow.* Boston: Houghton Mifflin, 1975.

Lucado, Max. *An Angel's Story.* Nashville, Thomas Nelson, 2002.

———. *When Christ Comes.* Nashville: Thomas Nelson, 1999.

Margolies, Morris R. *A Gathering of Angels: Angels in Jewish Life and Literature.* New York: Ballantine, 1994.

Martin, Malachi. *Hostage to the Devil.* New York: Reader's Digest Press, 1976.

Marus, Robert. "Army General's Comments Renew Controversy over Islam," *Biblical Recorder: North Carolina Baptists' News Journal,* October 24, 2003.

Mather, Increase. *Angelographia.* Boston: B. Green and J. Allen, 1696.

McConkie, Oscar W. *Angels.* Salt Lake City: Deseret, 1975.

McLaughlin, Corinne, and Gordon Davidson. *Spiritual Politics: Changing the World from the Inside Out.* New York: Ballantine, 1994.

Melville, Herman. *Moby Dick; or, The Whale.* 1851; Chicago: Encyclopedia Britannica, 1952.

Missionaries of the American Indian Bible Mission. *Satanic Forces at Work among the Navajos.* Farmington, NM: American Indian Bible Mission, 1970.

Moody, Raymond A., Jr., with an introduction by Elisabeth Kubler-Ross. *Life after Life: The Investigation of a Phenomenon—Survival after Bodily Death.* 1975; large print ed., New York: Walker and Company, 1987.

Otis, George, Jr. *The Last of the Giants.* Tarrytown, NY: Fleming H. Revell, 1991.

Peck, M. Scott. *Glimpses of the Devil: A Psychiatrist's Personal Account of Possession, Exorcism, and Redemption.* New York: Simon & Schuster, 2005.

Pentecost, J. Dwight. *Things to Come: A Study in Biblical Eschatology.* 1958; 19th printing, Grand Rapids, MI: Zondervan, 1980.

Peretti, Frank. *This Present Darkness.* Wheaton, IL: Crossway Books, 1986.

Phelps, Elizabeth Stuart. *The Gates Ajar.* 1868; Boston: Fields, Osgood, 1870.

Piper, Don, with Cecil Murphey. *90 Minutes in Heaven.* Grand Rapids, MI: Revell, 2004.

Prophet, Elizabeth Clare. *Fallen Angels and the Origins of Evil.* Corwin Springs, MT: Summit University Press, 2000.

Rhodes, Ron. *Angels among Us.* Eugene, OR: Harvest House, 1994.

Rice, Ann. *Memnoch the Devil.* New York: Alfred A. Knopf, 1995.

Richman, Michael. *Daniel Chester French: An American Sculptor.* New York: National Trust for Historic Preservation, 1976.

Robertson, Pat. *The New World Order.* Dallas: Word Publishing, 1991.

Sandford, John Loren. *Healing the Nations.* Grand Rapids, MI: Chosen Books, 2000.

Sardello, Robert, ed. *The Angels.* Dallas: Dallas Institute of Humanities and Culture, 1994.

Swedenborg, Emanuel. *Heaven and Hell.* Translated by George F. Dole, with an introduction by Bernhard Lang. West Chester, PA: Swedenborg Foundation, 2000.

Tazewell, Charles. *The Littlest Angel.* Illustrated by Paul Michich. 1946; Nashville, TN: Ideals Children's Books, 2002.

Twain, Mark. *The Mysterious Stranger and Other Stories.* New York: Harper & Row, 1922.

Virtue, Doreen. *Healing with the Angels.* Carlsbad, CA: Hay House, 1999.

———. *Messages from Your Angels Oracle Cards: What Your Angels Want You to Know.* Carlsbad, CA: Hay House, 2002.

Virtue, Doreen, and the Angelic Realm. *Angel Therapy: Healing Messages for Every Area of Your Life.* Carlsbad, CA: Hay House, 1997.

Warhol, Andy. *Angels, Angels, Angels.* Boston: Little, Brown, 1994.

Whitman, Walt. *Leaves of Grass.* 1892; New York: Bantam Books, 1983.

Wiese, Bill. *23 Minutes in Hell.* Lake Mary, FL: Charisma House, 2006.

Wink, Walter. *Unmasking the Powers.* Philadelphia: Fortress Press, 1986.

Worley, Win. *The Curse of Jezebel.* 1983; reprint, Mesquite, TX: WRW Publications, 1990.

———. *Curses and Soul Ties, Binding and Loosing Spirits.* 1983; reprint, Mesquite, TX: WRW Publications, 1993.

Index